THE OFFENSIVE ART

THE OFFENSIVE ART

Political Satire and Its Censorship around the World from Beerbohm to Borat

Leonard Freedman

 PRAEGER

Westport, Connecticut
London

Library of Congress Cataloging-in-Publication Data

Freedman, Leonard
   The offensive art : political satire and its censorship around the world from Beerbohm
   to Borat / Leonard Freedman.
     p. cm.
   Includes bibliographical references and index.
   ISBN 978–0–313-–35600–1 (alk. paper)
   1. Political satire—History and criticism. 2. Political satire—Censorship. I. Title
PN6149.P64 F74 2009
813'.54—dc22   2008032635

British Library Cataloguing in Publication Data is available.

Library of Congress Catalog Card Number: 2008032635
ISBN–978–0–313–35600–1

First published in 2009

Praeger Publishers, 88 Post Road West, Westport, CT 06881
An imprint of Greenwood Publishing Group, Inc.
www.praeger.com

Printed in the United States of America

The paper used in this book complies with the
Permanent Paper Standard issued by the National
Information Standards Organization (Z39.48–1984).

10 9 8 7 6 5 4 3 2 1

CONTENTS

FIGURES

PREFACE

This is a book about political satire and the efforts to constrain it within several countries with diverse political systems, from the beginning of the twentieth century to the present time.

There are many other books on political satire, some by the satirists themselves and some by commentators on the subject; there is also a large amount of literature on censorship, some of which draws examples from political satire. *The Offensive Art,* however, is the first effort to draw together material on the struggle between satirists and censors on an extensive, comparative basis.

Extensive—but, inevitably, far short of comprehensive. Readers may well complain that I have not included their favorite satirist, or overlooked countries with rich stores of political wit, or made only passing reference to the vast array of political satire that stretches from Aristophanes through Daumier. I can only plead that the material from which I have drawn is inexhaustible, with new absurdities bursting onto the political scene all around the world every day; and in undertaking to explore so much territory in one modestly sized volume, I have had to be highly selective. Even so, *The Offensive Art* provides substantial material on seven major countries, draws on examples from 20 more, and includes both democratic systems (Part I), and authoritarian regimes (Part II).

Sufficient, then, to illuminate three central points.

First: There has been political satire in most societies. The extent varies considerably, and in some extremely repressive regimes none of it is published, but always some jokesters, somewhere, will mock the rulers.

Second: There is considerably more satire in democratic than in authoritarian regimes. This, in fact, is part of the argument for democracy, and the bias of this book favors the relative openness of democracies—though, as this book makes abundantly clear, there is plenty to satirize in democracies.

Third: Nowhere are satirists completely free from censors of one kind or another. As compared with other dissenters, satirists enjoy a certain amount of protection by encasing their hostility in humor. And throughout history the jester has been allowed to speak truth to power. Yet few people enjoy being ridiculed, and retaliation by the powerful occurs often enough to make political satire a potentially uncomfortable trade in democracies, and a dangerous one in autocracies.

Of course, satirists face limits other than the censor. There are problems in finding and holding an audience, because most of the time, in most countries, most people are not deeply interested in politics, so political satire, except at the broadest level of personality traits or sexual scandal, is a minority taste. Then, too, topical references die very quickly, so satirists cannot rely for very long on well-tested quips.

But these, and the many other problems inherent in the satirist's craft, are not our subject here. Rather, we focus on the persisting struggle between the political jesters, whose work is presented with numerous lively examples from both old and new media, and those who try to suppress them.

Acknowledging all the innumerable sources for a survey such as this would stretch the preface beyond any possible bounds. I am especially appreciative of the support provided by grants from the UCLA Academic Senate and Political Science Department; the counsel contributed by my friends and colleagues, Professors David Rapoport and Richard Longaker; and Adena Schutzman's painstaking research assistance. I have gained invaluable insights from the participants in two UCLA Extension lecture courses, and have learned a great deal from the students in my Honors Colloquium seminars at UCLA, who have struggled through early drafts of this book. My wife, Vivian, and our sons Steven and David, provided indispensable help in preparing the manuscript and repairing my computer blunders. And I am grateful for the patience and thoughtful and witty counsel of Praeger's Senior Acquisitions Editor, Robert Hutchinson, and the publisher's production team.

INTRODUCTION: SATIRISTS AND CENSORS

Political satire, to be most effective
Is caustic, unfair, and never objective.
With all this in mind, you may ask why I'm for it.
The answer is simple: Tyrants abhor it.

Power breeds corruption. It also invites ridicule. The ridicule often provokes retaliation from the powerful.

This book is about the conflicts that exist between satirists—specialists in the art of ridicule—and their targets—the wielders of power—from the early twentieth century to the present day.

We begin by introducing the protagonists.

THE POLITICAL SATIRISTS

They include a remarkable range of artistic talent, expressed in a variety of media and drawn from many countries with widely divergent political systems.

But no matter what their medium of expression or their nationality, one characteristic is common to the work of almost all satirists: it expresses hostility and aggression. The satirist, according: to the late Victorian caricaturist and essayist Max Beerbohm, is "a fellow laying about him lustily, for the purpose of hurting, of injuring people who, in his opinion, ought to be hurt and injured."[1]

Hurting and injuring George W. Bush was certainly the intent of the massed ranks of satirists who poured furious scorn on the president as a willful, dangerous, inarticulate ignoramus. There were plenty of historical precedents for their anger. Daumier drew a caricature, "Gargantua," that depicted King Louis-Philippe sitting on a toilet throne, gorging tribute from the poor and excreting graft to his aristocratic friends.

Byron greeted the news of the suicide of a political leader he despised with:

So he has cut his throat at last—He! Who?
The man who cut his country's long ago.

H. L. Mencken was contemptuous of all politicians: "The only way to succeed in American public life lies in flattering and kowtowing to the mob."[2]

Not all satire is quite as bitter. Writers on satire commonly distinguish between the styles of two Roman poets: the Juvenalian—full of rage and disgust at universal corruption—and the Horatian—more mellow and amused, but not particularly appalled, by the follies of humankind. Art Buchwald's columns, for example, tend to the Horatian mood. Yet there is always an edge to his quips, and he himself says, "Satire is malicious."

Clearly political satire is an offensive art, and malice is its defining mood irrespective of the period[3] or the satirist's race or ethnicity. Or gender, for that matter. Women, having for so long been excluded from direct participation in politics, have recently been joining the ranks of political satirists as writers, cartoonists, and performers. Despite various studies indicating that women generally enjoy less aggressive humor than men, Maureen Dowd and Molly Ivins, for example, are as caustic as any of their male counterparts.[4]

The weapon of choice for all satirists is wit, a cerebral and cutting form of humor. Wit, according to Freud, is one of the means by which we release our repressed hostilities: "By belittling and humbling our enemy, by scorning and ridiculing him, we indirectly obtain the pleasure of his defeat by the laughter of the third person, the inactive spectator."[5]

Not surprisingly, then, satirists have had to put up with their own share of psychological scrutiny. We are told of Jonathan Swift's callous treatment of sick friends, his attacks of depression, and his repressed sexuality[6]; and of Mark Twain's lacerating view of himself: "Byron despised the human race because he despised himself. I feel as Byron did, and for the same reason." Art Buchwald's mother was committed to a private sanatorium for severe chronic depression soon after he was born, and Buchwald himself was hospitalized for depression. When asked what he was trying to do with his humor, he answered, "I'm getting even. I am constantly avenging hurts from the past."[7] The Russian satirist Mikhail Zoshchenko was a depressive who wrote an autobiography to try to answer the question: "I am unhappy and do not know why."[8] Some critics have read George Orwell's bleak prospectus of a totalitarian world in *1984* as the outcome of his miserable childhood in a despotic English prep school.[9] Of American political cartoonists it has been said: "Most cheerfully admit to being social misfits in their early days: a stutterer, nerd, or general adolescent ne'er-do-well who used his or her quick-draw humor to win friends and gain notoriety."[10]

But it would be unfortunate if we were to dismiss political satire as merely the neurotic venting of maladjusted personalities.

Jonathan Swift offered a *Modest Proposal*:[11] make the poor earn their keep by fattening their children as food for the rich. But this was no sick joke dragged out of his private torments. It was Swift's way of protesting the brutal disregard of a crushing Irish famine by the British government and landowners. Similarly, we should be wary of the tendency of some critics to judge Orwell's work in facile psychoanalytic terms: "Seeing 1984 as a reflection of Orwell's misery at prep school trivializes the very real political horrors he was writing about."[12] The same is true of satirists everywhere. Whatever their personal demons, most of them are writing about what they see as very real political evils.

Which particular evils they see depends on their political perspective. Some insist they don't have one, that their job is to entertain and not to proselytize.[13] But most of the political satirists discussed in this book do hold strong political beliefs.

Some have made their position clear by activism: Václav Havel, author of satirical anti-regime plays, spent four years in prison because of his open support of groups opposed to Czechoslovakia's Communist government after World War II. Dick Gregory was arrested several times, jailed for two months, and his nightclub and TV career badly damaged because of his role in civil rights demonstrations.[14] A few, like George Bernard Shaw, have written extensively about their political philosophies.

For the most part, however, satirists have been less explicit about their political doctrines, so if we're to see where they stand we have to look to their satire. Since satire is a negative art, it tells us what they're against rather than what they're for. Still, by examining their most frequent targets we can, in many cases, provide a rough assessment of their political perspectives.

In this book the predominant perspective will be that of the anti-authoritarian left: liberals[15] and an assortment of other critics of the status quo. They qualify as left of center because they have three favorite targets. The first is repressive governments that interfere with free expression and the right to privacy. The second is the super-rich, or plutocrats, who manipulate governments to preserve their privileged positions. The third is the "military establishment," the combination of armed services, politicians, and armament manufacturers that are accused of generating unnecessary wars.[16]

These ideas are a natural fit for an era of change and upheaval, and the left, with its post-Enlightenment irreverence towards established institutions and ideas, has produced a high proportion of all political satire during the past century.

But this is certainly not to say that liberals have had a monopoly of satire. There are satirists, as we'll see, all across the political spectrum from far left to far right.[17] There is always conservative satire.[18] Conservatives have one main target: the left. As conservative satirists see it, everyone on the left is hopelessly naive in refusing to recognize that liberty requires a framework of law and order; that societies are held together by a respect for tradition; that the prosperity of all depends on the energy and efforts of entrepreneurial capitalists; that without military strength there is international impotence.

Both sides in this debate have been relentlessly mocked: "Conservatives are not necessarily stupid, but most stupid people are conservatives." (John Stuart Mill) "The radical invents the views. When he has worn them out, the conservative adopts them." (Mark Twain) "The modern conservative is engaged in one of man's oldest exercises in moral philosophy, that is the search for a superior moral justification for selfishness."(John Kenneth Galbraith)

On the other hand: "Though I believe in liberalism, I find it difficult to believe in liberals." (G. K. Chesterton) "I can remember way back when a liberal was one who was generous with his own money." (Will Rogers) "Liberal — a power worshipper without the power." (George Orwell)[19]

There is no way of measuring which brand of satire is the funnier.[20] In general, what we find funny depends to a large extent on our own viewpoints as consumers of satire. We may admire, even enjoy, a witty thrust at the expense of our beliefs, but mostly we laugh loudest when the joke is on the other side and with more restraint when it's on us. Republicans are more likely than Democrats to laugh at jokes about the Clintons, and Democrats are more likely to buy volumes of so-called Bushisms. As the behavioral scientists put it, "humor appreciation varies inversely with the favorableness of the disposition toward the agent or entity being disparaged."[21]

But if we can't give the advantage in wisdom or wit to one side or the other, why do we give pride of place in this book to the liberals and other left-of-center anti-authoritarians? The answer is that our central theme is the struggle between the satirists and the censors; and it is the satirists of the left who, by mocking the political, economic, and military elites of their own regimes, are the most likely to provoke retaliation.

Conservative satirists, too, can claim to be anti-authoritarian because their targets include not only repressive communist regimes but also the rigid, "politically correct" dogmas of left-wing intellectuals.[22] Nonetheless, as exponents of law and order, the rights of property, and strong national defense, conservatives are usually defenders rather than opponents of the established order. This means that they are much less likely to face punitive sanctions from the authorities.

Consequently, in the chapters that follow we will find that it is the anti-authoritarians of the left who, more than any other brands, are in the thick of the battle with the censor.

THE CENSORS

Criticism and insults directed at the powerful are one thing; but ridicule cuts deeper. Some of those targeted suffer their humiliation in silence; better not draw more attention to the insult, and anyway you don't want to appear to lack a sense of humor. Other targets even pretend to enjoy the joke, welcoming the attention on the grounds that they would rather be ridiculed than ignored. So they appear on satirical TV shows, like Stephen Colbert's *The Colbert Report,* even though in his role as a self-important, right-wing pundit, he'll make them look like blundering fools. (One was the author of a proposed congressional law to require the posting of the Ten Commandments in every school who, when catechized by Colbert, was unable to remember several of the Commandments.)

Another reaction to satire is angry counterattack. This action is typically the response of authoritarian regimes. Not all of them, for some are relatively benign and tolerate a good deal of satire so long as it doesn't go too far. But more commonly despotic regimes cut out offending passages, or ban works entirely, and punish the satirists with imprisonment, ostracism, fines, exile, physical threats, even death.

The repression doesn't always work. In fact, some of the greatest satire has emerged from harshly authoritarian systems. For example, France generated ferocious satire even before the Revolution with lurid mocking of the alleged sexual licentiousness of King Louis and Marie Antoinette.[23] Then the nineteenth century brought France's classic period of political caricature, published in a profusion of journals, notably Charles Philipon's *La Caricature* and *Le Charivari,* whose stable of artists included the masterly Honoré-Victorin Daumier.[24]

As we'll see, the 1920s in the Soviet Union were another extraordinary period for political satire. Yet satirists in these systems were up against persistent repression. Philipon, Daumier, and several of their colleagues spent time in jail, and their magazines suffered repeated cuts and bans. Soviet satirists, even before Stalin clamped down on their efforts, worked within severe constraints. It could well be that these very constraints explain the high quality and intensity of much satire under authoritarian regimes, which provoked a deep indignation against profound injustice and required the ingenuity and subtlety need to outwit the censors.

In democracies, satirists fare much better, and they may even become well-paid celebrities. Yet they may face interference from commercial interests. Jon Stewart makes no bones about the corporate tie to his *Daily Show:* "To the extent we're not completely ineffectual, we're complicit in the corporate scheme, which is selling soap."[25]

Then, too, satirists face antagonism when they insult deeply entrenched ideas and traditions, breaking taboos on sex, gender, religion, race, ethnicity, and, especially in wartime, on patriotism. Satire's audiences enjoy the disrespectful treatment of sacred icons, but vast numbers cling to faith rather than skepticism, remain untouched by the Enlightenment, Darwin, and Freud, and resent having their beliefs mocked.

Faced with this hostility, some satirists pull back and, in effect, censor themselves. "We have met the enemy," said Walt Kelly's Pogo, "and not only may he be ours, he may be us."

Fortunately, most satirists have persisted. Daumier limned another *Gargantua* on his prison wall. Though satire in America practically stopped in the immediate aftermath of 9/11, and cartoonists replaced the lampooning of politicians with expressions of national grief, within a matter of weeks cartoonists, satirical magazines, and the rest were back in business. Almost everywhere satirists have used their ingenuity to find loopholes in oppressive laws and invented ways to ignore, bypass, or confuse the censors.

So, the satirists have played their cat-and-mouse game with the censors, and if the mouse has not won the game as regularly as in the Tom and Jerry cartoons, then it has prevailed often enough to ensure that satire could never be completely expunged and that, on the contrary, it continues to flourish.

Certainly satirists will never run out of material. Every day the headlines trumpet news that is at least as absurd as any of the more outlandish examples of satire in this book. Could any satirist have invented Watergate? Or imagined Bill and Monica? Or conjured up all those hopelessly scrambled Bushisms? Or put forward the idea of the Chinese Communists inviting capitalists to join their Party? Or dreamed up leaders as bizarre as Adolf Hitler and North Korea's Kim Jong Il?

As Art Buchwald has said, "You can't make anything up anymore. The world itself is a satire. All you're doing is recording it." Tom Lehrer finally tired of the effort. Satire became obsolete, he said, the day Henry Kissinger was awarded the Nobel Peace Prize.

Of course, satirists have not found absurdity only in politics. They see the ridiculous in every aspect of human behavior. In fact, the very foibles for which politicians are mocked—the hypocrisy, the watering down of principle, the vanity, the back-biting, the intense competitiveness for status and power—are all too common among businesspeople, doctors, lawyers, academics, journalists, and artists. But in politics the stakes are uniquely high, potentially affecting not only taxing and spending, health, and education, but also the fate of nations, even of the entire human race. Satirists work in a particularly fraught atmosphere when they take politics as their subject matter, and their caustic quips may lead to resentment, even to efforts to make them shut up.

To explore this tension between satirists and censors a natural place for this book to begin is democracy, for there exists more political satire in democracies than in any other system. For one thing, there is so much to ridicule in democracies. Satirists of every stripe find rich material in elections, political parties, interest groups, and so on—all of which prove to be rife with imperfections. Nor is democracy a guarantee against corruption, abuses of power, vast inequalities of income and status, or military and economic expansionism—all perennial subjects of angry satire.

Yet the fundamental reason that democracy is satirized so much is not merely that it is risible. All systems are. But it is in democracy that satirists face the fewest constraints on their caustic wit. The four chapters of Part I are devoted to satire in democracies. From the several countries rated as having democratic systems and press freedom, I have selected two for a detailed review: the United States and Britain. They are natural choices for me, having grown up in Britain and having spent most of my adult life in America. Apart from personal familiarity, however, these two countries can claim to be the oldest democracies, despite their serious historical blemishes (such as American slavery and segregation and British colonialism), and they have the longest history of relatively uninterrupted political satire. The two have much in common, yet there are sufficient differences in their political institutions and their cultures to give us a comparative perspective and prevent our associating democracy with any single system.

Chapter 1 demonstrates the extensive range of satire in the United States, focusing particularly on recent American presidents. Yet as Chapter 2 makes clear, satirists in America are not completely free from a complex of constraints, especially when they laugh at entrenched taboos. Chapter 3 shows how British political satire mocks prime ministers and royals, and Chapter 4 informs us that satirists in Britain, too, can face fierce resentment as they turn their wit against powerful taboos.

Part II moves the action from democracies to authoritarian states, which, by definition, are hostile to dissent and to political satire. Autocracy has been the common condition of mankind throughout history, and it survives even today over a large part of the human race. It has taken many forms: rule by a monarch, a prince, a sultan, a theocrat, a general, a charismatic leader, or a small oligarchy. In the twentieth century a new form, more repressive than any in the past, joined these traditional systems. This new form is more repressive not because its leaders were more brutal than earlier tyrants—brutal they were, but not more so than many of the monsters of the past. The difference was in organizational technique and technology and in the ability to dominate the lives and thinking of people, which led to these systems being called "totalitarian." The word is not quite accurate. They did not have *total* control. The technology available to them—radio, telephone, fast travel—was novel, but it lacked the ability Orwell posits in *1984* to reach everyone, everywhere, all the time. So these new-model dictators were no more than would-be totalitarians. Even so, Germany under Hitler in Chapter 5 and Russia and China under Stalin and Mao in Chapter 6 provide us with stultifying examples of the quasi-totalitarian model. While they ruled, dissent was dangerous. Political satire, where it existed at all, was either constantly circumscribed by official censorship or actually taken over by the regime to attack the regime's foreign and domestic opponents.

Chapters 7 and 8 explore political satire under more traditional forms of authoritarianism. Colonialism is almost dead now, but it was very much alive well into the twentieth century, by which time it was profoundly antithetical to the prevailing international attitudes and thus ripe for satire. Of all the empires of the era, the British Empire was the most extensive, and India, whose satirists are discussed in Chapter 7 (along with those of some of its neighboring countries), was the Jewel in the Crown.

If colonialism is essentially defunct, rule by monarchs, generals, and religious leaders is still a potent presence, as exemplified in Chapter 8 by the Muslim countries of the Middle East. Despite their vast oil wealth, they display little fundamental change from the models of power that have prevailed through the ages, and the rulers have not looked kindly on political satire.

The concluding chapter explores the prospects for political satire in the twenty-first century, for which purpose it was necessary to provide examples from a number of other countries. The chapter then addresses the final questions: Does political satire matter? And should it be subject to *any* limits?

part 1

(ALMOST) ANYTHING GOES: POLITICAL SATIRE IN AMERICA AND BRITAIN

chapter one

PUNCTURING THE IMPERIAL PRESIDENCY: FDR TO GEORGE W. BUSH

The President's role has impressively grown
Until it's attained an imperial tone.
But that makes a target that's bound to enthrall
Conrad, Art Buchwald, Jon Stewart, and all.

Long before Jon Stewart and Garry Trudeau's *Doonsebury* there was political satire in America. It was there in profusion during the struggle for independence, with some for it and some against it. Ben Franklin was cool to
the idea at first, but in time he turned his devastating wit against the bumbling British government. He proposed *Rules By Which a Great Empire
May be Reduced to a Small One,* including: quarter troops among the population, shoot down protesting mobs, impose intolerable taxes without representation, and treat complaints with contempt. As we know, these and
other rules proposed by Franklin were faithfully followed by the British.
Franklin also drew the first cartoon to appear in an American newspaper:
a snake divided into eight parts with the inscription "Join, or Die."

With his cartoon and his essays, Franklin proved to be a pioneer in two of
the principal formats used by American political satirists.

As costs of engraving and newsprint came down, political cartoons were
staple fare in daily newspapers as well as magazines by century's end, opening the way for the potent assaults on politicians and their policies by
Thomas Nast and an unending array of brilliant artists.

In the written word, Franklin was succeeded by James Russell Lowell
(*The Bigelow Papers*); Ambrose Bierce (*The Devil's Dictionary*); Peter Finley Dunne ("Mr.Dooley"), and America's master satirist, Mark Twain. In
the 1920s H. L. Mencken took devastating aim at the entire American population, and since Mencken there has been an abundance of prose satire in
the form of essays, newspaper columns, novels, and plays. Satirical magazines, notably *Monocle, The Realist, Onion,* and *American Humorist,*

have built on the youthful style and reputation of *Mad* and *The Harvard Lampoon.*

Individual performers have provided another popular form of political satire. Will Rogers set the pace; to be followed by Mort Sahl (who hated to be put in the same category as the folksy Will Rogers), Tom Lehrer, Paul Krassner, Dick Gregory, and Mark Russell. There were cabaret groups, too: *The Premise* and *Second City,* followed by *The Capitol Steps.*

Finally, there are the mass-media formats through which political satire reaches its widest audiences. Movies by Charlie Chaplin, Stanley Kubrick, and others have depicted political leaders and issues with scathing wit. Harry Shearer is among several radio satirists. After much doubt and hesitation, television entered the fray in the 1960s. Rowan and Martin's *Laugh In* included some rather tame political references, but it was the Smothers Brothers *Comedy Hour* that introduced political humor with a more acerbic tone from 1965 to 1967.[1] In 1975, television discovered the late-night youth audience with the still-running *Saturday Night Live,* and the way was prepared for the satirical programs of Jon Stewart, Stephen Colbert, Dennis Miller, and a number of other performers. The comedy and interview programs of Johnny Carson, David Letterman, and Jay Leno have also featured political jokes in their opening monologues, and *The Simpsons* mocked leaders at every level, including politicians.

At the century's end came the explosion of political satire on the Internet, with new satirical magazines springing up from all directions, including *The Borowitz Report, Jib Jab, The New York Slime,* and *The Washington Pox: A Plague on Both Your Houses,* as well as an exotic variety of Web logs.[2] Moreover, the Internet extended the producers of satire beyond the professionals to the Web logs, to YouTube postings, and to the e-mails of many thousands of amateurs.

Much of this, of course, had little — if any — staying power. Some of it was crude, obvious, and superficial. After its first seasons, *Saturday Night Live* always suffered under the assertion that it was not as funny as it used to be. Even so, there was more than enough lively and irreverent satire in the several media to refute the pessimistic view of one scholar of American humor who wrote in 1962 that political humor in America was "a suspended if not vanished art."[3]

American satirists have directed their art at every institution of American government and politics. Mark Twain on Congress:

It could probably be shown by facts and figures that there is no distinctly native American criminal class except Congress.

Reader, suppose you were an idiot; and suppose you were a member of Congress; but I repeat myself.

Will Rogers on political parties:

I am not a member of any organized party — I'm a Democrat.

Republicans take care of the big money, for big money takes care of them.

Thomas Nast drew New York's Boss Tweed of Tammany Hall as fat, repulsive, and corrupt. "Let's stop them damned pictures," said Tweed. "I don't care what the papers write about me — my constituents can't read; but . . . they can see pictures."

Election campaigns have always been an abundant source of satire. The 1972 campaign had inspired the "gonzo journalism" of Hunter Thompson,[4] and the 2008 primary campaigns of both parties were especially rich in material. Pollsters and interest groups have all attracted their share of the satirists' scorn.

Bureaucracies, seen as wasteful, incompetent, remote, and heartless institutions, are inevitable subjects of American satirists, as they are of satirists in every country.

That other great aggregation of resources and power, the military, has also attracted much satirical attention in, for example, the long-running TV series M*A*S*H, Joseph Heller's novel, *Catch 22;* and Stanley Kubrik's film, *Dr. Strangelove, or How I Learned to Stop Worrying and Love the Bomb.*

The solemn pronouncements of our highest court have not been immune. Peter Finley Dunne's Irish saloonkeeper Mr. Dooley commented that "th' supreme court follows th' iliction returns;" and this was amended by wits after November 2000 to suggest that the Supreme Court *determines* the election returns.

The media take a constant pounding from Jon Stewart, Stephen Colbert, and *The Simpsons.*

Nor have the American people at large been untouched by the satirists. H. L. Mencken railed against "the normal Americano:"

He has immovable opinions about all the great affairs of state, but nine-tenths of them are sheer imbecilities. He is violently jealous of what he conceives to be his rights, but brutally disregardful of the other fellow's.[5]

Yet nothing is more satisfying to satirists than to aim at the highest level of power, the apex of the political system. As cartoonist Bill Mauldin put it, "If it's big, hit it." In America the biggest, most common target of political satirists has been the President.

The presidency, because it combines both the nation's political and symbolic leadership, is an office that attracts deference, even awe. Satirists delight in debunking awesome subjects, and they have shown little respect for presidents.

Even Lincoln was battered in his time by angry humorists, sometimes as a bumbling fool, sometimes as a despot. Subsequently, historians have rated Lincoln as our greatest president. H. L. Mencken was not persuaded, dismissing Lincoln as "a shifty politician" and "the beau ideal of a rube."[6] Theodore Roosevelt, also highly rated by historians, was nonetheless a favorite target of satirists. Peter Finley Dunne's Mr. Dooley made wry fun of Roosevelt's account of how he, roaring ahead of his troops, had routed a Cuban army. Though Mencken admired T.R. as the Nietzschean man of action, he complained about his "quack" policies.

Satirists derided Woodrow Wilson as a self-righteous, puritanical bore and Warren Harding as a vacuous nonentity. Dorothy Parker asked the definitive question when the laconic Calvin Coolidge died: "How do they know?" The unfortunate Herbert Hoover, the paradigm of the efficient engineer, cut a pathetic figure as the economy collapsed around him.

Satire was to be provided with still more targets of opportunity with the arrival of the modern presidency — the enormously expanded office that was inaugurated by the New Deal, World War II, and the dropping of The Bomb on Hiroshima and Nagasaki.

SATIRE AND THE MODERN PRESIDENCY

Presidents of this new era have by no means been exempted from the convoluted checks and balances built into the constitutional system, and satirists have found plenty of material in the repeated deadlocks between the executive and legislative branches. (Jon Stewart: "The president can hold his breath and pound his fists and threaten to run away. But the president cannot make laws."[7])

Yet, as a leading scholar of the presidency has observed, despite all the constraints on the office: "The history of the presidency is a history of aggrandizement,"[8] and satirists have taken up the theme of ever-expanding presidential power with relish. Of all the presidents of the modern era, six in particular have been the targets of unremitting satire: Franklin D. Roosevelt, Lyndon Johnson, Richard Nixon, Ronald Reagan, Bill Clinton, and George W. Bush.

Not that the others have escaped the satirists' lash. Harry Truman was jeered for his inability to end the Korean War and for losing his temper when a music critic gave a bad review to a song recital by his daughter, Margaret.

Dwight Eisenhower had to endure repeated jibes at his horribly garbled replies at press conferences and his alleged lack of diligence and knowledge. One joke had him saying to Israeli Prime Minister David Ben Gurion, "It's a great inspiration. Despite all the anti-Semitism in the world, your country elected a Jewish president."[9] Cartoons by Herblock and Robert Osborn pummeled Eisenhower for his alleged ties to big business.

John F. Kennedy was mocked for the Bay of Pigs disaster, the glitz and glamour of his "Camelot" court, and his presidential campaign's dependence on his father's money. (Kennedy preempted the jokes by reading a purported telegram from his father: "Dear Jack: Don't buy a single vote more than is necessary. I'll be damned if I'm going to pay for a landslide.")

Gerald Ford, after an accidental fall on camera, inspired a weekly pratfall by Chevy Chase on *Saturday Night Live,* fixing Ford in the public mind as a clumsy oaf, unable to walk and chew gum at the same time.

Jimmy Carter was ridiculed for seeming to blame the problems of his administration on the "malaise" of the American public, for his aborted effort to free American hostages in Iran, and for his efforts to offset his rather prim image by telling *Playboy* magazine that he had "lusted in the heart."

George Herbert Walker Bush was laughed at for his scrambled syntax, his preppy manner, and his being forced to renege on his campaign promise of "Read my lips: no new taxes."

But the other six presidents had to undergo an even more rigorous ordeal by satire, directed on the one hand at their personal deficiencies and on the other at their policies.

Franklin D. Roosevelt is generally rated by historians as the second greatest of all our presidents, and easily the most impressive of the twentieth century.[10] Yet despite his vast popularity, which led to his being elected by landslide victories four times, satirists protested the vast power he had accumulated over the domestic economy. Cartoonists in the *Chicago Tribune* and *The Saturday Evening Post* drew the New Deal as a Trojan Horse tyranny aimed at the overthrow of the Constitution, bringing with it a ruinous tax burden, intolerable protections for labor, and utopian redistribution schemes. In the popular comic strip *Little Orphan Annie,* Daddy Warbucks was a benign plutocrat, and big government was the enemy. Don Marquis' character, Archy the cockroach, ridiculed the New Deal's alphabet soup of plans, agencies, and regulations.

Mencken weighed in. After initially admiring Roosevelt for his intelligence and courage, he soon turned against the New Deal's planned economy and was calling Roosevelt "the Führer," a charlatan, and a "snake oil vendor."

The right-wing columnist, Westbrook Pegler, pilloried FDR for abusing his power by attacking the rich, despite his own patrician background and lifestyle. After he "had done with nurses and tutors," said Pegler, Roosevelt "went to a dude school named Groton, which prepared him for Harvard; and after he had married and had taken his bride for a honeymoon tour of England, France, Italy, and Germany," he had returned home to go to

Columbia Law School. Pegler quoted Mrs. Roosevelt's account of how her mother-in-law had taken a house for them and engaged their servants, until she replaced the house with "an estate on Campobello Island, including a house completely furnished even to china, glass and linens." All this was in contrast to the self-made rich who "are proud to have taken care of their own parents, and every crack from him about well-fed clubmen and economic royalists evokes from them the soul-satisfying and contemptuous taunt, 'mama's boy.' "[11]

The next great expansion of federal power domestically came during the tenure of Lyndon Johnson. "Presidents," he said, "deal with power," and he dealt with it through the famous "Johnson treatment:" arm round the shoulder, wheedling, threatening, bargaining, bribing, and appealing to party and patriotism. It was all dedicated to creating his "Great Society," with its War on Poverty, Medicare, and civil rights programs.

In legislative terms, Johnson's achievements were extraordinary, yet he could never escape being lampooned as a sleazy manipulator. Cartoons reflected the impression of deviousness conveyed in his television appearances. He was also disdained for his crudeness. He would conduct long conversations with staff and visitors while seated on the toilet. After his gall bladder operation he opened his shirt to the press so they could see his scar, thereby providing David Levine with the inspiration for a cartoon where he drew the scar in the shape of Vietnam.

Initially there was broad public support for Johnson's decision to lead America ever more deeply into the morass of Vietnam. But as it became the first war in which the slaughter was brought home to people on their television screens, and as the prospects of victory became ever more elusive, the majority became disenchanted and more receptive to antiwar satire. The tone of the satire grew angrier. In the streets students mocked President Johnson with the chant, "Hey, Hey, LBJ, How many kids did you kill today?" Though Al Capp scoffed at the marchers in Li'l Abner as SWINE — Students Wildly Indignant About Everything — most other cartoonists were harsh in their condemnation of the war and a president who was obstinately unwilling to change course.

Some saw the war as an effort to impose the American business system on the world. A poster on the war proclaimed: "War is a good business investment. Invest your son." Abbie Hoffman, who had made a career of organizing public demonstrations parodying the American corporate culture, saw the Vietnam War as an extension of that culture, and with his "Yippies" held a riotous "Festival of Life" at the 1968 Democratic Convention.

Even these did not match the rancor of Barbara Garson's parody, *Macbird!* The play portrayed the Vietnam War as part of the plan to build a vast American empire, a "Pox Americana," and gruesome images were used to

"Our Position Hasn't Changed At All"

Lyndon Baines Johnson's remarkable legislative accomplishments might have led to his being rated by historians as one of our great presidents had he not, against all his political instincts, embroiled America in the Vietnam War, and then obstinately expanded it. Herbert Block (pen name Herblock) was one of the most trenchant critics of the Vietnam War, as we see from this Washington Post cartoon attacking Johnson's duplicitous justifications of his Vietnam policy. In a cartooning career that extended from 1928 until his death, and won him many awards, Herblock never wavered from the crusading liberalism inherited from the New Deal years. ["Our Position Hasn't Changed At All." A 1965 Herblock Cartoon, copyright by The Herb Block Foundation. Reproduced with permission.]

capture the horror of the war ("Sizzling skin of napalmed child") as the three witches stirred their cauldron.[12]

Of course, Vietnam was not solely Johnson's war. He had entered it with the gravest misgivings, his political caution being overwhelmed by a brilliant team inherited from Kennedy and drawn from the elite of corporate and academic life. As president, however, he was inevitably the prime satirical target, and the aura of mistrust he emanated was ferociously expressed in *Macbird!,* which shadowed Shakespeare's tragedy by showing Johnson plotting the death of his predecessor. The parody played to enthusiastic audiences.

Then came Richard Milhous Nixon. A profound dislike of Nixon had long been widespread in the press and among liberal satirists, dating from their belief that he had won his congressional and Senate seats by smearing his opponents with charges that they were soft on communism. Herblock showed him in one cartoon emerging from a sewer, dripping slime. "Would you buy a used car from this man?" was the constant jibe. Hunter Thompson dug deeper. Nixon spoke "for the Werewolf in us" as "America's answer to Mr. Hyde."

Norman Mailer was no less savage in his coverage of a Nixon press conference during his 1972 campaign for reelection to the presidency: He mocked his lack of authenticity:

> You could all but see the signal pass from his brain to his jaw, "SMILE," said the signal, and so he flashed his teeth in a painful kind of joyous grimace which spoke of some shrinkage in the liver, or the gut, which he would have to repair afterward by other medicine than good fellowship. (By winning the Presidency perhaps.) He had always had the ability to violate his own nature absolutely ... there had never been anyone in American life so resolutely phony as Richard Nixon, nor anyone so transcendentally successful by such means ... "[13]

In 1972, Nixon was indeed to be "transcendentally successful" again in winning a landslide reelection. Yet the rage against the presidency inspired by the Vietnam War was now transferred to Nixon, especially as he surreptitiously broadened the war into Cambodia.

The American incursions into Vietnam and Cambodia led Arthur Schlesinger Jr. to suggest that we had entered the era of the "imperial presidency." Presidents, he said, were extending their authority far beyond the limits set forth in the Constitution; as Chief of State as well as head of government, they had taken on an aura akin to that of a monarch or emperor. It is a theme much used by novelist Gore Vidal. In his novel *Empire,* he had Henry James wondering if the America of Boss Tweed was fit to rule the world: "How can we, who cannot honestly govern ourselves, take up the task of governing others? Are we to govern the Philippines from Tammany Hall?"[14] Tammany Hall was long gone, but the charge of imperial overreach was frequently hurled at Nixon. Edward Sorel drew Nixon swathed in imperial robes and holding a scepter.

That issue faded for a while as Nixon and his Secretary of State, Henry Kissinger, negotiated a peace treaty — the prelude to the occupation of the entire country by the communist regime in the north.

Richard Nixon, triumphantly re-elected in 1972, resigned in disgrace in 1974 to avoid being impeached, then tried desperately to salvage his reputation. But Pat Oliphant, the most widely syndicated of all cartoonists, is unforgiving. He portrays Nixon, furious that he is forgotten by later generations, planning his comeback from Hell. And Oliphant has a second target: through Punk, his sarcastic penguin commentator, we are reminded that "those who ignore history are the voters of tomorrow. [OLIPHANT (c) 1999 UNIVERSAL PRESS SYNDICATE. Reprinted with permission. All rights reserved.]

Satirists were then presented with a new and more dangerous source of trouble for the Nixon administration. During the reelection campaign, members of the White House staff had unleashed the absurd episode that came to be known as Watergate, a bungled effort to break into the Democrats' headquarters, apparently in the hope of finding some politically embarrassing documents. Whether or not Nixon directly authorized the break-in, beyond question he engaged in an elaborate cover-up during which he repeatedly lied in statements on television.

An Art Buchwald column has Nixon going on television to announce that, to counter the plots to force him out of office, he has ordered a military takeover of the U.S. government. But an aide informs him, "No one is impressed. We did an overnight poll, and it turns out your credibility is so low that the people don't even buy it when you say you're taking the government over by force."[15] Yet Buchwald complained that, despite his best efforts, he could not out-satirize the reality of Watergate. He dedicated one of his books to Richard Nixon, "who provided me with more stories than any other man who ever lived in the White House … From a humorous point of view, Mr. Nixon was a perfect President. Almost everything he did after the Watergate scandal lent itself to satire." And still, "the White House kept topping me with their statements as to the President's role in this intriguing affair."[16]

Satirists from several other genres joined Buchwald. David Levine variously portrayed Nixon as a demon from *The Exorcist,* as a Godfather, and as *The Caine Mutiny*'s Captain Queeg. There was a Gore Vidal play, *An Evening with Richard Nixon,* and a film by Emile de Antonio, *Milhouse: A White Comedy.* Philip Roth's novel, *Our Gang (Starring Tricky Dick and His Friends),* has Trick E. Dixon invading Denmark, being assassinated, and campaigning against Satan to become the ruler of Hell. Later Pat Oliphant was to show Nixon planning his comeback.

After Watergate there would be no coming back for Nixon. When at last — to avoid being removed from office by Congress — Nixon became the first president in history to resign, satirists showed their delight. They saw Watergate as but one manifestation of Nixon's contempt for constitutional constraints, and the personal characteristic they had repeatedly targeted — the phoniness, the lack of authenticity — had finally been exposed and rejected.

The most common depiction by satirists of Ronald Reagan as president was as an intellectual lightweight, prone to informational gaffes. Trudeau ran a conducted tour in *Doonesbury* of "Reagan's Brain." A publication of *Ronald Reagan's Reign of Error* included a number of actual Reagan quotes, including: "As for radiation, a coal-fired plant emits more radiation than a nuclear-powered plant. You even get more from watching TV or having your teeth X-rayed."[17]

Many jokes were made about his movie background, like Bob Hope's: "He doesn't know how to lie or cheat or steal. He always had an agent for that." Beyond a joke, however, was the fact that sometimes Reagan was unable to distinguish movies from reality. For example, he apparently believed that he had photographed the liberation of Nazi death camps, though he had never been out of the country during the war and had seen the camp horrors only on film.[18]

As a communicator Reagan built a towering reputation, for his training as an actor had prepared him to make masterly major speeches. Moreover, like Lincoln and Franklin D. Roosevelt, Reagan made superb use of humor. He deflected concerns about his age and his relaxed work schedule with self-deprecatory jokes, and he was a brilliant deliverer of the American art of wisecracks. During his first television debate with challenger Walter Mondale, Reagan seemed tired, and, since he was 73, the age issue was raised against him. In the second debate he was back on top of his form and seized the opportunity to declare: "I want you to know that I will not make age an issue in this campaign. I am not going to exploit, for political purposes, my opponent's youth and inexperience." Since Mondale was in his fifties and had been an effective senator and Carter's vice-president, he was hardly too young and inexperienced. But Mondale could only sit and laugh at the joke on himself, and see his slim hopes of unseating Reagan disappear.

Yet even as a communicator Reagan was vulnerable to satire, for when he was not delivering a set speech or a previously rehearsed riposte, his lack of knowledge often betrayed him. So his press conferences, like Eisenhower's, sometimes had to be followed by corrections by his staff.

Then there were Reagan's economic policies. With his election in 1980 the tide turned against government interference with business. Consequently, with business again in the saddle, the majority of political satirists turned their attention to the political policies favoring business corporations and the wealthy at the expense of less advantaged groups. The least advantaged of all were the poor, of course, and cartoonists portrayed Reagan's business-dominated policies as a kind of ruthless social Darwinism, with the poor as the victims.

Art Buchwald quoted Reagan's comment on unemployment in which he stated that he'd read 24 pages of "Help Wanted" ads in the *Washington Post*. Buchwald pointed this out to an unemployed man, who said he couldn't afford to buy the *Washington Post*, and anyway he wouldn't qualify for advertised positions as a research specialist on aerospace high-tension materials or as a neurosurgeon in Saudi Arabia.[19]

There was abundant satirical material, too, in the charges of "sleaze" resulting from the symbiotic links between private companies and members of the Reagan administration; in the collapse of the savings and loan industry leading to indictments and convictions of industry leaders; and in Reagan's business-friendly environmental policies.

On foreign policy, the satirists depicted him during his first term as an inflexible ideologue, denouncing the Soviets in movie script terms as an "Evil Empire," from whom we must be protected by a "Star Wars" anti-missile shield. On the Iran-Contra affair, satirists had to struggle to find ways of matching the absurdity of the clandestine sale of arms to Iran by agents of the Reagan administration to provide a secret source of funds for the "Contras" fighting to overthrow the Nicaraguan regime.

By the end of his eight years in office, the harshness of the satire directed at Reagan had eased considerably. He had softened his environmental policies. He had worked out a remarkable nuclear deal with Mikhail Gorbachev that signaled the end of the Cold War, and satirists had always found it difficult to harbor a personal distaste for a man so likeable and humorous. Still, there was enough sharp satire of Reagan in the White House to question the common verdict that his was a "Teflon Presidency," largely untouched by criticism.

Bill Clinton, unlike Nixon, was outgoing and affable, and unlike Reagan, he was unquestionably bright and deeply informed on a wide range of issues. Nonetheless, while personally popular with the media, he was subjected from the outset of his presidency to a steady stream of satire that, in his second term, was to increase to a raging torrent.

Always there had hung over his political career the sense that he was "Slick Willy," an opportunist lacking a moral compass. During the presidential campaign, word about his calculated efforts to avoid the Vietnam draft did not sit well with the image of a man who was to become the nation's commander-in-chief. As president he provided further evidence that he was driven primarily by political advantage, for, after a series of failed proposals on gays in the military and health care, followed by the Democrats' loss of their majority in the House of Representatives, Clinton turned abruptly to the right. His policies on balancing the budget and welfare reform were variations on traditional conservative themes, and cartoons on welfare programs showed Republicans and Democrats no longer attacking each other but joining in an onslaught on the poor.

Yet the changed direction, opportunistic or not, worked. The economy boomed, the stock market soared, and Clinton seemed to be on course to become one of the more successful presidents. But it was not to be.

Right-wing forces launched a nationwide vendetta fuelled by lavish funds from wealthy donors. First they succeeded in securing an official investigation of alleged financial shenanigans in Arkansas by Bill and Hillary Clinton, directed by the deeply conservative Kenneth Starr as the dubiously "Independent Prosecutor." When he was unable to secure any indictments, Starr turned his attention to allegations about Clinton's sexual philandering, which had dogged him during his Arkansas years. It was this issue, involving tangled charges of sexual harassment and perjury, that came close to destroying his presidency.

Clinton was far from the first president to have engaged in extramarital sex. Jefferson, we now know, fathered one of his slave's children. Grover Cleveland, accused of fathering a child out of wedlock, was taunted during a reelection campaign by opposition crowds jeering, "Ma, ma, where's my Pa?" (To which his supporters replied, "Gone to the White House, ha, ha, ha!") Harding, Franklin Roosevelt, and Eisenhower were all reputed to have had clandestine affairs.

Compared with Kennedy, Clinton was practically an ascetic. Kennedy as president engaged repeatedly in sexual liaisons in the White House with, among others, his wife's press secretary, two White House secretaries ("Fiddle and Faddle" to the insiders), a White House intern (who couldn't type), the mistress of a Mafia boss, and various "Hollywood stars and starlets and call girls paid by Dave Powers, the court jester and facilitator of Kennedy's indulgencies, who arranged trysts in hotels and swimming pools in California, Florida, and the White House."[20]

None of this was mentioned in the mainstream media,[21] nor was there a single published cartoon on the subject. Certainly some members of the Washington press knew what was going on, but in addition to Kennedy's enormous popularity with the press — whose members thoroughly enjoyed his witty ripostes to their questions — there was then an unspoken understanding that a president's sexual behavior was not a suitable subject for public comment. That understanding persisted during the Johnson presidency, though Johnson, always irritated by the Kennedy glamour, insisted that he'd bedded far more women than Kennedy (many of them in his "nooky room" in the Senate during his vice-presidency).[22]

However, some crucial changes had occurred between the Kennedy–Johnson and Clinton presidencies. Gary Hart had been the clear frontrunner for the Democratic 1988 presidential nomination until, accused of philandering, he challenged the press to follow him. When they did and caught him emerging from an extramarital tryst, his quest for the nomination was over. The rules of reporting had changed. Moreover, with 24-hour television news channels and Matt Drudge bringing the style of the tabloids to the Internet, presidents could no longer assume that the press would respect their sexual privacy.

Clinton was hardly unaware of this new, uninhibitedly intrusive atmosphere. Yet his affair with an intern, Monica Lewinsky, in the Oval Office and his denial that he had ever "had sex with that woman" (apparently convincing himself that, under Arkansas rules, oral sex was not really sexual intercourse) provided lurid fodder for a massive report to Congress by Starr's office. Though Starr's links to right-wing groups and the prurient sexual detailing of his report made Starr himself a target of satirists, the episode inflicted terrible damage on the Clinton presidency. The Senate, after the House impeached him, voted not to remove him from office. But the dress containing the President's semen (saved by Lewinsky as her conclusive evidence) as well as the charges of liaisons with other women had made him a figure of ridicule.[23]

Political satirists could only embellish the obvious. The audience for political satire is usually limited; but now politics was joined by that other, universal topic of satire — sex. There was a vast outpouring of cartoons. Many were brutal, depicting a leering, lascivious Clinton.

Even those satirists who resented the conservatives' unremitting attack on Clinton's person and policies, and who believed that lying under oath to cover personal embarrassment was no ground for impeachment, could only lament his reckless lack of restraint. Paul Conrad, for example, saw him as a great president — from the waist up.

Even Clinton's foreign policy was caught up in the satirical attack on his sexual peccadilloes. There have always been suspicions that presidents sometimes engage in foreign military adventures to divert attention from uncomfortable domestic problems. The movie, *Wag the Dog,* parodied this

12·1·98 THE PHILADELPHIA INQUIRER. UNIVERSAL PRESS SYNDICATE

Bill Clinton, like Nixon, faced the possibility of being removed from office by impeachment after being elected to a second term. Unlike Nixon, he actually was impeached by the House; but then remained in office after the Senate voted in his favor. Moreover, despite the sexual scandal that led to his impeachment, his poll ratings, boosted by a strong economy, remained high. Yet his reputation had always been shadowed by the charge that he was a devious "Slick Willy"; and his slippery responses to the inescapable evidence that he had had sex with an intern in the White House are nicely captured in this cartoon by Tony Auth, editorial cartoonist for the Philadelphia Inquirer since since 1971. [AUTH (c) 1998 The Philadelphia Inquirer. Reprinted with permission of UNIVERSAL PRESS SYNDICATE. All rights reserved.]

notion. A president facing reelection is accused of molesting a visiting "fire-fly girl" in the Oval Office. His aides bring in a Hollywood producer to invent a war against Albania, existing only on television, to blanket the news until election time. So when Clinton ordered a bombing attack on terrorist bases in Afghanistan and the Sudan just two days after his being forced to confess his affair with Monica Lewinsky, it was inevitable that skeptics would cry "Wag the Dog!"

Clinton closed his presidency by rubbing salt in his own wounds with a number of presidential pardons, including one for a financier who had fled the country to avoid being indicted for tax evasion and whose ex-wife had made large contributions to Clinton campaign funds. This event provoked a *Saturday Night Live* skit in which the new president, George W. Bush, tries to make a broadcast but is repeatedly interrupted by his predecessor offering advice and distributing pardons.

Ungraceful though this final action was, it was softened for satirists by a self-parody by Clinton and his staff before the assembled media of their reluctance to leave office. "In just eight years," he told them "I've given you enough material for 20 years," and he conceded that the first year of the TV series about the presidency, *West Wing,* "got a lot better ratings than mine did."

Jay Leno responded for the media, complaining that, like other satirists, he was inconsolable: "You bought my house! You bought my car!"

Leno need not have worried. Clinton's successor would buy many houses and cars for satirists. In fact, President George W. Bush was to be the target of the most extensive barrage of satire leveled at any American political leader. In part this was because of the emergence and maturing of the new media technologies. Televised political satire, which had come of age during the Clinton presidency, was featured in a growing number of programs. And while the Internet was already part of American life in the 1990s, it was not until the first years of the twenty-first century that a majority of Americans were connected to each other and the world of politics online.

But there were other reasons for the explosion of satire directed at G.W. Bush. His presidency brought together most of the vulnerabilities that satirists had fastened on when they ridiculed previous presidents from Franklin Roosevelt onward.

They would not, of course, find in Bush's relaxed, easygoing style any parallel to the tortured, near-paranoiac personality of Richard Nixon, and there would be no Clinton-like sexual gallivanting in the Bush Oval Office. But otherwise satirists could look to their previous presidential themes, some related to his personal attributes, some to his policies, and repeat them with a new zeal.

First there were the Bushisms. Eisenhower's fumbled responses to questions from the press had already made it clear that, though eloquence is normally considered an asset in a politician, it is not a prerequisite for the American presidency. Any doubts on this were disposed of by George W. Bush.

Actually, his problem seemed to be hereditary, for the fracturing of language that came to be known as "Bushisms" were first associated not with George W. Bush but with George Herbert Walker Bush. In 1992, the editors of the *New Republic* compiled Bushisms made up of the "staccato sentences with no pronouns. The long, meandering non-sentences that reverse course or get lost completely halfway through. The fractured syntax. The weird mixed metaphors and non sequiturs."[24] For example:

And I would say to those around the country, "Take a hard look now. Don't let that rabbit be pulled out of the hat by one hand and 25 other rabbits dumped on you in another."[25]

As he himself said: "Fluency in English is something that I'm often not accused of." Dana Carvey, on *Saturday Night Live,* and *The Capitol Steps* feasted on this lack of fluency.

George W. Bush carried on this family tradition of malapropisms with an equally bizarre, and much more extended, crop of Bushisms, including:

> They want the federal government controlling Social Security like it's some kind of federal program.

> More and more of our imports come from overseas.

> Rarely is the question asked: is our children learning?

> Our enemies ... never stop thinking about new ways to harm our country and our people, and neither do we.

> They misunderestimated me.[26]

Though the Bushisms stopped appearing on the Internet after 9/11, they resumed within a few months with no decline in the number of examples. Trudeau's *Doonesbury* provided an update every April, "The Year in Bushisms." The Internet also carried a profusion of Web sites, including *georgewbush.com* (as distinguished from the official *GeorgeWBush.com*), in which Bush's mangled language was incessantly under attack. Bushisms provided ample material, too, for Christmas gifts popular among Democrats: a daily tear-off calendar and a talking doll. On *Saturday Night Live* Will Ferrell's impersonation of George W. Bush's semantic fumbling took up where Dana Carvey had left the father.

Bush worked hard to defuse the ridicule by satirizing his own garbled performances. At the 2001 White House Correspondents dinner he declared, "In my sentences I go where no man has gone before." He recalled some of his gaffes: "I know the human being and the fish can coexist peacefully ... You see, anyone can give you a coherent sentence. But this takes you to an entirely new dimension." And: "I understand small business growth. I was one ... I don't have the slightest idea what I was saying." (However, the tactic has to be used with care. At the annual Radio-TV Correspondents' Dinner in 2004 Bush pretended to be looking for weapons of mass destruction under cabinets and desks in the Oval Office. When this hit the cable news programs, there were protests from families of troops in Iraq. Bush stood accused of the same offense commonly hurled at satirists: tastelessness.)

Bushisms were only one aspect of the charge that George W. Bush was an intellectual lightweight. Like Reagan, said the critics, Bush was hopelessly ignorant of world affairs. *National Lampoon* had him responding to a Colin Powell proposal for the creation of a Palestinian state in the Mideast, and finding himself unable to see "how we could possibly squeeze in a state for the Palestinians anywhere in the mideast given how closely packed together Virginia, Maryland and Delaware are."[27]

Even *National Lampoon* could not have contrived an instance of Bush's intellectual limitations to compare with his response to a question by a TV interviewer on why he hadn't demanded more wartime sacrifices of the people other than the troops and their families. Bush pondered, then insisted that the people do indeed sacrifice. They "sacrifice peace of mind when they see the terrible images of violence on TV every night."

Like Reagan, who had been derided for working a four-day week and taking an afternoon nap, George W. Bush was no workaholic, and satirists scorned him for taking long and frequent vacations. When he was slow in returning from vacation to address the disastrous Katrina hurricane in August 2005, he was subjected to a barrage of ridicule. A *New Yorker* cover had Bush and his cabinet sitting haplessly in the Oval Office almost inundated by rising waters.[28]

Just as there had been satire directed at Franklin Roosevelt's upper-class heritage in reaching the presidency, so now satirists could hardly ignore the close proximity in the presidential succession of the two Bushes. While the first Bush had come to the office with an impressive background in the highest levels of public service, his son had a far more limited political experience. This, together with his personal shortcomings, created an impression seized on by satirists of a man promoted far beyond his intelligence and capabilities through his family money and connections.

After Bush's election in 2000 a transatlantic assessment appeared on-line.[29] It began:

> To the citizens of the United States of America. In the light of your failure to elect a competent President of the USA and thus to govern yourselves, we hereby give notice of the revocation of your independence, effective today. Her sovereign Majesty Queen Elizabeth II will resume monarchical duties over all states, commonwealths and other territories. Except Utah, which she does not fancy.

Bush's various idiosyncrasies provided satirists with an exceptionally easy target. By portraying him as an incoherent, incompetent fool, they could invite us to treat him with disdain, even contempt.

But his policies are another matter. However much we may disagree with a president's programs, they are never the products of one person alone. In this case Vice President Dick Cheney, political adviser Karl Rove, Defense Secretary Donald Rumsfeld, and the administration's cabal of "neoconservatives" were all deeply involved in the decision-making process. They might be criticized as terribly mistaken, ruthless, and blinded by ideology, but they could not, like the president, be dismissed as uninformed, inarticulate, and indolent.

Much of the policy satire, therefore, was more serious, cut deeper, and was angrier in tone than jokes about the personal quirks of the president. Some of it was directed at others in the administration. In fact, Vice President Cheney became the satirical target of the week when he accidentally shot a close friend and political donor standing behind him during a quail hunt in February 2006. But long before this mishap (compounded when the unfortunate victim actually apologized) satirists had lampooned him for being the real power behind the throne. Rumsfeld, too, was a favorite target of the satirists, who were consequently among the very few regretting his resignation after the 2006 midterm elections.

Yet, whether or not, as Bush has claimed, "I'm the decider," the record is that of *his* presidency, and satirists have fastened their biting wit on his policies as the product ultimately of the president himself. As was true of his personal traits, much of the satire echoed themes directed at earlier presidents.

Thus, Bush's economic policies were reminiscent of the Reagan years. Aaron McGruder's *Boondocks* has Bush addressing critics who say his policies favor the rich: "Everyone knows that the poor will receive all the infinite gifts of heaven after they die. I don't know why they can't be satisfied with that and stop being so greedy here on earth."[30]

Bush's tax cuts included the abolition of estate taxes; and if he succeeded in his plan to end them permanently it would further increase the already significant role of inherited wealth in America.

As many satirists saw it, this policy tilt toward the affluent classes was also reminiscent of the Reagan administration's cosy relationship with the top executives in American business, but on an even more egregious scale. In 2002, it was revealed that the CEOs and other top leaders of business corporations and auditing firms were manipulating their accounts to hide serious financial problems, in some cases selling their stocks and clearing millions of dollars just before the stocks plummeted and destroying the pension plans of their employees. Prime targets were WorldCom and other companies that had suffered massive losses while their CEOs made huge gains, and most especially Enron, a Texas energy corporation. Enron had close ties to members of the administration, including President Bush himself, to whom the company's CEO, Kenneth Lay, was "Kenny boy."

Molly Ivins, whose columns and books had flayed "the shrub" from his days as governor of Texas, was enthralled by this affair:

I love the Enron scandal. Did you know that Enron's board of directors twice voted to suspend its own ethics code in order to create private partnerships? Wasn't that thoughtful of them? If they hadn't voted to suspend the ethics code, they would have been in violation of it. Why didn't we think of that?[31]

"Now, now ... we have to get used to wearing this stuff in case
the inheritance tax gets repealed."

One of the principles on which the United States was founded was the rejection of an
inherited aristocracy. So when Congress passed a tax bill early in the George W.
Bush presidency eliminating the inheritance tax—a penalty paid by little more than
one per cent of taxpayers—it was inevitable that critics would protest. The tax was
to phase out in 2010, and Senate filibusters prevented its permanent repeal. In this
cartoon Bruce Beattie suggests the social consequences of a permanent repeal for
an America in which there is already a wide gulf between the top and bottom of
the income and wealth scales. Bruce Beattie, Dayton Beach News-Journal. Copely News.

For a while, said Ivins, we have been living in "The United States of
Enron."[32] Maureen Dowd went further, describing a "Planet Enron...a
planet of the privileged," in which the atmosphere was "so rarefied that its
inhabitants were blissfully oblivious to how privileged they were." Only
when the scandal had set off massive public outrage had Bush, "distancing
himself light-years...ordered the U.S. government to look into cutting off
all business with the planet..."[33]

Yet all these jibes at the Bush domestic policies did not approach the
fury of the satirical onslaught on his foreign policies, especially the invasion
of Iraq.

Just as other presidents had been accused of twisting the truth in times of
war, so skepticism was called for when the Bush administration offered a
changing variety of reasons for the invasion of Iraq. The initial emphasis
was on weapons of mass destruction (WMDs). Despite the assurances of
the *New York Times* and other organs of the allegedly liberal press, the

WMDs were nowhere to be found after the conquest of Iraq, and allegations of Iraq's importing nuclear materials from Niger turned out to be based on forged documents. The government's credibility was badly damaged, and a fury of satirical resentment was unleashed.

Art Buchwald, in talking about the various causes of his depression, said: "I get depressed over the Iraq War, but my psychiatrist friends say if I weren't depressed over that I would be sick."[34] Michael Moore was offended that Bush had not even bothered to plant any WMDs. Johnson and Nixon would at least have tried to cover up their lies, said Moore, but:

> Your blatant refusal to back up your verbal deception with the kind of fake evidence we have become used to is a slap at our collective American face. It's as if you are saying, "These Americans are so apathetic and lazy, we don't have to produce any weapons to back up our claims!"[35]

On the Internet thousands received the e-mail message: "NO ONE DIED WHEN CLINTON LIED." Cartoon after cartoon excoriated the Pentagon for the gross treatment of Iraqi prisoners at the Abu Ghraib compound in Iraq and the CIA for "outsourcing" interrogations to countries known to use torture as well as maintaining its own network of prisons in several other countries. Amnesty International took out a magazine ad headed: "The U.S. has learned the benefits of outsourcing certain jobs. Torture, for example."

Cartoonists attacking the war far outnumbered those rallying to its defense. Satirical magazines, columnists, TV comedians, and innumerable authors of blogs, joined in the assault, as did rock performers Eminem, the Rolling Stones, and Neil Young. E-mails were crowded with anti-Bush and antiwar jokes. In 2003, in cities in America and other countries, women demonstrated their hostility to the expected war by readings of Aristophanes' *Lysistrata* (though it is not recorded that they followed the example of the women in the play by withholding sex from their husbands until the war was ended). As more and more commentators drew analogies between Iraq and Vietnam, one cartoon showed Bush gradually morphing into Lyndon Johnson.[36]

A connection to Bush's domestic policies was seen in the profits made from the war by American corporations. In particular, the postwar contracts given to the former company of Vice President Cheney were an irresistible target for *Saturday Night Live,* which lauded "the brave Halliburton executives that stormed Baghdad."

Moreover, satirists tied some of their main war themes back to the personal attributes of George W. Bush. Like other presidents, Bush enjoyed creating a strong, martial impression, landing on an aircraft carrier in full airman's regalia after the initial occupation of Baghdad under a sign

There is no more unremitting critic of George W. Bush and the Iraq War than G. B. Trudeau. Through his "Doonesbury" comic strip he has symbolized Bush first as an intellectual lightweight—a feather, then an empty Texas hat—and finally as the mock warrior, conveyed by a Roman centurion's helmet. In this strip the warrior responds to the media's questions about a time-table for leaving Iraq with his usual hopelessly garbled responses. [DOONESBURY (c) 2007 G.B. Trudeau. Reprinted with permission of UNIVERSAL PRESS SYNDICATE. All rights reserved.]

declaring "Mission Accomplished!" This was unfortunate not only because it proved to be profoundly premature, but also because it encouraged satirists to draw attention to the fact that Bush had chosen to serve at home in the Texas National Guard rather than see active service in Vietnam. His cause was not helped when a colonel who had served with him in the National Guard insisted that "we were answering 3 AM scrambles for who-knows-what inbound threat over the shark-filled Gulf of Mexico."

A Bush action doll, complete with airman's uniform, became a popular derisory gift. In *Doonsebury* the symbol for Bush had previously been a feather wafting in the breeze, then an empty Texas hat; now it became a Roman centurion's helmet.

Then there was the connection to Bush's religiosity. Domestically this was an important part of his appeal to the Republican base of religious fundamentalists. Internationally, he followed the example of Woodrow Wilson and other former presidents in invoking the Deity to justify their policies. While insisting that he was not declaring a Christian war against Muslims, he believed he was called to the presidency to do God's work. General William Boykin, a deputy undersecretary of defense for intelligence, went further: "George Bush was not elected by a majority of voters in the United States. He was appointed by God." Boykin, who saw the Muslim world as a satanic force, declared from a pulpit that a dark mark appearing on a photograph he took from a helicopter over Mogadishu, Somalia, after 18 Americans had been killed there, was not a blemish on the photo, but in fact, " the principalities of darkness . . . a demonic spirit over Mogadishu." Satirists could not compete with the reality. An online satirical journal could only suggest he was "a bit daft," a "General Strangelove" of our time.[37] Boykin remained in the government.

Finally, the criticism that America, launched on a never-ending war against terrorism and contaminated by the arrogance of power, reached a new level during the Bush years. In satirical columns and cartoons came the suggestion that Bush, even more than Nixon, was using the terrorist threat to override the clear provisions of the Constitution. So Garry Trudeau asked, "Which president should be impeached? The one who had an affair with an intern? Or the other who subverted the Constitution?"

In the international context, as the concept of an American Empire, albeit without the formal apparatus of colonialism, appeared in several books and articles, satirists leapt on the idea of Bush asserting the imperial view as a war leader. Ted Rall presented him in a demented version as Generalissimo el Busho.

For cartoonists abroad, however, Bush simply did not fit the image of Emperor or Generalissimo, and they changed the analogy to that of a Texas gunslinger, contemptuous of any country that did not meekly follow America's instructions.

As *the Onion* headline put it:

Bush Seeks U.N. Support for "U.S. Does Whatever It Wants" Plan[38]

UNFAIR TO PRESIDENTS

Of course, this is all extremely unfair. Overwhelmingly these satirical examples present a distorted picture, overstating failures and ignoring accomplishments.

They do not take account of Johnson's Medicare program and his forcing through a Voting Rights bill despite his awareness that it would erode his party's fortunes in the South; or Nixon's environmental programs and opening to China; or Carter's brokering of peace between Israel and Egypt; or the elder Bush's forging an alliance that won the Gulf War. And so on.

With respect to the presidents' personal qualities, we now know that Eisenhower was much more involved and knowledgeable than it appeared while he was in office. On Reagan, Harvard psychologist Howard Gardner has suggested that though he might not do well on the kind of analytical intelligence measured by IQ and SAT tests there are other kinds of intelligence, and Reagan possessed formidable interpersonal and language intelligences. As for George W. Bush, even the persistent Bush critic, Molly Ivins, has conceded that he is not stupid, "but he's smart on a very narrow bandwidth." So perhaps he was misunderestimated.[39]

These are all reasonable arguments. Yet there is no shortage of courtiers to trumpet the accomplishments of presidents or of historians to give us a balanced view. Satirists have a different function. Their focus on the deficiencies of presidents — unfair though it must be by the very nature of satire — performs a necessary and proper service. It acts as a protection against abuses of power, lapses in integrity, and failures by presidents to carry out the promises they made so blithely when they were elected.

chapter two

CENSORSHIP, AMERICAN STYLE

> We're the land of the free; speak your mind as you may!
> But in wartime, we're told, better watch what you say!
> And even in peacetime, don't let them detect
> A hint you're politically not quite correct.

Apparently American satirists have a considerable degree of freedom in hurling disrespectful abuse at presidents.

Thus, Lyndon Johnson couldn't do anything about his portrayal as Kennedy's murderer in *MacBird!* and the *New York Times* drama critic's speculation that the play "may even be suppressed by some government agency" proved to be nonsense.

When Nixon had Paul Conrad placed on his "enemies list," whose purpose was to punish dissenters by subjecting them to the scrutiny of the IRS and other government agencies, Conrad took this move as a badge of honor and made a cartoon out of it.

While the annual White House Correspondents' Dinners[1] provide presidents with an opportunity to display their own (or their scriptwriter's) wit, they must also be good sports and submit to being roasted by professional comedians. Usually the roasting is amiable, but TV satirist Stephen Colbert's commentary in 2006 was more sharp-edged than was customary, and Bush's smile wore thin. Yet Bush must not show his displeasure too obviously, and there was no evidence that Colbert's career suffered.[2] (However, the White House took no chances the following year. They chose the longtime presidential impersonator, Rich Little, who indicated that he would not "even mention the word 'Iraq.'")

Does this mean that satirists face no constraints on their work? Not quite.

Mort Sahl, for example, has charged that he was bullied by the Kennedys, especially the president's father, and that this severely damaged his career as a performer. Sahl had lampooned Eisenhower and Nixon, and for a while worked for Kennedy as one of his scriptwriters. When he began to introduce quips about Kennedy into his routine, he was told: "You're not loyal, the Old Man said you're not loyal." He responded by increasing his Kennedy jokes and saying: "You're trying to tell me that the man who faced the Cuban missile crisis and the problems of the Berlin Wall is worried about a

His Own Worst Enemy

Cartoonist and sculptor Paul Conrad roasted every contemporary American president during his tenure as chief editorial cartoonist for the *Los Angeles Times* from 1964 to 1993. None aroused his ire more than Richard Nixon, who tried to hit back by putting Conrad on his notorious "enemies list" of citizens subject to a variety of federal investigations. But it was Conrad who had the last word on who was the real enemy. [CONartist: Paul Conrad 30 Years With the *Los Angeles Times* (Los Angeles Times, 1993), 46.]

nightclub comedian. I find that hard to accept, even with my ego." He claims he was then told: "The ambassador (Joseph Kennedy) says if you don't cooperate, you'll never work again in the United States," after which the work began to dry up, and he was dropped by his agent.[3]

Satirists may have to face protective coverage for presidents from the owners or editors of media outlets. For example, the *Los Angeles Times* refused to carry a *Doonesbury* series on alleged sleaze in the Reagan administration, and other papers cancelled the *Doonesbury* derisive tour through "Reagan's Brain."[4] Again, corporate interests intervened in the 1980s, when Detroit and Miami newspapers, seeking favorable operating agreements from Reagan's Attorney General, Ed Meese, turned down cartoons criticizing Meese.

Moreover, in America as in all societies, there are a number of taboos — near-sacred beliefs and attitudes — and challenging them, as satirists will, arouses strong resentments. These taboos may be reinforced by both official and unofficial pressures: presidents through speeches, press conferences, and executive agencies like the U.S. Federal Communications Commission; congressional laws and investigations, which rarely challenge the prevailing standards of taste and propriety; business organizations through industry-wide regulators, such as the Hays Office established in 1934 to monitor the movies; newspaper advertisers and TV and radio sponsors, watching closely over media content to ensure it doesn't threaten the commercial climate in general and their products in particular;[5] and organized constituencies speaking for a great range of interests, who launch avalanches of complaints when they believe that their constituencies have been slighted.

These pressures, sometimes separately but more often in combination, have imposed restraints on satire, especially as satirists have mocked prevailing attitudes on wartime patriotism, sex, religion, ethnicity, and race. As we'll see, however, the intensity of these restraints has changed markedly over the years as public attitudes in America have evolved.

PATRIOTIC GORE

Wartime is when presidents are at their most powerful. It is also when satirists who oppose the war run up against widespread aversion to their jibes. Yet every war has also generated protest and an audience for satire, and the extent to which satire has been inhibited by mass opinion and the censor has varied from war to war.

The Philippine War

After the 1898 Spanish-American war, critics and satirists were angered by a three-year colonial war against a Philippine insurrection. Striking back against ferocious guerrilla attacks, American forces burned villages, gunned down men, women, and children, shot up a wedding party, and resorted to torture.[6]

Mark Twain spoke out against the war in essays, speeches, and interviews.[7] While he would rally to the flag if the country's existence were threatened, it was very different

> when there is no question that the nation is in any way in danger, but only some little war away off, it may be that on the question of politics the nation is divided, half patriot and half traitors, and no man can tell which from which.[8]

Even in the aftermath of the war he recognized that his views were abhorrent to many Americans. Consider *The War Prayer*,[9] in which Twain tells of a church service the day before the battalions leave for the front. The preacher offers an impassioned prayer that the Almighty protect our noble young soldiers and help them crush the foe. The prayer is interrupted by an ancient robed stranger who takes the preacher's place and says he bears a message from God — that their prayer will be granted if they are sure they understand that what they were asking for contained an "unspoken part of the prayer."

> O lord our God, help us to tear their soldiers to bloody shreds with our shells; help us to cover their smiling fields with the pale forms of their patriot dead; help us to drown the thunder of the guns with the shrieks of their wounded, writhing in pain; help us to lay waste their humble homes with a hurricane of fire...We ask it, in the spirit of love, of Him Who is the Source of Love ... Amen."

It was believed afterward that the man was a lunatic, because there was no sense in what he said.

The *War Prayer* was written in 1905, but not published until 1916 — before America entered World War I. Undoubtedly it would have caused a furor in 1905.

World War I

Once America had entered the war, satirists, if they were to ply their trade at all, were expected to do it as part of the war effort. Cartoonists were encouraged to join the government-sponsored Bureau of Cartoons, whose patriotic task was to "inspire in every man a keen sense of his obligation to the cause of democracy and stimulate public opinion as few other forces in this country can."[10]

A few cartoonists defied the pressure and insisted on taking a strong anti-war stand, but they came up against powerful resistances. Robert Minor drew cartoons for the *New York Herald* on the theme that the conflict was for the benefit of banking and business interests. He continued to do so as long as the paper opposed the war; but when the *Herald* switched to supporting the war, Minor was fired. He also worked for the socialist *Masses*, along with Art Young and other radical cartoonists, but the *Masses* was no safe haven. Young and four other members of the magazine were indicted by the government under the 1917 Espionage Act, which made it a crime to say or write anything opposed to the war, and Young's cartoons were specifically cited. The trials ended in hung juries, but *Masses* went under (though it was later reincarnated as *New Masses*).

The wartime atmosphere persisted as Attorney General A. Mitchell Palmer, fearful that the 1917 Russian Revolution would spread to America, ordered a series of raids on radicals and anarchists between 1918 and 1921 that led to arrests, jail sentences, and deportations. Humorist Robert Benchley mocked Palmer with a satirical tale of a conventional, patriotic supporter of the war, who, in a lecture on interurban highways, had opined that public improvements generally did better in peacetime than in wartime — and found himself included in a newspaper story under the blaring headline: "PRO-GERMAN LIST BARED BY ARMY SLEUTH."[11] But no satirist could outdo the purple prose of Palmer's own warning that "tongues of revolutionary heat were licking the alters of the churches, leaping into the belfry of the school bell, crawling into the sacred corners of American homes, seeking to replace marriage vows with libertine laws, burning up the foundations of society."[12]

World War II

As the war clouds gathered again, Charlie Chaplin announced his plans for a movie lampooning Hitler, *The Great Dictator*. The German government tried to bring pressure to bear. So did the British, fearing that their appeasement of Hitler would be undermined. Chaplin ignored the pressures, the war had broken out by the time it was finished, and the film opened to international acclaim — other than the bans imposed in Germany, Japan, Spain, Peru, Ireland, and the city of Chicago, which didn't want to offend its large German population.

During the war there was no need for agencies like the Bureau of Cartoonists, for most American satirists enthusiastically directed their fire at the enemy. Particularly ferocious were their depictions of Japanese troops as monkeys during the early part of the war, and later as apes. Theodore Geisel (Dr. Seuss), whose cartoons raged against the subordination of African Americans, drew demeaning renderings of all Japanese Americans as dangerous traitors and spies.

Some of the core antiwar satirical themes did appear in Joseph Heller's novel about World War II, *Catch 22*. Heller depicts the military's insistence on obedience to orders as bureaucratic, inhuman, and irrational to the point of insanity: Lieutenant Scheisskopf, discovering from his research that the hands of marchers should not swing freely but only three inches from the thigh, regretfully decides against tying their wrists to their thighs with copper wire and instead wins a competition by teaching them to march without swinging their hands.[13] The main protagonist, Yassourian, is told he must keep flying after completing his assigned limit of 40 bombing missions, decides he has had enough of glory, and eventually deserts. And Milo forms a syndicate that gleefully trades with both sides and has its own planes that could launch a sneak attack on German targets, but could also "alert the German anti-aircraft gunners in time for them to begin firing accurately the moment the planes came into range."[14]

However, the novel appeared several years after the war was over. Had it been published during the war, the debunking of military bureaucracy might have passed muster, especially among the rank-and-file troops, but an anti-hero who, at the end, deserts, and a character who manipulates the war to get rich, would have been very much out of step with the mood of the time.

The Cold War

World War II had barely ended when a tense standoff emerged between the Soviet Union and the West. Fear of the Soviets and communism loomed large in America, and limits on the free expression of political ideas were particularly severe in the early 1950s, when Senator Joe McCarthy, echoing the House Un-American Activities Committee, stigmatized anyone left of center as an agent or dupe of the international communist conspiracy.

Though a number of commentators complained that political satire had gone into remission during this era, the art was by no means defunct. There was Mort Sahl, delighting his nightclub audiences with his anti-McCarthy, anti-Eisenhower quips, and the *Second City* revue included sketches aimed at the same targets. However, much wider audiences were reached by the anti-McCarthy onslaught in cartoons by Walt Kelly, Robert Osborn, Bill Mauldin, and Herblock. Though they also directed their ridicule at the Soviet Union, they were closely watched by the FBI and subjected to economic sanctions.

Walt Kelly introduced Joe McCarthy into his *Pogo* comic strip in May 1953 as Senator Simple J. Malarkey. Some of the newspapers subscribing to *Pogo* dropped particular strips in the Malarkey series or cancelled their subscription entirely.

Bill Mauldin, whose wartime cartoons of ordinary soldiers, Willy and Joe, had been enormously popular, found that turning his attention after the war to the House Un-American Activities Committee and racism was not a smart career move. With cancellations pouring in, Mauldin wrote: "It was explained to me by the syndicate . . . that selling cartoons on a nationwide basis was big business and that it was damn poor business I was doing."[15]

At last McCarthy overreached by attacking the army, and the investigative fervor waned. Yet the confrontation with the Soviets became ever more dangerous as the stockpiles of thermo-nuclear weapons grew on both sides. Feiffer, Mauldin, Herblock, and Osborn all drew fierce warnings about the possible breakdown into the ultimate conflagration. Tom Lehrer had grisly fun with the end-of-the-world theme: "We will all fry together when we fry."[16]

The most powerful satirical expression of the danger came in Kubrick's movie, *Dr. Strangelove.* The film features an insane general, Jack D. Ripper, who orders an unauthorized nuclear attack on the Soviet Union to crush the communist plot to sap our "precious bodily fluids" through fluoridation; a

"Pogo," Walt Kelly, Hall Syndicate, May 7, 1953.

Pogo, a possum, was the lead character in a daily comic strip by Walt Kelly that was widely syndicated from 1948 to 1975. The setting was the Okefenokee Swamp that featured several animal characters who conveyed Kelly's satirical view of his world. Kelly was at his most biting when opposing the investigations of the Senate committee headed by Senator Joseph McCarthy. In this cartoon Deacon Muskrat, an unctuous preacher who has brought Simple J. Malarkey to the swamp, finds himself denied his constitutional right to protest by the sinister Malarkey. Malarky-McCarthy caused considerable anxiety among newspapers carrying Pogo, some of which dropped the sequence. [Walt Kelly "Pogo," Hall Syndicate, May 7, 1953. © OGPI. Used by permission.]

Joint Chief of Staff who argues that, if we go all out, we can win the resulting war at a manageable cost in American lives of "10 to 20 million, tops;" and the mad scientist, Dr. Strangelove himself, who claims that America could survive and win a thermo-nuclear war.[17] Despite frantic efforts to work with the Soviets in stopping the attack, one bomber, though crippled, gets through, and its captain, with a wild cowboy whoop, mounts his only remaining bomb and guides it to his target — thereby automatically setting off the Soviets' cataclysmic Doomsday Machine. As the movie ends in a thermo-nuclear Armageddon, mushroom clouds cascade across the screen, and we hear a World War II saccharin song assuring us that we'll meet again some sunny day.

The film caused considerable anxiety among its Colombia Pictures producers, and Bosley Crowther of the *New York Times* accused it of being tasteless, a scare-mongering sick joke. Others, however, received it warmly. Fortunately, Senator McCarthy was gone from the scene, and in the aftermath of the 1963 Nuclear Test Ban Treaty the satire seemed less ominous.

Korea

On the other hand, the era of the allegedly cold war encompassed some very hot confrontations between America and the communist countries. North Korea had invaded South Korea in 1950, and the United States, after securing a United Nations condemnation of the invasion, entered the war. The war dragged on, becoming intensely unpopular, and a prime target for satirists was the struggle for supremacy between the president and the commander of the United Nations forces, General Douglas MacArthur, pictured by some cartoonists as a strutting megalomaniac but by others as a magnetic hero, a giant towering over the diminutive Truman.

There was a very different kind of satire depicting the Korean war as it was fought not by the generals but by the ordinary GIs: *M*A*S*H*, a movie and then a long-running television program, featured a medical team keeping itself sane by gossiping, wisecracking, and flirting, as they worked to stem the flow of blood from a never-ending succession of dreadfully wounded soldiers. In fact, however, though the setting of the series was the Korean War, the movie appeared in 1970, 17 years after the end of the Korean War, and the TV series ran from 1972 to 1983. Thus, the war in Vietnam and Cambodia was still in progress during the early years of the television program, and Larry Gelbart, the principal writer for *M*A*S*H*, has made it clear that Vietnam was very much on the minds of the program's creators and audience.

Vietnam

The prevailing mood of M*A*S*H was antiwar. If the medics showed distress at the death of a patient, their colonel pointed out there are only two rules about war: "Rule 1: Young men die. Rule 2: Doctors can't change Rule 1."[18] Most of the lead characters — Hawkeye, B. J. Honeycutt, Radar, Klinger — were profoundly casual and antimilitaristic, whereas Frank, the stickler for discipline and formality, was an inept clown.

"To its credit, CBS never once asked us to tone down the political content of the show or deemphasize the humanism we tried to emphasize,"[19] said Gelbart; and though the network's euphemistically named Department of

Program Practices sometimes registered discomfort with political references, the only censorship actually imposed related to expletives and sex.

One critic has suggested that *M*A*S*H* was far from radical. Rather than addressing "the militarism and bureaucratic irrationality of an imperial superpower," the show emphasized "universal values — helping others in need, recognizing the commonality of the human condition, and preferring peace and life over war and death."[20] Yet it is surely a testimonial to the persistence of its writers and performers, as well as the temper of the times, that week after week a sitcom on commercial television provided witty putdowns of military bureaucracy, McCarthy-like loyalty investigations, and a pervasive preference for "peace and life over war and death."

Tommy Smothers, of the *Smothers Brothers* TV series, was less sanguine than Gelbart about the freedom to satirize the Vietnam War on TV. "Nixon came in," he said, "and we were off. We were thrown off the air because of our viewpoint on Vietnam."[21] Otherwise, once the American public had turned decisively against the Vietnam War, there were few effective constraints on the explosion of antiwar satire, which even invaded the army newspaper, *Stars and Stripes,* through the Doonsebury comic strip. The army dropped the strip in 1973, but it was soon reinstated after a flood of protests from readers.

9/11

A dramatic illustration of wartime's stultifying impact on satire came on September 11, 2001. Though there was at the time no formal declaration of war, the Bush administration announced that we were, in fact, engaged in a long-term war against terrorism. So profound was the shock of this first attack on the American mainland since the war for independence that criticism was essentially suspended, and satire abandoned.

This, according to Attorney General John Ashcroft, was entirely proper. Critics of the government "only aid terrorists" and "give ammunition to America's enemies." Since the war was expected to continue indefinitely, the prospect for critics was gloomy indeed.

New legislation, the Patriot Act, was passed, suspending some of the rights of individuals accused of terrorist activities. President Bush's ratings, which had been slipping, now soared to almost unprecedented levels. Flags flew everywhere. Patriotism surged. Football commentators avoided their usual language of violence and mayhem. Pop music songs about planes, explosions, and death were put aside.

Over and over columnists declared that "nihilistic irony" was out. Most cartoonists seemed to agree; putting aside their usual jibes, several of them drew a weeping Statue of Liberty. Mike Luckovich of the *Atlanta Journal-Constitution* changed his depiction of President Bush.

It's not going to be the little tiny guy with the gigantic ears that I have been drawing . . . our patriotism comes first. The president is our president and we want him to be successful, and this trumps all the other stuff we've been hammering him about."[22]

Said a *Saturday Night Live* writer:

For a decent number of weeks we'd test the waters in dress rehearsal with your basic, straightforward "Bush isn't that smart" joke, and it would always get a decidedly negative response, so we had to toss it out.[23]

A *Comedy Central* show, *That's My Bush,* was pulled off the air. The satirical weekly, *Onion,* suspended publication. Another weekly, *Modern Humorist,* abandoned its satire for the time being at least:

Understandably some of you might not want to think about comedy right now. We hope, though, that you will eventually return. Our comedy serves two functions: escapism and satire. Satire — our means of mocking the news and our leaders — may not feel as appropriate now, but escape is needed more than ever.[24]

A few satirists who cut against the grain felt the pressure. In a discussion on Bill Maher's television show, *Politically Incorrect,* Maher said that, while suicidal hijackers are wicked, he could not agree with the common assertion that they are cowardly; whereas it is cowardly for the United States to launch cruise missiles against targets thousands of miles away. The station was inundated with outraged protests. Ari Fleischer, the president's press secretary, observed that Americans "need to watch what they say." Maher apologized profusely, but advertisers cancelled and *Politically Incorrect* went off the air.

In Aaron McGruder's *Boondocks* comic strip on Thanksgiving Day 2001, its character Huey Freeman offered a satirical prayer giving thanks that we were not led by "the spoiled son of a powerful politician from a wealthy oil family who is supported by religious fundamentalists" and who has no respect for democracy and civil liberties. Some newspapers refused to carry the strip.

When, nearly five months after the tragedy, the *Concord Monitor*'s Mike Marland drew a cartoon of the President flying a "Bush Budget" plane into twin towers labeled "Social" and "Security," the resulting uproar led to an apology by the editor and then by Marland himself, who said he should have listened to his wife's counsel not to run the cartoon.[25]

In a gathering of comedians at the New York Friars' Club on September 29, 2001, roasting the guest of honor, Hugh Heffner, comedian Gilbert Gottfried joked: "I have a flight to California. I can't get a direct flight. They said they have to stop at the Empire State Building first." Amidst the boos and hisses a voice called out "Too soon!" Quickly Gottfried changed course and found a safe haven in the Friars' Club specialty — a dirty joke. The mood changed immediately. The audience howled with laughter.[26]

It was indeed too soon for Empire State Building jokes, yet the chilling effect on satire gradually weakened. The totemic standing of the calamity and its impact on political attitudes remained, and there was overwhelmingly support for the subsequent attack on Afghanistan. Even so, the prime political beneficiary of these events, the Bush administration, did not succeed for very long in uniting the country behind its policies. The simmering resentment of a substantial segment of the public at Bush's disputed election was intensified by his tax and environmental programs at home and his cavalier, even contemptuous, attitude toward the international community. Protests grew against the post-9/11 antiterrorist legislation and the repressive tone of some administration leaders.

So satire began to find its way back. *Onion,* in fact, resumed publication after a week, irreverent as ever about the president and his administration. Under the headlines, "U.S. Vows to Defeat Whoever We're at War With," and "Security Beefed up at Cedar Rapids Public Library," the magazine attributed to Attorney General Ashcroft the decisive comment that, "To whoever did this, wherever you are, I say to you: Justice will be served, swiftly and hopefully."[27] Other satirists followed, tentatively at first, then with increasing enthusiasm.

As one gag-writer commented:

> It seems the time that elapses between catastrophes and the comic takes on them grows shorter and shorter. It took almost 100 years for jokes to emerge about Lincoln's assassination — as in "What did you think of the play, Mrs. Lincoln?" — and less than a decade about John F. Kennedy's death."[28]

Bill Maher returned to television with a program on a cable station. For Aaron McGruder's *Boondocks,* 9/11 provoked a harsher, more sharply political tone. It brought home to him

> how valuable that little piece of real estate in the newspapers had become when the so-called free press lost their minds and started censoring themselves ... and I made the decision that I would use my little space to scream out louder against the great injustices the United States government was about to unleash upon the planet."[29]

A *New Yorker* cartoon showed an ad in the window of a bookstore proclaiming "Now With 50% Less Irony."[30] Apparently the announcements of the death of irony were premature.

Iraq[31]

When the attack on Iraq began most of the American public rallied around the flag and behind the troops in the field. Media correspondents were embedded with the troops, themselves becoming part of the action. Jokes on television were mostly patriotic. Saddam Hussein was the standard butt of jokes, and comedians and their audiences were convulsed by the Saddam spokesman who kept insisting that American troops had been hurled back from the approaches to Baghdad even as they took over the city. Conservative satirists made their case for the war and against the United Nations, Michael Ramirez showing a series of ineffectual UN resolutions imprinted on a roll of toilet paper.[32]

Those who were not for us were against us, so the French became popular targets. In the congressional cafeteria Republicans renamed French fries "patriot fries." On *The Simpsons* the French became "cheese-eating surrender monkeys." *Fox*'s Bill O'Reilly told critics that it was their patriotic duty to "shut up."

Mike Luckovich, an editorial cartoonist for the *Atlanta Journal-Constitution* since 1989, had been unsparing in his lampooning of George W. Bush—until September 2001, after which, Luckovich said, humor was out of place. Four years later, however, he was aroused to bitter wit in this cartoon painstakingly incorporating the names of every one of the 2,000 American soldiers who had then been killed in the Iraq War—a figure which was to double by the spring of 2008. [Mike Luckovich, *Atlanta Journal-Constitution*, October, 26, 2005. By permission of Mike Luckovich and Creators Syndicate, Inc.).]

Yet very quickly the predisposition of a large part of the American public to be deeply suspicious of Bush's policies took over. There had been clamorous opposition to his decision to act without UN approval. As a result, once the initial fighting was over, a flood of satire burst forth in every medium. In fact, as noted earlier, it came on an unprecedented scale in every medium from newspaper columns and cartoons to the Internet and street protests.

Conservatives were resentful. When Trudeau's *Doonesbury* included a strip listing the names of all the U.S. dead in Iraq, they accused him of using their names for his personal profit and pressured newspapers not to carry the strip. A few complied; most did not. Mike Luckovich, who had called for a time-out on anti-Bush satire after 9/11, drew a cartoon in November 2005 on the same theme.

Michael Moore's antiwar documentary satire, *Fahrenheit 9/11,* initially ran into a problem when its producer, Miramax, a Disney company, decided not to distribute it. This decision generated a great burst of publicity for the film, and Moore quickly found other distributors. *Fahrenheit 9/11* became the highest-grossing documentary in movie history. Bitter attacks on the movie appeared on an anti-Moore Web site and elsewhere. A Ramirez cartoon showed Mr. USA, tired of watching reality programs, asking for "something that has nothing to do with reality." His wife's answer: "How about a Michael Moore film?"[33] But anti-Moore groups failed to generate support for censorship. Claiming that the movie distorted the truth by taking facts and statements out of context and used crude cinematic tricks to distort reality, they launched an Internet campaign to pressure theater owners not to show the film. The president of a national theater owners' group rejected the pressure: "Exhibitors, as a whole, are probably more conservative than Hollywood, as a whole, but they're also believers in the First Amendment . . . "[34]

Evidently, wartime censorship of satire today is not as intrusive as it used to be, particularly in the case of unpopular wars like Vietnam and Iraq. Yet some of the other examples remind us that in the atmosphere generated by wars, satirists will have to contend with the hostility not only of the administration and the military but also of a large segment of the public. For satirists are bringing into question widely admired values and rituals, and mocking them requires strong convictions and considerable tenacity. It is safer in such times to turn the satiric weapons against the nation's enemies and to win plaudits by demonstrating that all the cruelty and barbarism is on the other side, never on one's own.

SEX: FROM PROHIBITION TO LIBERATION

From the time of Aristophanes sexual byplay has been closely allied with political satire. This is certainly true today in America, yet the present openness about sex is in startling, — some would say shocking — contrast to the situation that prevailed until quite recently.

In the nineteeth century Anthony Comstock's New York Society for the Suppression of Vice, crusading against books, articles, and pictures "ruinous to the public morals," inspired a state law, followed by the federal Comstock Law of 1873 banning obscenity sent through the mails.

These attitudes persisted well into the twentieth century. In the movies they were inscribed in a code written by the Hays Office. Though the Office was acutely sensitive to any "un-American" slur, overwhelmingly the cuts it imposed on movies were based on objections not to politics but to the most oblique references to sex.[35] The movie code banned "lustful and open-mouthed kissing," "indecent or undue exposure," the word abortion, any intimation of "sex perversion," and vulgar expressions such as "chippie, fairy, goose, nuts, pansy, S.O.B, son-of-a-." The consequence was that movie after movie had to remove any hint of adultery, homosexuality, or even marital sex, for married couples had to occupy twin beds. Chaplin's *Modern Times,* for all its indictment of industrial oppression, was approved without demur once a few sexually suggestive lines had been deleted. Even Ronald Reagan's *Bedtime for Bonzo* had to remove some mildly off-color lines before it could be approved[36]

As the twentieth century advanced these attitudes could not hold. First, literature was liberated. H. L. Mencken helped prepare for the change in the 1920s. This archetypal reactionary, who longed for a return to a mythical aristocracy, was also an obstinate and courageous champion of free speech. The Boston Watch and Ward Society accused Mencken's *Mercury* magazine of obscenity for publishing an article about an amateur prostitute and the aphrodisiac effect of revival sermons. The issue was banned in Boston. Mencken deliberately invited arrest; he was found not guilty, then lost on a technicality when the Postmaster General prevented the sale of the magazine through the mails. Nonetheless, the case laid the groundwork for subsequent Supreme Court decisions freeing magazines from interference with their mailing privileges and paving the way for the publication of James Joyce's *Ulysses* and the detailed sexual adventures in the novel *Fanny Hill.*

In 1988 the case of *Hustler v Falwell* provided specific protection for even the most outrageous satire. *Hustler* magazine had run a "parody advertisement" alleging that the Reverend Jerry Falwell's first sexual encounter was with his mother in an outhouse. A jury awarded Falwell $150,000 for emotional distress. This judgment was appealed to the Supreme Court, and the Association of American Editorial Cartoonists filed a friend-of-the-court brief citing cartoons depicting Washington as an ass and Thomas Nast's onslaught on Boss Tweed. During oral arguments several justices cited the cartoons, and the unanimous decision announced by Chief Justice William Rehnquist overturned the jury award. A defamation suit by a public figure, said Rehnquist, must prove that it is based on a deliberate or reckless false-hood — "and a lampoon could not be factually false."[37]

There were still some bitter battles to fight over public expressions of obscenity. Lenny Bruce, using his stand-up routines to shock the sensibilities of his mostly liberal audiences, was arrested for obscenity after including the word "cocksucker" in a San Francisco nightclub act. The jury acquitted him, but he was arrested in Chicago and other cities. He managed to stay out of jail, but in 1964 he was tried on a charge of obscenity before a three-judge panel in New York, found guilty after a six-month trial, and sentenced to four months in the workhouse.[38] Where Bruce led, many others have followed, and his verbal outrageousness soon became the norm in his profession. No evening at a Comedy Club is complete without a series of verbal barrages echoing a George Carlin routine featuring the "Seven Dirty Words."[39]

There were dramatic changes, too, in the mass media. By the end of the 1960s the movie codes were gone, transmuted into age-related ratings, and even movies now rated acceptable for 13-year-olds might have been regarded as unacceptably raunchy in the 1970s.[40]

On television some of America's most popular comedy sitcoms are built around the themes of promiscuity and homosexuality, and cable channels are even less inhibited. A few prohibitions persist on the networks. The f-word is forbidden, though it has slipped out occasionally, always followed by profuse apologies by the broadcasters and appropriate sanctions against the perpetrators.

Moreover, the sanctions against the use of profane language on TV and radio have in recent years been backed by government censorship. Using a 1978 Supreme Court decision that the Federal Communications Commission (FCC) could punish the Pacifica Foundation for airing George Carlin's "Seven Dirty Words" routine,[41] the FCC has used its power enthusiastically during the George W. Bush presidency, imposing heavy fines for the airing of allegedly indecent material. Clear Channel Communications (owned by the ABC network) was fined $1.75 million on various indecency charges, especially the lewd references to every possible bodily function regularly issuing from Howard Stern's radio programs, and an FCC fine of $550,000 followed a Super Bowl half-time show in 2004 that included the (unscripted) baring of a female performer's breast, though it was thrown out in July 2008 by a federal appeals court.

However, other media outlets may be available to bypass the censors. Stern, dropped by the six stations on which he was carried by Clear Channel, turned his profanity virulently against the Bush administration and switched to satellite radio, where his audience would be smaller but he'd be free of the FCC and its regulations. And whatever is bleeped out by the networks may still find its way onto the Internet. In a 2006 *Saturday Night Live* parody in which a rapper group sings about sending a gift box to their girlfriends containing their genitalia, the lyrics were bleeped in the show but were heard unbleeped on YouTube.[42] Thus, sexual censorship is still possible in mainstream media, but it is now impossible to prevent the appearance of the most detailed and explicit sexual humor in a medium accessible to anyone.

The transformation of prevailing attitudes on sex has had a liberating effect on political satire. Joseph Heller's *Catch 22* could include graphic brothel scenes and the details of a nurse's anatomy that make Yossarian "sick with lust." Hunter Thompson, in *Fear and Loathing on the Campaign Trail,'72*, could draw on similes and metaphors not available to political satirists of an earlier era:

> A man on the scent of the White House is rarely rational. He is more like a beast in heat: a bull elk in the rut, crashing blindly through the timber in a fever for something to fuck. Anything![43]

In 2001, *Onion* magazine could blithely introduce its first issue after 9/11 with "Holy fucking shit." When David Rees's comic strip protested against the attack on Afghanistan in 2001, under its slogan "Operation: Enduring Freedom" he used a drumbeat of expletives as a prime technique of attack, as in "Oh yeah! Operation: Enduring Our Freedom is in the motherfucking house!" and "Oh yeah! Operation: Enduring Our Enron is in the motherfucking house!"[44]

Yet cartoonists have not been completely freed from the sexual taboo. A Clinton cartoon by Clay Bennett, showing him wearing a tee-shirt with the inscription "I'm With Stupid" and an arrow pointing below his belt, was axed by the *St. Petersburg Times* in 1994. The *Los Angeles Times* refused to include a Paul Conrad cartoon in 1999 that mocked congressional bipartisanship by drawing a Republican elephant humping a Democratic donkey.[45] Editors have killed various other cartoons for being too vividly sexual or anal, but if there are still some limits on sexual expression by satirists, the change from the past is enormous and irreversible. Yesterday, explicit mention of sex was considered bad for business. Today, sex sells.

HANDS OFF RELIGION

Attitudes toward religion, too, have undergone change. The strong anti-Catholic prejudice that doomed Democrat Al Smith's presidential bid in 1928 was laid to rest by the election of John F. Kennedy in 1960. More recently, satirists have not hesitated to aim their fire at Pat Robertson and other fundamentalist leaders as well as at George W. Bush's basing his electoral strategy on the support of religious fundamentalists. The scandals involving child molestation by considerable numbers of priests enabled television wits to use sharp-edged humor, as in Jay Leno's:

The pope has asked all the cardinals to return to Rome. You know how they got them all to come back? They told them there was going to be a performance by the Vienna Boy's Choir."

Nonetheless, the receptivity of the satirist's thrusts at religion is limited by the fact that Americans are more religious than the people of any other industrialized country. Various polls in 2004 showed that 90% or more of Americans believed in God, close to 80% in heaven and angels, and 70% in hell and the devil.

During the 1924 Scopes trial in Dayton, Ohio, Mencken hurled his satiric brickbats at the anti-Darwin arguments of William Jennings Bryan. Eighty years later, one-third or more of the population believe that every word of the Bible is literally true, and two-thirds believe that creationism should be given equal time with evolution in the school curriculum.[46] When Republicans vying for the 2008 presidential nomination aired the issue, Maureen Dowd commented:

The world is globalizing, nuclear weapons are proliferating, the Middle East is seething, but Republicans are still arguing the Scopes trial.[47]

Proposals by some local school boards to replace evolution with creationism, however, went too far for most people, and satirists declared open season on the school boards. In general, though, the mainstream media have been extremely wary of satire on religion. Doug Marlette has had his cartoons critical of the failure of both Protestant and Catholic churches to live up to the teachings of Christ rejected by editors who believed they made fun of religion.[48] One of his cartoons published by *Long Island Newsday* took issue with the pope's refusal to accept women priests. A number of readers complained, and the paper apologized: "We regret that many readers were given an unintended message."[49]

CBS's discomfort with the *Smothers Brothers*'s sniping at the Vietnam War was compounded by the show's insistence on including a routine by David Steinberg in which he laughed at literal interpretations of the Bible. The routine never made it on the air, for the show was cancelled.[50] *Saturday Night Live* was the arena of a fierce battle between NBC's Standards department and producer Lorne Michaels in 1979 over a proposed skit, the "Nerds Nativity," to be aired three days before Christmas. Said the Standards representative: "The nativity is central to an entire religion. You cannot spoof the nativity."[51] Michaels contended they were only spoofing high school nativity pageants, but the advertisers threatened to pull out, and the battle raged. The skit went on the air, but with a number of cuts that did nothing to stem the flood of letters from outraged viewers.

So, for all but the mildest digs at religion, we have to look outside the mainstream. In the 1960s Paul Krassner's *Realist* magazine mocked religion, especially the Catholic Church, in terms calculated to infuriate believers. More recently, *Onion* magazine showed its usual lack of respect, as in its headline on the dying Pope John II: "Pope Died As He Lived: Propped Up for Public Viewing."[52] Jon Stewart's *Daily Show* gets away with a regular "This Week in God" feature making fun impartially of all religions, and Bill Maher enjoys mocking religion on his TV programs. But these are cable shows, unlikely to be tolerated by a mainline network.

RACE, ETHNICITY, AND POLITICAL CORRECTNESS

With race and ethnicity we arrive at a brand of political satire which, rather than ridiculing the wielders of power and authority, is directed at less powerful groups.

Historically in America each successive group of immigrants has been the butt of demeaning humor, with published collections in the nineteenth century of "Jew Jokes," "New Dutch Jokes," and "Chop Suey" jokes. Those with the longest staying power, however, have been the "Dark Town Jokes" directed at America's one group of forced immigrants that have been denigrated first as slaves and then as perennial losers in the American system.

In the 1930s, the Hays code declared that there must be no inciting to racial, religious, or ethnic bigotry, including such words as chink, dago, nigger, and kike. Still, it was many years before movies went beyond earlier stereotypes of black Americans.

Newspaper editors handled race relations nervously, especially during the McCarthy House-Un-American-Activities-Committee years. Ollie Harrington, a cartoonist for African American papers until he set up the public relations department of the NAACP, came under investigation by the House Un-American Activities Committee and spent 40 years in exile in Europe, sending his work home to be published by papers in Chicago and Pittsburgh.

Bill Mauldin, Jules Feiffer, and Herblock, too, raged against racism in their cartoons. Tom Lehrer mocked the Ku Klux Klan and the lynchings in "I Wanna Go Back to Dixie." Most newspapers, however, fearful of giving offense, shied away from biting depictions of the civil rights struggle of the 1950s and 1960s. Subsequently satirists have worked hard to correct this deficiency. Richard Pryor and Dick Gregory were among several African Americans who have used their bitter wit to confront white America with the reality of life for most blacks. In Aaron McGruder's *The Boondocks* comic strip and cable TV show, two young boys, Huey and Riley, who lived with their curmudgeonly grandfather, commented outrageously about almost every aspect of American society, but most especially about the utter incomprehension of black life by whites, including liberals.[53]

This point of view can evoke hostile reactions. Periodically, editors have dropped *The Boondocks* strip when McGruder's intention "to provide a daily foot in the ass of The Man" was "achieved a little too vividly." In fact, a dozen editors dropped the strip completely, and others moved it to the op-ed page.[54]

Race issues came to television in the 1970s in the form of an enormously popular comedy show, *All in the Family*, that ran from 1971 to 1979 featuring Archie Bunker, the prototypical blue-collar worker engaged in fierce arguments with his counter-cultural daughter and son-in-law. The show laughed at Bunker's bigoted, racist, anti-Semitic, and sexist pronouncements. However, Archie was portrayed an endearing character, and his views were close to those of many in his audience. Even today people tell racist jokes, which have a wide following on the Internet and via e-mail.

Still, for satirists working in mainstream publications or on network television, derogatory humor about African Americans and other minorities is now off limits. To most reasonable people this is surely a change for the better, a movement in the direction of a more civil, tolerant society. Yet satirists and others worry that this insistence on respect for others has been pushed to the point at which it creates a new kind of conformity.

Consider the example of *Huckleberry Finn,* which was banned soon after its publication in 1876 by the trustees of the Concord, Massachusetts, public library as "trash and suitable only for the slums."[55] Several other public libraries imposed bans on similar grounds. However, from the 1950s a very different kind of protest against *Huckleberry Finn* was heard. The NAACP and the National Urban League condemned the book as "racially offensive" because of its use of the word "nigger," and that same year the novel was banned from New York City schools. In 1976, the book was removed from the required reading list of the state of Illinois. According to one reviewer, "It constitutes mental cruelty, harassment, and outright racial intimidation to force black students to sit in the classroom with their white peers and read Huckleberry Finn."[56] Another African American critic defended the book as representing "the brief flowering of Mark Twain's dream of brotherhood."[57] Just the same, for the decision-makers in some school districts, their students had to be protected from one of the masterworks of American literature. Later the issue surfaced again when Aaron McGruder was subjected to complaints from African American viewers of his TV show, who objected to Huey's use of the "n-word."

Nor was the problem limited to comments on African Americans. Stephen Hess and Sandy Northrop observe that, "As each minority group demanded a reconfiguration of its image and appellation in the mainstream press in the 1990s, 'political correctness' had become more than a trend for cartoonists: it had become a bad joke."[58]

Latin Americans, already outnumbering African Americans early in the twenty-first century, were prominent among the groups demanding "a

This cartoon does not include the title character of the Mallard Fillmore comic strip, a duck working as a TV reporter. But it does convey a central political theme of the strip: a conservative view of American politics and a dislike of the "political correctness" propagated by a "Liberal Establishment." Tinsley was fired from his first job at the Charlottsville, Virginia, *The Daily Progress,* because of his duck's aggressively conservative views. However, he has been nationally syndicated since 1992. [Bruce Tinsley, "Mallard Fillmore" Mallard Fillmore©King Features Syndicate.]

reconfiguration of its image." Once cartoonists had depicted them as indolent and shiftless, putting off problems until mañana. When the manifest absurdity of this image became clear, it was replaced with other demeaning comments on their cultural background. Hence, Latin American organizations refused to see the joke when comedian Barry Humphries' alter ego, Dame Edna, in an article in a spoof advice column, advised readers not to bother to learn Spanish because there was nothing worth reading in that language.[59]

Then, after 9/11, satirists had to undertake a delicate balancing act in deriding the fundamentalist Muslim attacks on American and Western culture while not appearing to be hostile to Muslims at home and abroad.[60] Consequently, there was a remarkable degree of unanimity in the media in 2006 against reprinting a group of cartoons mocking Mohammed commissioned by the Danish newspaper *Jyllands-Posten,* despite the fact that it had already appeared in several other countries and had provoked an international uproar.

There were a few exceptions, however. One of the cartoons appeared in the *Philadelphia Inquirer* after an elaborate process of consulting with Muslim theologians and experts on press freedom, explaining why the images could be offensive to Muslims and inviting op-ed pieces from the local Muslim community, all this in an effort "to inform our readers, not to inflame them."[61] Some of the cartoons also appeared in the *Philadelphia Jewish Voice* and were shown on American television newscasts. Student newspapers at Harvard, Wisconsin, Northern Illinois, and Illinois State published some of the cartoons, and the editor-in-chief of the University of Illinois newspaper was suspended for doing so.

But much more common were expressions of lukewarm editorial support for *Jyllands-Posten* while, like the *Los Angeles Times,* explaining that it

> has not reprinted these insensitive images, even as a means of shedding light on the controversy in Europe. But it is not necessary to agree with these cartoons to defend another's right to publish them.[62]

To the editorial staff of the alternative weekly *New York Express,* this was hypocrisy. When the newpaper's management agreed to an editorial supporting the Danish newspaper but vetoed the cartoons, all the editors resigned in protest.

A far more blatant double standard was adopted on television's *Comedy Channel.* In April 2006, a proposed cartoon episode that was to have included an image of Mohammed was cut, yet in the same program President Bush and Jesus were shown pelting each other with excrement.[63]

Conservatives found this kind of discrimination offensive. A Bruce Tinsley cartoon issued a "breaking news bulletin: for the past 14 minutes, NO Muslims anywhere have been OUTRAGED about anything."[64] It was all, said the conservatives, one more example of the stultifying political correctness that increasingly pervades the media. They argued that, as radical left dogmas on race and gender take over university liberal arts departments, a hostile atmosphere has developed for anyone who believes, for example, that the great leaders of the American past should not be dismissed as irrelevant "dead white men."[65]

So hostile is this atmosphere, conservatives alleged, that conservative speakers who dare to appear at the country's most prestigious universities are likely to be heckled mercilessly and even driven off the stage. Moreover, the radical attitudes embedded in universities were disseminated to the broad public through the mass media, whose employees, according to a number of studies, are predominately left of center.[66]

Liberals hit back. The real threat to free expression in the universities, they argued, has always come from the anti-intellectualism long associated in America with conservatives and their business supporters. Back in the 1920s Sinclair Lewis made the point, when he put an anti-intellectual rant into the mouth of his typical American businessman booster, George F. Babbitt. Said Babbitt, there are too many left-wing, "blab-mouth, fault-finding, pessimistic, cynical university teachers" subverting the minds of our youth.[67] Today, say the liberals, Babbitry is alive and all too well. As for the media, if they are so dominated by liberals, why are we subjected to such a drumbeat of hostile comments from innumerable conservative columnists and TV pundits, radio talk show hosts like Rush Limbaugh, and TV's Fox News?

Al Franken led the charge against the claim of Rupert Murdoch's Fox News to be "fair and balanced" with his book *Lies and the Lying Liars Who Tell Them.*[68] The book's subtitle, *A Fair and Balanced Look at the Right,* led the network and its anchorman, Bill O'Reilly, to sue Frankel for copyright infringement of the program's slogan. The judge threw the case out. There are hard cases, he said, and easy cases. This was an easy case.

Liberals also contend that, though it is true that working journalists mostly lean toward liberal views, this is more than offset by the conservative attitudes of most of the corporate owners of the media.[69] As the American wit, A. J. Liebling, put it: "Freedom of the press is guaranteed only to those who own one."

Nonetheless, it is not only conservative satirists who worry about the pressure for political correctness. While liberal satirists are themselves unlikely to jibe at blacks, minorities, and women, they are generally protective of the right of others to do so. No less than conservatives they agree with cartoonist David Low:

> The limitation imposed by the necessity of conforming to the genteel code of taboos which constitute the average man's 'good taste' are such that they cramp the style of any satirist worth his salt."[70]

Satire, after all, is no respecter of orthodox views, whether conservative, liberal, or radical. Taboos of all kinds are inviting targets for political satirists and will inevitably be the subject of ridicule no matter how many people subscribe to them, or how sacred their devotion.

chapter three

BRITAIN: FROM BULLDOGS
TO POODLES

In Britain Prime Ministers govern indeed.
Monarchs and Parliament follow their lead.
But out in the world their glow seems to fade
As they bring up the rear in the U.S. parade.

There is a vast heritage of British political satire. In literature the roster of authors who have played with political wit includes novelists Jonathan Swift, Charles Dickens, Anthony Trollope, George Orwell, and Evelyn Waugh; playwrights from Shakespeare to Shaw; among the poets, Dryden, Swift and Byron; Hilaire Belloc, writer of light verse; essayist and caricaturist, Max Beerbohm; and historian Lytton Strachey. In the graphic arts, there were superb lithographs on political themes by Hogarth, Rowlandson, and Gilray in the eighteenth century, followed by Tenniel and other *Punch* cartoonists in the nineteenth century, and a plethora of cartoonists, including David Low, Vicky, Giles, Gerald Scarfe, and Steve Bell, in the twentieth century.[1] Satirical magazines have included *Punch,* which ceased publication in 2002 after "more than 150 years of baiting the establishment,"[2] and the more caustic, and still very much alive, *Private Eye.*

In the 1960s there was a new burst of political satire in England in the form of stage revues, particularly *Beyond the Fringe* and *The Establishment,* featuring talented young men who began performing while they were at Oxford and Cambridge, including Jonathan Miller, Dudley Moore, Peter Cook, Alan Bennett, John Bird, John Fortune, and David Frost. The success of these revues led directly to television: *That Was The Week That Was (TWTW),* featuring many of the *Establishment* performers, followed over the years by a number of successful programs, including *Yes, Minister* and *Yes, Prime Minister;* the raucous puppet program, *Spitting Image,* and the brilliantly satirical, though only occasionally political, *Monty Python's Flying Circus.* More recently Rory Bremner, John Bird, and Stephen Fry have kept the satirical art alive on TV and radio in several programs; the long-running quiz show, *Have I Got News For You,* features political humor and often includes well-known politicians. Chris Morris has outraged viewers with spoof interviews with politicians on subjects like child abuse and drugs, and Sacha Baron Cohen's *Da Ali G Show* has scandalized people of all parties, professions, beliefs, and races even before his American debut on HBO television and his hit movie, *Borat.*

There is also a growing use of political satire on the Internet, with *The Brains Trust,* touted by the *Guardian* newspaper as the "British son of the Onion," *DeadBrain* ("News, Satire, Spoof, Parody, Humor, Donald Rumsfeld"), and a weekly podcast, *The Bugle,* carried by *The Times* online.

Yet one more venue for satire must be mentioned, this one within the political system itself, the House of Commons.

The U.S. Congress has produced some masters of political wit, but the physical setting of the houses of Congress, where members speak from a podium, does not encourage the cut and thrust of debate that is inescapable in the British Parliament. For there, behind the rows of government and opposition benches facing each other across an aisle, members speak from wherever they happen to be sitting. So the debates and question periods are forced confrontations, jousting matches in which a high premium is placed on verbal dexterity and on the ability to think fast on one's feet. Using wit to score political points off political opponents becomes a frequent part of the legislative process.

Consequently, the annals of political satire in Britain included Benjamin Disraeli's eloquence and caustic wit in House of Commons debates in the nineteenth century, and in the twentieth century Winston Churchill was the great master of parliamentary wit. In 1933, ridiculing Labour Prime Minister Ramsay Macdonald from the floor of the House of Commons, Churchill declared:

> I remember, when I was a child being taken to the celebrated Barnum's Circus, which contained an exhibition of freaks and monstrosities, but the exhibit on the program which I most desired to see was the one described as "The Boneless Wonder." My parents judged that the spectacle would be too revolting and demoralizing for my youthful eyes, and I have waited 50 years to see the Boneless Wonder sitting on the Treasury Bench.

Furious with the Conservative governments of Baldwin and Chamberlain for failing to rearm adequately against the threat from Nazi Germany, Churchill alleged:

> They are decided only to be undecided, resolved to be irresolute, adamant for drift, solid for fluidity, all powerful for impotence.

The twenty-first century has not yet produced any Churchills. Still, Prime Minister Gordon Brown was the victim of a lethal thrust in the House of Commons in November 2007. Previously accused of being autocratic, he had suffered a series of humiliations opening him to charges of incompetence. These were encapsulated in an opposition quip: "The House has noticed the Prime Minister's remarkable transformation in the past few weeks — from Stalin to Mr. Bean."[3]

As in the United States, satirists aim their fire at every aspect of the political process. Parliament has been the daily target of humorous barbs from columnist Mathew Parris in the *London Times* and Simon Hoggart in the *Guardian.*

The two-party system has come in for its share of ridicule. Dickens in *Pickwick Papers* tells us that every man in Eatanswill "felt himself bound to unite, heart and soul, with one of the two great parties that divided the town, the Blues and the Buffs," with no possible meeting of minds. "There were Blue shops and Buff shops, Blue inns and Buff inns; there was a Blue aisle and a Buff aisle in the very church itself."

In the television programs, *Yes Minister* and *Yes Prime Minister,* the bureaucracy was the target, the political chief being regularly outwitted by his civil servants. In a typical program the minister is told about a hospital with an administrative staff of 500 — but no doctors, nurses, or patients because of funding cutbacks after the hospital was built. The minister proposes that the staff be fired, but Sir Humphrey, his department's senior civil servant, is appalled: the administrators will be busy at their bureaucratic chores, collecting data, purchasing equipment, and so on — all much more expeditiously done without patients.[4] A skit in *Monty Python* took the charge of bureaucratic superfluity to its ultimate absurdity with John Cleese's creation of a Ministry of Silly Walks.

The military suffer their share of lampooning. Cartoonist David Low created Colonel Blimp, an elderly, bloated symbol of imperial reaction and stupidity.[5] So the targets of British political satirists are as plentiful as those of their American counterparts, but in Britain, as in America, satirists have reserved their sharpest sallies for the apex of the system: the Prime Minister.

THE MOCKING OF PRIME MINISTERS

Unlike some American presidents, no British prime ministers have been mocked because of their hopelessly garbled vocabulary and syntax. They have all been at least reasonably articulate, and a joint appearance by George W. Bush and Tony Blair could only be embarrassing to Americans. (Blair's Deputy Prime Minister, John Prescott, was so prone to malapropisms that if he were to become prime minister there would be volumes of Prescottisms. This was one of the reasons he could never become prime minister.)

As for sexual appetite, the last British leader whose conduct in office suggests comparisons with Kennedy and Clinton was Lloyd George, prime minister during World War I. He was known as "The Goat" because of his inability to keep his hands off any woman within his reach. Since then several members of the cabinet and parliament have been caught in steamy sexual escapades, but no prime ministers during their time in 10 Downing Street. There was a long affair in Prime Minister Harold Macmillan's household, but it was his wife's with another Conservative Party leader, and the affair was not outed until much later. In 2002, a former cabinet member revealed in her memoirs that she and John Major had a four-year extramarital affair, but it was over before Major became a cabinet minister and then prime minister. (Of course, after the later revelations of his extramarital affair, the satirists were able to let loose with a vengeance, one cartoonist regretting that he had spent years "drawing Major as a hopeless gawk" when, in fact, "he was also a sex-romping superstud."[6])

Still, there have been other themes that echo the satire of presidential idiosyncrasies. For example, Harold Wilson, elected prime minister three times, was sometimes derided as the British Richard Nixon, paranoid and fearful that his political foes were conspiring to oust him as prime minister.[7]

Yet satirists had to stretch to make Wilson seem more than a pale shadow of Nixon. When it came to the issue of hereditary advantage, on the other hand, British satire cut much deeper than the American version. The jibes at the privileged background of Franklin Roosevelt, Jack Kennedy, and George W. Bush were tame stuff compared with the vitriolic assessments of Sir Alexander Douglas-Home, the last of the aristocratic prime ministers.

Class, and the dominance of a hereditary upper class, had long been a British obsession, and a perennial subject of satire was "The Old Boy's Club," whose members had attended exclusive private schools, then moved on to Oxford or Cambridge, followed by senior positions in the army, the Church of England, and the government. Home's predecessors — Churchill, Eden, Macmillan, and even the Labour leader, Clement Attlee — were all members of this class.

Unfortunately for Home, the power of the privileged circle had been fading since the last two decades of the nineteenth century. A Hilaire Belloc verse told the tale of the late Lord Lundy, who in 1889 was appointed governor of New South Wales at the age of 27. The Duke, his grandfather, had intended him to be "the next prime minister but three," only to find that Lord Lundy's propensity to weep at the slightest provocation made this impossible, leaving Australia as the only option.[8]

By the 1960s the time was long past when any duke could plan to make his progeny "the next prime minister but three." Little remains today of the deference vital to the maintenance of an aristocracy. Hereditary titles no longer qualify even for membership in the upper legislative chamber,[9] derisively known as "life after death." Satirists treat the upper class as absurd anachronisms. Their refined accent (much admired in America) has become a staple fare of British comic imitators. A *Monty Python* skit had them as mental defectives, taking part in a foot race in which they engage in frantic but unsuccessful efforts to jump over a stick on the ground.

Prime Minister Harold Macmillan had not understood how much things had changed when, compelled by ill health to resign, he maneuvered Home into the post of prime minister as his successor.[10] Home had been an able foreign secretary, but as prime minister he was, in Harold Wilson's words, an "elegant anachronism," to be ridiculed in cartoons and on television as an absurd relic of a long past era.

Home lasted barely a year as prime minister, then lost the next election. After him as Conservative prime ministers came Edward Heath, a builder's son, Margaret Thatcher, daughter of a grocer and definitely not a member of the old boy's club, and John Major, son of a trapeze artist and failed garden gnome maker. True, David Cameron, elected Conservative Party leader in 2005, had an Eton and Oxford background, so an advantaged birth and education still counted for something in the new Britain. But Cameron knew that his hopes to become prime minister depended on avoiding the mannerisms and style that were no longer appealing to most of the British public and that had provided so much fodder to the satirists.[11]

Satire, then, has reflected some major stylistic differences between presidents and prime ministers. Yet in both countries the heart of the matter for satirists has been power, and the arrogance of power.

THE RISE OF PRIME MINISTERIAL POWER

Over time, power in the British system has shifted from the Parliament to the government's executive committee, the cabinet, and then to the head of the cabinet, the prime minister. Today prime ministers commonly have more power over the governmental process than presidents exercise in the American constitutional structure. Unlike American presidents, prime ministers rarely face the frustration of having their proposals ignored or butchered by the legislature.

Of course, prime ministers are not dictators. Their initiatives are usually modified in the two houses of Parliament. Being regular members of the House of Commons, they face constant debates and a regular weekly barrage of questions from the floor, very different from the pomp and formality of a president's once-a-year State of the Union visit to Congress.

Further, prime ministers hold onto office only as long as they retain the support of a majority of members of the House of Commons.[12] If their party has no clear majority, as in the 1970s under James Callaghan, or if the majority is very small, as was the fate of John Major in the 1990s, they are the butts of satirical jeers about their frantic efforts to hold their parties in line and prevent being voted down and out. More commonly, prime ministers have had majorities big enough to ensure that the only vote they had to fear was that of the people at the next election (though their power might also be affected by the polls).[13] Consequently, satirists have often depicted prime ministerial power as dangerously excessive. That critique has applied especially to three prime ministers since the 1940s: Churchill, Thatcher, and Blair.

Churchill's period of concentrated authority was atypical, however, for he first became the prime minister when his country faced the strong possibility of invasion. The normal partisan skirmishing was suspended, the opposition Labour and Liberal parties joined a coalition government, and elections were postponed until the end of the war against Germany. So, only a few voices questioned his unprecedented powers, notably that of a Welsh socialist M. P, Aneurin Bevan,[14] who accused Churchill of being "a man suffering from petrified adolescence" and who mistook "verbal felicities for mental inspirations." Otherwise, the most biting criticism of Churchill's wartime leadership came after the war, as in *Private Eye*'s review of a new biography of the "Great Bumpkin...Rudolph Rednose" (Churchill's capacity for drink was legendary), in which the magazine summed up a career that included breaking strikes, suppressing India, and being responsible for various military disasters ("Only 5,000 dead! You should have seen what we did at Gallipoli.")[15]

In any case, when the war ended Churchill led his Conservative Party to ignominious defeat. In opposition he was still a formidable and witty foe, opposing the Labour government's nationalization of key industries and deriding the able but extraordinarily uncharismatic Prime Minister Attlee as "a sheep in sheep's clothing" and "a modest little man with much to be modest about."[16](According to a joke that some attributed to Churchill, he and Attlee were in adjoining urinals, and Churchill moved two stalls away on the grounds that "whenever Attlee sees something big, he wants to nationalize it.")

In 1951 Churchill became prime minister again, but with his health failing he was no longer the wartime Churchill, no longer an example of extraordinary power concentrated in the prime minister's office. Hence, for more typical illustrations of the trend toward the aggrandizement of prime ministerial power we turn to the experience of Margaret Thatcher and Tony Blair.

Churchill was Margaret Thatcher's great hero, and though she lacked his intellectual force, sweeping oratory, and brilliant wit, she, too, was to exercise a remarkable personal and political dominance over the British system. Before this could happen, however, she had to benefit from two sets of ironic, almost farcical, circumstances.

The first was the incredibly inept calculations of the grandees of the Conservative Party in the leadership struggle following the defeat of the

Margaret Thatcher

Margaret Thatcher, Prime Minister from 1979 to 1990, was an assertive, transforming leader. Her assertiveness is conveyed here by British cartoonist Nicky Taylor: Thatcher's upraised finger and stern, scolding expression making it clear that she will brook no opposition within her governing ranks. Though she aroused strong resentments even among her colleagues, her single-minded determination produced profound changes in the British economy. Thatcher was reelected twice by large majorities—but was finally ousted by her own party because of her obstinate refusal to change course on the deeply unpopular poll tax. [Nicky Taylor, Cartoonstock.]

Edward Heath government in the 1974 election. When Heath made a bid to continue as Leader, his erstwhile colleagues were too gentlemanly to campaign vigorously against him until it was too late. It was too late because they did not take seriously the candidacy of Margaret Thatcher, a woman in a deeply male-chauvinistic party who refused to play by their gentlemanly rules and who, to their astonishment and dismay, was elected Conservative Party Leader.

Now she had to lead her party to victory in an election, and once again her opponents, this time the Labour government, played into her hands with a remarkable display of self-defeating bungling. In the bitter winter of 1978–1979 British unions engaged in a series of crippling strikes. Cartoonists thrived on the havoc caused by uncollected garbage and unburied bodies in cemeteries, but satire could not keep up with the irony of a union movement — the organizational and financial mainstay of the Labour Party — committing political suicide by bringing down the Labour government.

Once in office Thatcher displayed from the beginning an extraordinary self-assurance and force of personality. For a time she was limited by the fact that her cabinet included several members of Heath's cabinet, who advised caution in the face of a series of political crises. Each time she decided against them, and, one by one, they were removed until the cabinet consisted almost entirely of reliable Thatcherites.

She had become a formidable figure indeed, her power backed by an extremely assertive personality that cried out for the ministrations of the satirists. Cartoonists portrayed her as a scolding, chastising figure, much given to dressing down even her closest associates.

Now, male leaders are admired rather than resented for being strong and assertive, and some of the criticism aimed at Thatcher, with constant references to her ubiquitous handbag as a potential weapon, undoubtedly smacked of sexism. Yet it remains true that no male prime minister has ever been as high-handed or abrasive as Thatcher in dealing with colleagues as well as foes. So, there was an abundance of jokes about her aggressive personality:[17]

She took her Cabinet members out for dinner. She ordered steak for herself. "And how about the vegetables, madam?" They'll have steak too."

Definition of the word "unnecessary" — it's as unnecessary as Margaret Thatcher taking an assertiveness course.

Matthew Parris, her former assistant, described her as "a cross between a B2 bomber and a sabre-toothed tiger."[18] Columnist Simon Hoggart spoke of her "growing conviction that she is actually the Queen, and that the woman in Buckingham Palace is a pretender, an irrelevance like ex-King Zog of Albania."[19] *Private Eye* offered a cartoon series in 1986 in which Thatcher was featured as a Hitlerite Führer.

The ruthlessness of her policies matched her personality. Previous Conservative governments had differed with Labour governments only in degree. Thatcher put an end to temporizing. Union power was confronted directly, a yearlong miner's strike crushed. Spending on social services was cut. Nationalized industries were privatized.

Anti-Tory cartoonists drew her as heartless, but she brushed aside criticism. Ignoring the faint hearts in her own party, she prevailed against the miners and defeated Argentina in the Falklands war. She won reelection twice by large majorities. She rejected suggestions that she might consider resting on her laurels and retiring; instead, since there are no constitutionally mandated term limits in Britain, she declared she would "go on and on."

But, even in a system that gives so much power to prime ministers, hubris can be fatal. Believing herself invincible, she introduced a deeply unpopular

The Offensive Art

effort to change the system of local taxes from a residential charge to a "poll tax." Despite massive opposition she refused to compromise, and this time she did not prevail. Faced with a requirement for reelection as Conservative Party leader, she was narrowly defeated. No longer leader of her party, she was no longer prime minister.

Across the Atlantic, Thatcher still had a devoted public. A two-ton, eight-foot marble statue of her could not yet be installed in the House of Commons because of a rule preventing installation until the subject has been dead for five years. So the Lake Havasu Tourism Board, which had previously arranged the transplanting of London Bridge, offered to provide a temporary home for the statue in the Arizona town's new City Hall. Labour firebrand Dennis Skinner would be happy to see the statue stay in the United States: "Although working-class people in the UK can't stand the sight of her, I know you love her in the United States." As it turned out, the statue would have been safer in Lake Havasu; for when it went on display in a London art gallery in February 2003, a protester decapitated the statue as "an act of satirical humor." He went to jail for three months.

Whatever the plaudits for her in America, at home the theme of obstinate self-assurance was taken up with a vengeance by the satirists, and *Spitting Image* depicted her as a crazed hag trying to interfere in the administration of her successor, John Major.

Tony Blair had none of Thatcher's imperious public personality. His style was down-to-earth, ordinary middle-class, devoid of any suggestion of putting on airs. Yet, after an initial period in which his youth and earnestness led to his being depicted as "Bambi," critics and satirists shifted to depicting him as a "control freak" intent on concentrating near total power in the prime ministership.

His cabinet, said his accusers, consisted mostly of people he could control, with the sole exception of Gordon Brown, the chancellor of the Exchequer, a longtime colleague, rival, and eventual successor. In the House of Commons, Blair, after his first two election victories, had a Labour majority so large that he could survive revolts by resentful back-benchers, and he had little to fear from a weak Conservative opposition. As for his party, Blair had become its unchallenged leader by overturning the policies of the Labour left, accepting Thatcher's privatizations and a reduced role for the unions (though he passed some pro-union legislation, introduced and raised minimum wages, and plunged much more money than did Thatcher into health and education). After that he contemptuously swept aside attacks on his policies from both left and right. Simon Hoggart wrote of his accusing his critics of an unpatriotic refusal to recognize the extraordinary achievements of his government which, he constantly claimed, has ended forever the curse of unemployment, inflation and high interest rates, while turning sink schools into groves of academe worthy of ancient Greece, ending crime, curing the sick, and handing out a bag of gold to every household in Britain.[20]

Satirists further mocked Blair for trying to control public opinion through the "spinning" of news by his media director, Alastair Campbell. *The Times* ran a weekly strip about a spin doctor called "Alisdair." A radio program won awards for a comedy about a hapless cabinet minister harassed by the prime minister's spin doctor. In a stage farce called *Feelgood,* Campbell was portrayed as a demonic spinmeister, with Blair as Divine Light, his ventriloquist dummy, mouthing platitudes. The show played at a fringe theater to sold-out audiences of people who roared with laughter, even though most would be voting for Blair in the forthcoming election.

Other devastating satires on Blair and his associates were presented in the Rory Bremner-Two Johns television series. In one program Blair is depicted (like Wilson) as utterly lacking in political beliefs and driven only by polls and focus groups. Then he is shown bemoaning the fact that he has to share the spotlight with the Queen; and when Clinton arrives for a clandestine visit, Blair observes enviously that, unlike prime ministers, presidents are constantly greeted with "Hail to the Chief!" Clinton's purpose is to tell Blair that the United States has discovered life in outer space; and that since he is about to retire, he is planning to blast into space in a quest for new electorates and more flesh to press. At the end, Blair, hoping for his own kingdom, decides to accompany Clinton.

Bremner's imitation of Blair on this program was projected into election campaigns. He would appear at scheduled campaign events and, in a convincing impersonation, deliver mock speeches before Blair arrived.

Still more lampooning of the Blair government came in the 2005 series, *The Thick Of It,* which ridiculed the prime minister, his cabinet members, and Alastair Campbell as devoid of principle, manipulators of public opinion, and totally obsessed with their image.

Satirists mocked Blair's domestic policies, ridiculing his enthusiastically courting the approval and financial contributions of the business community. While he was Leader of the Opposition, Blair had made a particular point of attacking the government of John Major for alleged conflicts of interest and for accepting donations from dubious sources. Inevitably, then, satirists took after Blair when, eager to reduce his party's dependence on the unions, he began assiduously seeking money from business interests. The whiff of hypocrisy was in the air. Satirists delighted in tarnishing his squeaky-clean image, as in *Private Eye*'s depiction of him as the vicar of St. Albion's parish, full of unctuous praise of his own impeccable standards. At the annual Labour Party conference *Private Eye* observed "the corporate posse of company directors, sidling up to ministers and lecturing delegates at every opportunity."[21] The satire intensified in 2006 when a police inquiry was launched into allegations of a relationship between large preelection loans to the Labour Party and the subsequent appointment of the donors to the House of Lords.[22]

The American practice of granting huge salaries to top corporate executives was replicated in Britain. Columnist John O'Farrell had the chairmen of the board establishing the criteria for executive salaries: "What's the most outrageous and exorbitant pay rise I can give myself? Right, I'll have that much then."[23] The gap between the rich and the poor, and between the top one percent and the rest, was wider than it had been since the 1930s. So critics asked: Was Blair fundamentally different from Thatcher? Not according to *Private Eye,* which placed, next to a photo of Blair, a current picture of Thatcher, under the heading: "Tony Blair: How He Has Aged."[24]

At last Blair, like Thatcher, found that his longevity in office brought him up against the limits of his power. The unpopularity of his support of the Iraq War, the substantial reduction of his third election majority, his decision not to run again for the prime ministership, and the accusations of loans-for-peerages all produced a drastic decline of his standing in the polls and a serious weakening of his authority. When he retired, making way at last for Gordon Brown, his departure was not the occasion for national mourning.

The experience of Thatcher and Blair makes it clear that prime ministers who overreach, who see themselves as the sole exponents of sound and intelligent policy, and therefore above the tedious necessity of negotiation and compromise, will eventually reach the limits of their power. Nonetheless, it took several years to reach those limits. Within the British system, it appears, a very great deal of latitude is provided to strong-minded prime ministers who possess substantial majorities in the House of Commons.

Yet this remarkable degree of power holds true only as long as it operates *within* the British system. In the context of the larger world outside, satirists in the past half-century have fastened less on the expansion than on the decline of the power of British prime ministers.

THE DECLINE OF PRIME MINISTERIAL POWER

Once Britain bestrode the world, its empire extending over more than a quarter of the world's land surface. Since World War II, however, American power has replaced British power, and prime ministers have played a subordinate role to American presidents. Constantly the British speak of the Anglo-American "special relationship," but it is not a relationship of equals.

This became evident in the Churchill–Roosevelt relationship. They enjoyed and admired each other, and Churchill believed he was a full partner with his friend in the White House. Yet Roosevelt was beyond question the senior partner, and soon he made it clear that he had no sympathy with Churchill's war aim of preserving of the British Empire.

Churchill's successor, Anthony Eden, plotted with the French and Israelis in 1956 to take over the Suez Canal by force after Egypt had nationalized it. But the United States had not been consulted, so Eisenhower demanded that the plan be cancelled. The troops were recalled, and a humiliated and ailing Eden resigned soon after. The shock waves of the Suez crisis reverberated throughout the British system, compelling both elites and the general public to face the decline of Britain's international status. Suez was also a "particularly important factor in undermining Britain's apparently instinctive deference to its leaders," thereby opening the way to a burst of political satire.[25]

Eden was succeeded by Harold Macmillan, who relied heavily on personal diplomacy in his foreign policy. Playing against his customary role as the languid Edwardian gentleman, he jetted around the world so frenetically that the cartoonist Vicky fixed him in the public mind as "Supermac," an elderly version of Superman.[26] Macmillan was hardly a Superman when, with his country unable to afford to produce new nuclear missiles, he went to Washington to ask President Kennedy to sell Britain the Skybolt missile. Skybolt, he discovered, was being cancelled, and Kennedy offered the new Polaris as a replacement, but only as part of a multilateral, NATO force. Macmillan pleaded, Kennedy relented, and Britain was allowed to buy Polaris missiles to mount on its own submarines with its own warheads — which everyone knew could not be fired without American approval. Peter Cook imitated Macmillan in a *Beyond the Fringe* sketch. The president, he said, had thoughtfully shown him beautiful photographs of the missile:

> A very handsome weapon, we shall be very proud to have them; the photographs, that is; we don't get the missiles till round about 1970 — in the meantime we shall just have to keep our fingers crossed, sit very quietly and try not to alienate anyone.[27]

The former U.S. Secretary of State, Dean Acheson, infuriated Macmillan when he said, "Britain has lost an Empire and has not yet found a role." A cartoon by Vicky indicated that Acheson had a point. As Acheson looks on, Kennedy is shown as the front part of a music-hall horse, while Macmillan pleads to be allowed to be the hind legs.[28]

Harold Wilson, prime minister during the Vietnam years, agonized over the dilemma posed by the American connection. At home he was confronted by huge demonstrations against any British involvement in the war, while Lyndon Johnson was applying fierce pressure for at least a token British presence in Vietnam, telling Wilson that "even a platoon of bagpipers would be sufficient, it was the British flag that was wanted."[29] Wilson desperately tried to find a middle ground. Though he rejected Johnson's request for British troops, he avoided direct condemnation of the war and proposed himself

Steve Bell, *Guardian* cartoonist since 1985, has taken gleeful aim at British prime ministers from Margaret Thatcher to Gordon Brown. Tony Blair, as we see here, was a prime target of Bell's derision. This cartoon contains several characteristic Steve Bell features. First, there is his fury at the impending Iraq war (for which the drums began beating right after September 11, 2001). Next, he shows his contempt for Blair's eager acceptance of a humiliating role assigned by Iraq war enthusiast, Vice-President Cheney. There is the use of toilet humor to convey the degradation of politics. A typical Bell touch is Blair's allegedly mad left eye. (Bell had noted the same phenomenon in Thatcher.) Finally, a simian George W. Bush, perched on the Republican elephant, points the way to Iraq. [Steve Bell, The *Guardian*, December 12, 2001 (© Steve Bell 2001–All Rights Reserved.]

instead as an intermediary to negotiate an end to the war. Johnson treated this characteristic Wilsonian balancing act with contempt. At a banquet when Wilson came to Washington for economic and foreign policy talks, Johnson allegedly arranged for the band to play "I Got Plenty o' Nuttin."

Under Thatcher the balance was corrected somewhat, for Reagan doted on her and sometimes bowed to the advice of the "Iron Lady," as she was delighted to be called. Yet it was American power she depended on for facing the Soviets, and whose aid was indispensable to the British victory over Argentina in the Falklands. Moreover, when Reagan launched an invasion of Grenada, still nominally under the authority of the British Queen, he did not seek Thatcher's approval. *A Private Eye* cover showed Thatcher trying to phone Reagan, and hearing: "This is President Reagan's answering machine. We're going in again. Have a nice day."[30]

During the Blair years satirists returned in full force to the charge that Britain was subservient to the United States, especially after Blair's commitment to the Iraq War. Blair made the same assertions as Bush about Saddam's weapons of mass destruction, going even further with a claim that Iraq had the capacity to launch chemical weapons with only 45 minutes notice. Two investigations, the first by Lord Hutton, the second by Lord Butler, examined these claims. They exonerated Blair of "sexing up" an intelligence report or of any intention to deceive. Skeptics suggested that an investigation conducted by such members of the Old Boy's Club as Lords Hutton and Butler would never ruin a prime minister. And Blair's standing in the polls sank to a level similar to those of Bush, as antiwar demonstrators carried posters with the one word: BLIAR.

Cartoonists piled on, replacing the stalwart British bulldog — once the representation of the nation's assertive role in the world — with a new symbol: America's poodle. Steve Bell depicted Blair glowing with "intense pride" as Vice President Cheney informs him of the important task America was assigning to Britain in the Iraq War.

NO RESPECT FOR ROYALTY

Prime ministers are the centers of political power in Britain, but they are not the nation's ceremonial leaders. That role is still vested in a hereditary monarchy which, replete with palaces and huge staffs underwritten by public funds, is much more lavishly endowed than its counterparts in Scandinavia and the Netherlands. Consequently, the displays of pomp and grandiloquence, and the antiquarian absurdity of Lords High Chamberlain, Masters of the Horse, and Ladies of the Queen's Bedchamber, provide splendid material for satirists,

Most especially, there is the contrast between the quasi-religious veneration lavished on the monarchy and the triviality of its responsibilities. Constitutionally, the Crown today has little choice but to endorse and register the decisions of the elected government.

Until the seventeenth century this was not the case; dominant power resided in the hands of the king or queen. But step by step (one step involving the beheading of Charles I, another the expulsion of James II) the power moved away until by the Victorian era the queen could be no more than a nuisance to be placated by her ministers, whose ascendancy was clear.

A residual political influence does remain in the hands of the monarch, who usually outlasts a succession of prime ministers and is regularly informed and consulted by each of them. Most observers believe that Elizabeth II has not tried to affect government policy other than to declare her very strong concern about global warming. Her son and prospective successor, Prince Charles, is another matter, going public with anti-modernist views on the countryside and architecture as well as complaints (delivered without any sense of irony) about people being brought up to believe they can attain any position "without ever putting in the necessary work or having the natural ability." Repeatedly he has used his position to send missives to government ministers informing them urgently of his views on a variety of issues, both major and minor. *Private Eye* had him writing an indignant protest about "one of our biggest problems"— the replacement of milk glass bottles by newfangled cardboard cartons that can't be opened without spilling milk on your waistcoat.

> With a sigh of contentment Charles sat back and reread his latest missive. Yes, this would get Blair's government back on the right track.[31]

In his comedy, *The Apple Cart*, George Bernard Shaw plays with the theoretical possibility that royal influence might be transformed into real power. The prime minister confronts King Magnus with an ultimatum: either he stop making speeches about current policy issues (which, according to the largely unwritten British constitution he is not supposed to do) or the government will resign. The king, after a long display of Shavian wit, concedes that they have won. However, rather than be reduced to a cipher, he will abdicate and run for parliament as a commoner at the head of his own party. The terrified government capitulates.

This is all good Shavian fun, but the clever Magnus (Shaw, himself, of course) is quite unlike any past or prospective British monarch. None since Elizabeth I, except for George III between his bouts of madness, seem to have had more than average intelligence, and some have had less. In any case, the British monarch reigns but does not rule, and reigning is largely a matter of ceremony and formality.

The essayist and caricaturist Max Beerbohm was closer to the mark than Shaw with "Some Words on Royalty."[32] He spun the tale of a European Emperor who narrowly survived an assassin's bullet, then displayed remarkable courage, smiling and continuing to salute the cheering crowd as though nothing had happened. His coolness under fire proved to be less surprising when it transpired that, as a security measure, the Emperor had been replaced in the imperial carriage by a wax automaton, constructed to turn its head slowly from side to side and salute. So here we had "a mob doffing its headgear, day after day, to a dummy!"

Queen Charlotte in Alan Bennett's play and movie, *The Madness of King George,* makes the same point when she scolds the Prince of Wales as they ride past the cheering crowds in the royal carriage: "George, smile, you lazy hound. It's what you're paid for. Smile and wave. Come on, everybody, smile and wave. Everybody, smile and wave, smile and wave."[33]

To a considerable extent, the bite of the satire on the monarchy has depended on the popularity of the monarch and the royal family. For example, there was little taunting of Victoria until, after her husband Prince Albert died, she went into a long period of seclusion, refusing to "smile and wave" to the public as she was paid to do. As soon as she resumed her ceremonial duties, derision was replaced by adulation. Later there was the bad publicity engendered by the abdication of Edward VIII in 1938. Forced by his marriage to a divorced woman, the abdication should have provoked an outburst of satirical scorn celebrating the departure of a foolish and trivial man who had a soft spot for Hitler and the Nazis. (Churchill, ever the romantic, fought to keep him on the throne.) Instead, the press treated the matter with portentous gravity as a great national crisis.

The royals' reputation recovered when George VI and his wife, Queen Elizabeth, refused to leave London during the Blitz; and the coronation of the young Elizabeth II, followed by the equally splendid spectacle of her marriage to Prince Phillip, generated unbounded public enthusiasm.

However, the 1960s ushered in the era of declining deference and inevitably brought the royals into the sights of the disrespectful young performers of *The Establishment* and *TWTW*:

> The Royal Barge is, as it were, sinking. The sleek, royal-blue hull of the barge is sliding, gracefully, almost regally, beneath the waters of the Pool of London ... And now the Queen, smiling radiantly, is swimming for her life. Her Majesty is wearing a silk ensemble in canary yellow.[34]

The writers of this piece admitted that "none of our items dealing with the Royal Family had the cutting edge that those with political or religious content sported." But the ridicule became more caustic with the *Sex Pistols* 1977 single, "God Save the Queen," packaged in a record sleeve depicting the queen with a safety-pinned lip.

In the 1980s stories began to surface about marital tensions between princes and princesses, and *Spitting Image* portrayed the royals week after week as a ludicrously dysfunctional family. It was in the 1990s that the deferential dam gave way completely as a result of a succession of royal scandals. One after another royal marriages, embarked on with such splendor and pageantry, broke up. Most damaging was the highly publicized antagonism between Prince Charles and his wife Diana. Both were involved in extramarital affairs, the sexually explicit details of which were captured on tapes of telephone conversations and spread all over the tabloids. With the unhappy couple separated and tabloid headlines blaring — Queen Mum Saw Di Suicide Attempt; Diana Has Betrayed Me; The Camilla Conspiracy — the royals had succeeded in making themselves more ridiculous than any satirist could hope to achieve.

Nor was this the end of the family's humiliations, including steamy accounts in the tabloids of the sexual behavior of the royal staffs. Prince Charles's valet also revealed that among his responsibilities was squeezing the toothpaste onto his master's toothbrush. Little seemed to be left of the magic of monarchy.

To some extent the criticism subsided as the public came to accept Charles's remarriage to his longtime mistress, Camilla Parker-Bowles. However, the tabloid press was full of feeble jokes and cartoons about Camilla's unprepossessing looks.

For all the derision now being heaped upon it, the monarchy will no doubt survive, for the adoration heaped on royals from Victoria to Elizabeth and Diana is now lavished on Prince William, with the media competing fiercely for even a glimpse of the photogenic young heir to the throne.[35] Columnist John O'Farrell caught the mood nicely, suggesting that, though the media should leave William alone,

> intelligent critics on media intrusion are excepted; it's important for commentators such as myself to examine the conflict between private life and public duty ... Anyway, doesn't he look like his mum? Aaah bless him, I hope he settles in alright. I wonder of he'll get a girlfriend? More pictures, pages 7, 8, and 9.[36]

Max Beerbohm, despite his disdainful fiction of the mechanical bowing emperor, explained why he thinks the monarchy is necessary. It is, he said,

> a rather absurd institution, no doubt ... But then humanity itself is rather absurd ... man is not rational, and the spirit of idolatry is strong in him. And, if you take away his idol, that energy which would otherwise be spent in kotowing will probably be spent in some less harmless manner.[37]

Still, it is all flummery. The power is gone, and the decline in the power of the monarch matches the decline in the power of the prime minister, for it is part of the decline of Britain in the world. Even King Magnus, fresh from his victory over the elected government in *The Apple Cart*, is brought down to earth at the end of the play. The American ambassador joyfully brings him the great news that America has cancelled the Declaration of Independence and decided to rejoin the British Empire. Magnus knows that rejoining the Empire means the end of British independence.

chapter four

CENSORSHIP, BRITISH STYLE

> Milton and John Stuart Mill said it clearly:
> Liberty's cause must be cherished most dearly.
> I suspect they'd regard as a dangerous error
> The erosion of freedom by laws against terror.

In Britain, as in America, the satirists' disrespectful treatment of their political elites doesn't mean they're entirely free from restrictions.

In fact, the British system provides prime ministers some potent weapons not available to American presidents. For one thing, they can apply pressure on the British Broadcasting Corporation (BBC), the public television and radio system underwritten by a license fee levied on every owner of a TV set; and the government makes the decisions on the size and duration of the fee as well as appoints the members of the BBC's board. Moreover, as a public agency, the BBC is required to provide balanced political coverage,[1] especially in an election period, and, as the BBC's director-general said, "You can't balance laughter."

There was an inevitable furor in 1964 when David Frost, dressed as former Conservative Prime Minister Benjamin Disraeli on *That Was The Week That Was,* launched into a savage parody of Sir Alec Douglas-Home:

> Just as you are the holder of an ancient earldom through no intention of your own, so stage by stage you have been raised up the ladder of our public life . . . You are the dupe and unwitting tool of a conspiracy — the conspiracy of a tiny group of desperate men who have seen in you their last slippery chance of keeping the levers of power and influence within their privileged circle.[2]

This came in the midst of an election campaign, and as one commentator put it: "For the BBC to mount a program which is politically satirical is tantamount to a tightrope walker inviting a group of jesters to bounce up and down on the tightrope."[3] In this case the tightrope walker fell, and TWTW did not survive.

In 2005 the BBC cut the word "lying" from the radio satire, *Absolute Power.* The script called for a PR man to say there was nothing he could "teach this prime minister about deception, manipulation, and lying. Except how to do it properly." The program's writer alleged he was told, "It has been pulled because you can't call Tony Blair a liar in the current climate."[4] Still, there was no embargo on the efforts to make Blair look ridiculous. One program by Rory Bremner and company produced a standard complaint from a senior member of Blair's cabinet: "I'm all in favour of being able to laugh at ourselves and for satire to keep our feet on the ground. What I worry about is when satire masquerades as serious comment." But, of course, effective satire always does.

Prime ministers also have more leeway than presidents in withholding information. Embedded in the British governmental culture has always been a passion for secrecy, and the 1911 Official Secrets Act made it an offense to reveal without permission anything that happened in government agencies, conceivably including their staff cafeteria menus. The Act was made less ludicrous by new legislation in 1989, but journalists must still be wary of some of its provisions.

Then, too, prime ministers might have recourse to a legal weapon that is particularly potent in the British system: the libel suit. The laws of libel place a much greater burden of proof on the alleged libeler than in America, with the result that *Private Eye* must allot almost one-quarter of its budget to paying out libel defeats,[5] and the online version of *Punch* was sued 41 times in three years, losing seven times. This situation encouraged John Major, Thatcher's chosen successor, to sue the obscure satirical magazine *Scallywag* and the socialist weekly the *New Statesman* for printing an allegation that Major was having an affair with the lady in charge of official catering.[6] The case was settled out of court, with costs that put *Scallywag* out of business and brought the *New Statesman* to the edge of bankruptcy.

Generally speaking, however, prime ministers are ill advised to use the libel weapon, and though satirists are as unfair to prime ministers as they are to presidents, the system requires prime ministers to grin and bear it as best they may.

So must the members of the royal family today. There was a time when the kind of ribald jokes leveled at them could have led to the stocks, as happened in the eighteenth century to Daniel Defoe, or to jail, as in the case of the indomitably scandalous writer-politician John Wilkes. Even in the twentieth century the monarchy was protected from the playwrights' wit by the office of the Lord Chamberlain, charged since 1824 with ensuring that stage productions did not offend Britain's major institutions and morality.[7] But the Lord Chamberlain's office was abolished in 1968, and there are no longer any penalties incurred for making rude comments on stage about the monarchy.

When "comedy terrorist" Aaron Barshchak, dressed in his stage Osama bin Laden costume, scaled the walls of Windsor castle, interrupted Prince William's 21st birthday speech, and then went to the bar to order champagne, the Home Secretary expressed "deep concern" over the breakdown of security. But no charges were filed.

Private Eye knew that it could jeer at Prince Charles as well as the Blairs with impunity. One of its covers featured the Blairs visiting Prince Charles on his yacht, the Prince saying, "Welcome Aboard, Your Majesty," Tony saying, "Carry On, Windsor," and Cherie Blair telling Tony to "give him a pound, darling."[8]

Nonetheless, as in America, there are subjects shielded by long-established taboos, and satirists have run up against considerable resistance as they launch their derisive missiles at patriotism in wartime and at attitudes on sex, religion, and race.

NO MORE WAR?

Like America, Britain has been engaged in a number of wars in the past two centuries. In the nineteenth century the country fought on the one hand to maintain a balance of power in Europe and on the other hand to expand its empire, especially in Africa.

To each of these wars there was opposition. In fact, opponents of the Crimean war in the 1850s and the war against the Boers in South Africa at the end of the century included influential senior politicians, arguing trenchantly in heated parliamentary debates. In the twentieth century antiwar sentiment has, at various times, inspired the passions of a mass movement.

Satirists have added their wit to the solemnity of the opposition, deriding the arguments for vainglorious colonial adventures and illusory efforts to balance power. Preferring antiheroes to heroes, their favorite Shakespearean character is Falstaff, who resists Prince Hal's admonition that "thou owest God a death:"

> 'Tis not due yet; I would be loath to pay him before his day. What need I be so forward with him that calls not on me? Well, 'tis no matter; honour pricks me on. Yes, but how if honour pricks me off when I do come on? How then? Can honour set to a leg? no; or an arm? no . . . What is honour? a word. What is in that word honour? what is that honour? air . . . Therefore I'll none of it . . .

Yet satirists are cutting against the grain of a culture that glories in martial triumphs — Drake over the Spanish Armada, Nelson at Trafalgar, Wellington at Waterloo, and so on. Even the dubious involvement in the Crimea and Africa stirred strong patriotic support fanned by the popular press. If Shakespeare could offer skepticism through Falstaff, he could also evoke patriotic glory through Henry V's summoning up the courage of his troops as they prepare for Agincourt:

Dishonor not your mothers; now attest
That those whom you call'd fathers did beget you.
Be copy now to men of grosser blood
And teach them how to war ...
Follow your spirit, and upon this charge
Cry 'God for Harry, England, and Saint George!"

The conflict between these two attitudes has appeared in every British war over the past century, sometimes stifling satire and sometimes unleashing great floods of derisive opposition.

World War I

Perhaps no war in history has been as horrifyingly absurd as the first of the world wars — ridiculous in its origins; obscure in its war aims; ludicrous in its strategy of back-and-forth fighting to control a few hundred yards of torn-up dirt; shocking in the fatuous mismanagement by its generals; and barbarous in the massacre and maiming of the youth of several nations by advanced weapons of mass destruction: gas, tanks, artillery, and machine guns.

Yet in Britain patriotism surged. Young males who didn't volunteer (or were in civilian clothes after being invalided out) might receive a white feather from members of patriotic organizations. *Punch* magazine believed that, by providing humor, it was doing its patriotic duty:

When all allowance is made for shirkers and slackers and scaremongers, callous pleasure-seekers, faint-hearted pacifists, rebels and traitors, the great majority so bore themselves as to convince Mr. Punch that it was not only a privilege but a duty to minister to mirth even at times when one hastened to laugh for fear of being obliged to weep.[9]

Antiwar satirists were subjected to harassment and ostracism. Among them was George Bernard Shaw, whose views on war and heroism had already been set forth in 1894 in his *Arms and the Man*. The play's antihero, Blunchli, is dubbed "the chocolate cream soldier" because he has chocolates in his ammunition pouches on the principle that only young soldiers carry cartridges and pistols, whereas old soldiers carry food.[10] During the war Shaw was furiously attacked when he wrote the essay "Common Sense About the War" and when, objecting to the sentences of prison with hard labor on two pacifists, which he feared they might not survive, he made a modest proposal: Why not "shoot them out of hand and have done with it?"[11]

The historian Lytton Strachey registered as a conscientious objector. When Strachey, a homosexual, was asked the standard question: "What would you do if you saw a German soldier trying to rape your sister?" he replied: "I should endeavor to interpose my body between them". The board was outraged, and only his frail health saved him from prison. Some of his friends were less fortunate.

The most trenchant of all the British satires on World War I was a musical revue, Joan Littleton's *Oh! What A Lovely War*.[12] The show featured songs sung during World War I in sardonic verses fashioned by troops in the trenches. French, German, British, and Russian industrialists are shown discussing how to send military materials to each other's countries during the war and conspiring together to put an end to "peace scares."[13] The British commanding general defends his strategy of grinding them down. Since his country has the bigger population and the enemy is suffering greater losses, he explains, at the end he will have 10,000 men left to their 5,000, so he will have won.[14]

But *Oh! What A Lovely War* appeared in 1963. Its reception would have been less rapturous had it been presented during World War I.[15]

World War II

This time there was no debate about Britain's central war aim: survival. As in all wars, there were conscientious objectors; but their view did not find its way into published satire, which was directed mostly at Germany and Italy until Japan came in, after which even David Low initially drew the Japanese as monkeys (but refused to continue doing so).

So the draconian censorship that the war effort required did not bother British satirists — with one major exception: George Orwell. Charged with the responsibility of running a BBC program of talks by prominent figures, he was denied permission to use anyone who fell outside the mainstream, including Labourite Aneurin Bevan and the left-wing scientist, J. B. S. Haldane.[16]

But a still greater problem arose in connection with Orwell's *Animal Farm*. The novel was a poor fit for the war effort because it was a brilliant dissection not of an enemy of his government but of an ally, the Soviet Union. Orwell was a socialist, but a bitter opponent of Stalinism. He had fought on the government side against Franco's fascist forces in the Spanish civil war, but he had become deeply disillusioned with the ruthlessness and slavish subordination to Moscow of his fellow anti-fascists, the Communist party members. *Animal Farm* expressed his loathing of the Communists and the Soviet system in the form of a fable in which the animals revolt against the farmer in the name of freedom and equality until the revolution is taken over and corrupted by the pigs and their leader, Napoleon.

The analogy to the Russian Revolution, and to the specific characters of Stalin and Trotsky, is unmistakable. Today this would hardly seem controversial, but Orwell knew that, given the time in which *Animal Farm* was written, publication could be a problem. World War II was in its climactic stages, and the Soviet Union under Stalin was engaged in a deadly struggle against Nazi Germany and suffering massive losses.

Victor Gollancz, the usual publisher of Orwell's fiction and the main publisher of left-wing books, sent back the manuscript with the comment: "I am highly critical of many aspects of internal and external Soviet policy; but I could not possibly publish . . . a general attack of this nature." Another publisher, after asking the advice of the Ministry of Information, turned the book down on the grounds that it would be "highly ill-advised to publish at the present time" because it was too directly pointed at the Soviet Union and because "the choice of pigs as the ruling caste will no doubt give offense to many people, and particularly to anyone who is a bit touchy, as undoubtedly the Russians are . . . " (To the suggestion that a different animal might be used, Orwell wrote in the margin of the letter: "balls.") T. S. Eliot, as a director of the conservative Faber and Faber, found that the novel was "a distinguished piece of writing," but that "the effect is simply one of negation." For T. S. Eliot to rule against a fine novel for its lack of positive thinking was, to say the least, unconvincing. More to the point was Eliot's comment that, in any case, "it is not our kind of book."

After an American publisher had rejected it on the grounds that "it was impossible to sell animal stories in the USA," Orwell turned to Frederick Warburg, who hesitated, then decided to publish. There was a paper shortage and various other wartime production problems, so publication took over a year. At last *Animal Farm* was published in August 1945. The war in Europe was over.[17]

The Falklands

From 1958 the Campaign for Nuclear Disarmament, calling for unilateral British abandonment of nuclear weapons, had attracted the involvement of a high proportion of the country's intellectual, religious, and artistic elite, who participated in a huge annual protest march.[18] There were vociferous protests, too, against the Vietnam War, undoubtedly a factor in Harold Wilson's refusal to commit British troops. In 1981 Women for Life on Earth established a camp at Greenham Common with the intention of blockading a NATO (i.e., American) Cruise Missile base.

But any notion that British policy would shift toward pacifism was rudely dispelled in 1982 when Britain went to war to recapture the Falkland Islands after they had been invaded by Argentina.

Today this adventure seems like something out of the theater of the absurd, profuse with raw material for satire.[19] Said the Argentine writer,

Jorge Luis Borges, "The Falklands thing was a fight between two bald men over a comb."[20]

The stakes were indeed miniscule: control of the Falklands, one of the last tiny remnants of the British Empire, population 1,800, located 8,000 miles from London but 300 miles from Argentina, which called them the Malvinas and which had a long-standing claim to them at the UN. Various efforts at reaching a compromise settlement of the dispute failed because of intransigence on both sides. One proposal suggested by the Thatcher government was literally shouted down in the House of Commons by a die-hard group of right-wing Conservative back-benchers, the "Falklands lobby." Later proposals put forward by America ran afoul of Argentina President Galtieri's desire for military glory and Thatcher's temperamental dislike of half-measures.

The consequence was that, in response to an Argentine invasion of the island, a huge British flotilla of ships, submarines, troops, helicopters, and jets set out on a 50-day, 8,000-mile journey — a prodigious organizational feat culminating, after fierce, closely fought engagements, in the defeat and withdrawal of the Argentine forces.

Despite this enormous effort, the Falklands was a relatively small war, concluded in six weeks after some uncertain moments and spilling less blood than most wars. Still, for antiwar satirists there were more than enough casualties from fierce, brutal fighting to fuel their anger. British losses included 255 dead, 800 injured, 34 planes, and six ships. Argentina suffered 655 dead, including 358 in the sinking of the cruiser Belgrano by a submarine one day after the war began.

Finally, there was satirical material in the jingoistic blaring of much of the British popular press and the triumphalism at war's end. Tabloids screamed for the blood of the "Argies." The headline announcing the sinking of the Belgrano in Rupert Murdoch's *Sun* was beyond parody: "Gotcha!" *Private Eye* mocked the frenzied headlines with its own version of the *Sun*'s front page: "What the Sun Says, Kill All the Argies,"[21] and had Thatcher launching "a massive air-and-ground assault on the BBC" because of its scandalously evenhanded coverage of the war."[22]

Thatcher had no patience with those who dwelled too much on the war's cost or the projections that to keep the Falklands after the war would be absurdly expensive for Britain. Flak might be coming at her from all sides, but she was unmoved.

"Rejoice! Rejoice!" Thatcher proclaimed when it became clear that Britain would win; and she was furious when, at a service of thanksgiving after the war, the Archbishop of Canterbury gave a solemn sermon mourning the dead on both sides.

The majority were ready to "Rejoice!" with Thatcher. Though polls at the outset indicated mixed feelings about going to war to defend these far-off islands, once the flotilla was launched, pride in the embarked troops

Kevin Kallaugher (KAL), editorial cartoonist for *The Economist* and *The Baltimore Sun*, shows us that as prime minister Margaret Thatcher always saw herself as embattled, fighting for her convictions against enemies from every side. This cartoon dates from her first term, when she had to fend off attacks not only from the opposition parties and the media, but also from "wet" cabinet members inherited from past Conservative governments. A year later she was truly to assume the warrior's role in spearheading the Falklands War—again in the face of fierce criticism. [KAL, June 20, 1981 (Courtesy of Kevin Kallaugher).]

dominated. The only kind of satire most of the public was ready to respond to was that easiest of targets — Galtieri, one of the more obnoxious of the Latin American dictators of the period.

As was the case with some earlier wars, the most biting satire did not appear until the war was over. A John Mortimer novel in 1986 told of members of a local Conservative Association who didn't know where the Falkland Islands were, yet thoroughly enjoyed a war "which brought back irresistible memories of the Empire . . . and newspapers full of distant campaigns which didn't put them in the slightest danger."[23] In 1986, too, came Steve Berkhoff's verse play, *Sink the Belgrano*.[24] An official inquiry after the war confirmed that, despite Thatcher's denials, when the Belgrano was sunk it was not a threat to the arriving British forces but was outside a British-announced exclusion zone of 200 miles around the Islands and heading toward the mainland. Enraged by this event, Berkhoff's play mocked not only Thatcher ("Maggott Scratcher") and her war cabinet, but also the chauvinism of the British working class. Two decades later the issue was brought to life again in Tim Binding's novel, *The Anthem:*

> No matter that the land was no bigger than a back garden, a thumbnail scrap of unwanted scrub ... with penguins and sheep and a flying flag, denoting, like all the discarded baggage of yesteryear, a Gibraltar-like refusal to be dislodged.[25]

There were still conservative reviewers to be outraged by such reflections, but by then it was ancient history and no longer likely to stir widespread hostility.[26]

9/11

In Britain the initial reaction after 9/11 was a general empathy with American mourning, as British subjects were among the dead and there was concern about possible terrorists among Britain's Muslim population. The Blair government followed the American example of introducing anti-terrorist laws. Cartoonist Martin Rowson told of the same dilemma that had faced his American peers when submitting a cartoon for the *Scotsman* newspaper. Cartoons, he said, gained their power through the use of humor. But 9/ll wasn't funny, and he couldn't go after Bush on any related topics because

> for a couple of days at least, a cartoon was too blunt an instrument to say these things adequately without causing huge offence, and without making me feel like an insensitive schmuck.

Instead he drew a Statue of Liberty engulfed in a cloud from Lower Manhattan, then telephoned the editor to confess that the cartoon was meaningless. "That's about the right tone for the moment," the editor replied.[27]

However, the British satirists' restraint did not last as long as in the United States. The British, after all, were not newcomers to disaster striking from abroad, and the majority had no use for George W. Bush. Though most British cartoonists were as subdued as Martin Rowson immediately after the event, they soon returned to the attack. In any case, the *Guardian*'s Steve Bell never shared Rowson's example. In fact, said Rowson, he had been "soundly told off by Steve Bell for my hackneyed cowardice."

Muslim comic Shazia Mirza who, as a woman, was already defying her culture's taboos, had been scared to go on stage when the tragedy struck. "When 9/11 happened, I thought I'm never going to be able to do stand-up comedy ever again," she said. Yet just three weeks after 9/11 she appeared in a London club, opening with: "Hello, my name's Shazia Mirza, at least that's what it says on my pilot's license." The audience gasped, then laughed. "There was so much tension in that room when I'd walked on that people were actually quite relieved that they could laugh."[28]

Iraq

In Britain a still larger proportion of the public than in America was infuriated by the Iraq War. The deep unpopularity of Blair's unwavering support of the war and his commitment of over 40,000 British troops[29] — far more than any other U.S. ally — infused a new vigor into the long tradition of antiwar protest in Britain.

This time Martin Rowson was not be outdone by Steve Bell in the savagery of his portrayals of Blair and the war. As for Bell, he was not among the journalists embedded with the troops in Iraq. "I believe passionately in the idea of cartoon reportage," he said, but "certainly not in the present circumstances with the military breathing down my neck."[30] So he continued his ferocious depictions of Bush, Blair, and their war.

What about censorship during the war? "Personally speaking," said Bell, "there is no more 'censorship' than usual." The only thing he had to adapt slightly was the "turd count" in one cartoon. He agreed to "remove three splattered turds" from a version that appeared in the printed newspaper; but he was pleased to report that all the turds remained in the version that appeared on the Web.[31] Having to remove a few turds from a cartoon is one of the least oppressive examples in the chronicle of wartime censorship.

SEX AFTER THE VICTORIANS

Sexual behavior in Britain during the Victorian era was not quite the same as the "Victorian" myth. Nonetheless, the censor was intervening busily to prevent open discussion of sex and sexuality. The 1857 Obscene Publications Act empowered magistrates to order the destruction of offending books and prints, which led to a magistrate's declaring in 1915 that D. H. Lawrence's *The Rainbow* was "utter filth" and ordering all copies destroyed. Vaudeville and music hall comedians thrived on sexual innuendoes and off-color jokes, but in more proper venues a puritanical attitude persisted well into the twentieth century, monitored by censorship agencies.

Among them was the British movie industry's Board of Censors. While firmly outlawing "Bolshevist propaganda" and "white men in state of degradation amidst native surroundings," the Board regarded sex as a still greater menace. There must be no nude or semi-nude figures, no mention of marital infidelity, "passionate and unrestrained embraces," and "lecherous old men."[32] In the theater, the Lord Chamberlain blue-penciled innumerable references to homosexuals ("perverts"), including some camp lines in a production of *Beyond the Fringe*.[33] In play after play it took out words like "piss off," "buggered," "short-arsed," and references to pubic hair and "excessive lovemaking."[34]

The BBC from its creation in the 1920s avoided sexual references that might give offense to the Church of England; and a 1948 policy placed an absolute ban on jokes about "lavatories, effeminacy in men, and immorality of any kind" as well as honeymoon couples, chambermaids, fig leaves, prostitution, and "ladies underwear, e.g., winter draws on."[35]

Eventually a profound cultural shift produced new, permissive legislation in 1959, and a jury verdict on Lawrence's *Lady Chatterly's Lover* removed any inhibitions from the publication of sexually explicit material, as well as the previously forbidden language used to convey it.

The transformation of what could appear in print was followed by changes in other media. By the end of the 1960s the movie codes were gone, transmuted into age-related ratings. With the abolition of the Lord Chamberlain, film and theater knew almost no sexual limits. On television everything changed for the BBC in 1956, when commercial TV and radio were allowed to enter the field. In the ratings war that followed, the BBC could no longer be straitlaced; one of its top-rated TV comedians for several years, Benny Hill, was as lewd as Aristophanes.

Censorship of nude performances has also been lifted. During World War II, the Windmill Theater in London was able to defy the ban on nudity onstage by arguing that the law did not apply to stationary nude tableaux, for these were artistic expressions. Today no such subterfuges are necessary. Whereas American TV stations did not show repeats of the Super Bowl bared breast, British TV did. *The Economist,* tongue in cheek, deplored this degradation of the British press, and "as a service to American readers, who should know how low it has fallen," it reprinted the offending picture.[36]

In any case, the British are inured to the sight. A daily feature on page 3 of Rupert Murdoch's *Sun* newspaper is a lubricious pair of bare breasts. Apparently Murdoch, as a conservative, has had periodic pangs of conscience about these displays. However, any qualms have been overwhelmed by business considerations, for the page 3 photos are immensely popular.

As in America, a few prohibitions persist. The f-word is forbidden in prime time on television, though it has slipped out a few times. To protect children, potentially offensive programs are scheduled after 9 PM, and a warning is issued "if we judge some people may find a particular broadcast distressing."

Certainly in July 2001 some people found the satirical TV program, *Brass Eye,* distressing. The program presented a spoof of the media's hyping of pedophile cases, inveigling celebrities into reciting absurd "facts" such as, "We have footage, too alarming to show you, of a little boy being interfered with by a penis-shaped sound wave generated by an online pedophile." The program concluded with a fictional crowd capturing a pedophile and burning him on a 25-foot phallus. There was a wave of protest from the public and rebukes from government ministers, showing that there are still topics, such as rape and child molestation, that are generally regarded as unfit subjects for publicly expressed humor.

Even so, it is all a far cry from the Victorian era when it was said of *Punch* magazine: "It will provoke a hearty laugh, but never bring a blush to the most innocent cheek."

RACE AND RELIGION: TESTING THE LIMITS

In Britain religion had been central to Victorian values. Even in the twentieth century, the British movie codes banned irreverent quotations of religious texts, travesties of religious services and well-known hymns, comic treatment of incidents connected with death and the materialized figure of Christ.[37] In the theater, too, the Lord Chamberlain maintained a watchful attitude to prevent blasphemy, and there was a blanket prohibition against "the impersonation of Christ or the Deity on the stage."[38]

Today, however, despite the existence of an official, "Established" Church of England, the British tend to be irregular in their religious observance and somewhat relaxed in their beliefs. So, there is a sharp contrast between British and American attitudes on organized religion. Whereas in America almost 60 percent insist that to be a moral person one must believe in God, only a quarter of the British public agree. Overwhelmingly, British ministers of religion reject a literal interpretation of the Bible. There is no effective equivalent in British politics of the fundamentalist right wing in America. In 2005 a new law authorized civil partnerships that gave gays legal rights comparable to those in marriages.

Blair, a faithful churchgoer, has referred to his religion as his moral guide to his policies. *Private Eye,* always unconvinced of the purity of his motives, scoffed at Lord Hutton's report clearing him of deceiving the public over Iraq and cast Blair again as the sanctimonious Vicar of St. Albion Parish: "Vicar Innocent — It's Official!!!"[39] Even so, Blair as prime minister did not mention his faith as often as Bush, did not end every speech with "God bless Britain," and avoided any suggestion that on Iraq he was carrying out God's purpose. As his spokesperson Alastair Campbell pointed out, in Britain "we don't do God."[40]

So the climate of opinion for satire on religion in Britain is very different from the one prevailing in the United States. The Church of England was fair game for *Monty Python,* and a number of comedians have featured farcical impersonations of clergymen in their routines. An *Establishment* revue sketch in the 1960s even mocked the new, highly praised Coventry Cathedral, which replaced the one destroyed by German bombs in World War II. The sketch congratulated the people of the city for choosing a cathedral, where they can "pray for such things as hospitals, schools, and houses" rather than spending the money on hospitals, schools, and houses.[41]

However, the prevailing attitude of tolerance toward satire on religion was severely tested by a storm of protest when the BBC proposed a television version of the London stage show, *Jerry Springer: The Opera,* a send-up of the raucous American TV interview program. Christian groups insisted that a publicly supported network should not be presenting a program that was profoundly blasphemous, featuring a gay Jesus and the Devil in a swearing tirade against each other. The show went on as scheduled, provoking thousands of complaints.[42]

Clearly, however, *Jerry Springer* came close to the limits of what the BBC would tolerate. Those limits had already been passed the previous year, when Catholic groups forced the cancellation of a cartoon satire, *Popetown,* which included the pope on a pogo stick surrounded by backstabbing cardinals.

Whereas religious conflict goes back into centuries of British history, there was no overt race problem in Britain until the 1950s. This was because, apart from Chinese who ran laundries and small restaurants and a few blacks in port cities, there was only one race. There had been no major wave of immigration since 1066.[43]

This changed after World War II, when a shortage of unskilled and semi-skilled labor prompted Britain to recruit from the populations of its soon-to-collapse Empire, first from the West Indies and Africa, then from the Indian subcontinent. Though both parties took turns at tightening the requirements for immigration, the numbers increased until, by the millennia's end, close to 1 in 12 of the British population were nonwhite.

In the wake of this rapid growth of immigrants, satire was sure to follow, for satire feeds on irony, of which there was no shortage. There was irony as the immigrants, initially welcomed to do the dirty jobs that no one else wanted, faced resentment when the job market tightened and there was competition for scarce housing. There was irony, too, as the insular British, who had previously looked down on American-style prejudice, showed some of the same symptoms of racism.

In 1968, a prominent Conservative, Enoch Powell, made an extraordinary speech on the subject. A classical scholar, Powell warned portentously: "As I look ahead, I am filled with foreboding. Like the Roman, I seem to see "the River Tiber foaming with much blood.""

Edward Heath, the Conservative Party leader in opposition, was outraged, and he fired Powell from his leadership team. Cartoonists jumped on Powell's message and his fiery "rivers of blood" imagery.[44]

However, while party leaders and satirists deplored Powell's speech, it touched a chord among large numbers of people who inundated Powell with letters of support. Tabloid newspapers weighed in with demands for less immigration and tougher laws against the alleged high crime rates among the new populations. Ten years after Powell's speech and before she became prime minister, Margaret Thatcher spoke for many in a TV interview when she worried that if the rate of immigration continued "the British character ... might be swamped." On their side, immigrants resented the prejudice which, they believed, kept so many of them unemployed and in poverty. In the 1980s there were racially driven riots in a number of cities.

However, the rivers did not foam with blood. Race Relations Acts were passed that brought a measure of relief to the immigrants, many of whom began to do well economically and educationally. Though deep racial prejudices remained, along with continued hostility to high rates of immigration (directed by century's end at east Europeans as much as people of color), there were rising hopes that, in time, Britain would become a reasonably tolerant, multiracial society.

As the experience of Muslim comedienne Shazia Mirrza made clear, however, a new, dangerous dimension was thrust into the issue after 9/11, which was to be intensified after the bombing of London underground trains and buses in 2005. The Blair government responded with still more stringent antiterrorist laws, and inescapably the focus of attention was on Britain's Muslim population. This meant that tensions over race and ethnicity were now interwoven with controversies over religion.

Accordingly, in 2004 the Blair government, eager to demonstrate that its antiterrorist drive was not driven by animus toward Muslims, proposed legislation against "incitement to racial or religious hatred."

Civil liberties organizations led a coalition against government interference. Included were a number of popular comedians who complained that the law could be interpreted to inhibit their routines on religion. The government minister in charge of the legislation rejected the complaint. It was not true, he said, that the proposal would prohibit gags about religion. "Here's the punch line," he said. "Nothing I've suggested is an attack on people's rights to legitimately criticize religion or make jokes about it."[45]

Opponents of the bill were not mollified, and the government suffered two defeats on the issue on the floor of the House. When a bill finally passed in 2006, it was in considerably modified form.[46] Even then members from all parties expressed doubts, and a Labour MP asked the government spokesman if the proposed law could result in the prosecution of anyone who published the cartoons from Denmark lampooning Mohammed. The answer, said the minister, was yes "if there was an intention to stir up hatred."

In fact, the British media, like their American counterparts, were almost unanimous in deciding not to reproduce the Danish cartoons.[47] The BBC did show them, but only in one telecast in the context of its coverage of the storm erupting when they appeared in a French humor journal. The conservative weekly, *The Spectator,* though repeatedly arguing that the pressures against honest discussion of racial and ethnic issues, especially by Muslims, had become intolerable, nonetheless withdrew the cartoons from its Web site after showing them once. Only the far-right British National Party and *Wikipedia*,[48] the online encyclopedia, published the cartoons on their Web sites.

The liberal media were especially reluctant to support a right-wing Danish newspaper and to join a cause that was enthusiastically endorsed by anti-immigrant parties. They balked at ridiculing the beliefs of what they saw as a politically weak minority. Said the *Guardian,* the most liberal of the British dailies:

> The Guardian believes uncompromisingly in freedom of expression, but not in any duty gratuitously to offend. It would be senselessly provocative to reproduce a set of images, of no intrinsic value, which pander to the worst prejudices about Muslims . . . even if the intention was satirical rather than blasphemous.[49]

However, the *Guardian*'s online edition told its readers that they could find the gratuitously offending cartoons by going to *Wikipedia*.

Another British liberal daily, the *Independent,* also declared itself in favor of free speech, but it decided not to reproduce the cartoons after chiding *France Soir,* which had printed the cartoons, for "throwing petrol on the flames of a fire that shows every sign of turning into an international conflagration."[50] As the *Independent* saw it, "there is an important distinction to be made between having a right and choosing to exercise it." Yet the paper had chosen to exercise its right to publish a highly provocative cartoon by David Brown, which went on to win the 2003 Cartoon of the Year award of the Political Cartoon Society of the United Kingdom. Based on Goya's "Saturn Devouring One of His Children," the cartoon portrayed a naked Ariel Sharon biting off the head of a Palestinian child, with Sharon inquiring, "What's wrong? You never seen a politician kissing babies before?" It was published on January 27, Britain's Holocaust Memorial Day.

Evidently, civil liberties in a multicultural society has become an even more complicated issue than when the battles were being fought by John Milton and John Stuart Mill.

part 2

A DANGEROUS GAME: POLITICAL SATIRE IN AUTHORITARIAN SYSTEMS

chapter five

WHAT'S FUNNY ABOUT HITLER?

Hitler: haranguing his lunatic views
Of Germany ruined by villainous Jews.
What kind of image should satire evoke?
A monster? Or simply a farcical joke?

No political leader has been the subject of as much ridicule over a longer period than Adolf Hitler. While he was in power he was immune from public criticism within Germany. Yet because he had to win office by election he was a prime target of bitter wit even before he became Der Führer. Once in office he was laughed at from abroad by his exiled nationals and by satirists in other countries. After the ignominious overthrow of the "Thousand Year Reich," 988 years short of its goal, Hitler was established as the ultimate satirical icon, the perpetual target of derisive scorn.

HITLER DURING WEIMAR

The end of World War I ushered in a heady period for free spirits of all kinds in Germany. For the first time they were liberated from a long history of censorship. The 1819 Carlsbad Decrees had codified the censorship systems of the several German states into the most elaborate, highly structured system of censorship in Europe. Satire existed, but only by virtue of a constant effort by satirists and publishers to circumvent the censors, moving their publications from less to more lenient states, playing one censor off against another, sending books off in delivery wagons in all directions so they would be sold before the bureaucratic machinery could catch up with them. Though the Decrees were repealed in 1848 and the 1874 Reich Press Law further extended the right to publish freely, a number of restrictive laws remained on the books under which satirical journals were periodically closed down, their writers and artists fined and even jailed.

All that was gone under Weimar. Literature and the arts knew no bounds, and everywhere there was experimentation and the testing of sexual and political limits. Yet, delight in freedom from former restraints was soon dampened by the bitter realities that followed the war. The humiliation of defeat, the harsh sanctions imposed by the victorious allies, and the runaway

Adolf

*Der Häuptling vom Stamm der wilden Kopfjäger nach der
Schlacht von Leipzig — in vollem Kriegsschmuck*

This is one of the many cartoons lampooning Hitler before he came to power. The caption reads: "The corporal from the tribe of wild headhunters after the battle of Leipzig—in full war regalia." Hitler had been a corporal in Germany's defeated World War I army, and here he is mocked as a barbarian celebrating a victory from the past. (The Battle of Leipzig refers to the massive war of 1813, which Napoleon lost to an army drawn from Austria, Prussia, Sweden, and Russia.) The head on the spear refers to one of Hitler's threats that, once he came to power, some of the Weimar "heads" would be taken care of. [Berlin October 7, 1930. Cited in Randall L. Bytwerk, German Propaganda Archive: Hitler in Caricature, http://www.calvin.edu/academic/cas/gpa/caric.htm, from Ernst Hanftsaengl, Hitler in der Karikatur der Welt.Tat gegen Tinte (Berlin: Verlag Braune Bücher, Carl Rentsch, 1933).]

inflation followed by economic depression created a national mood of profound anxiety and resentment against the government parties.

It set the stage for the emergence of Adolf Hitler. The myth of the strong man who could lead his nation to salvation was strongly rooted in German culture. Heinrich Mann's 1914 satirical novel, *Der Untertan* ("The Loyal Subject"), had warned against this myth. Mann had his principal character cheer the Kaiser as he passes in a parade:

> There on the horse rode Power... The Power that transcends us and whose hooves we kiss, the Power which is beyond the reach of hunger, spite and mockery!... Which we have in our blood, for in our blood is submission... In it we live and have our being, merciless toward those who are remote beneath us, and triumphing even when we ourselves are crushed, for thus does power justify our love for it.[1]

To more and more of Germany's Loyal Subjects, Hitler's frenzied message of a nation regenerated at home, reasserting itself abroad, and eliminating the alleged domination of the Jews seemed the answer. As his appeal spread, satirists began their mockery. Caricaturists fastened not only on his odd appearance and mannerisms but also on his insatiable drive for total power. They warned that if he came to power, the result would be total disaster for Germany. One cartoon mocked Hitler's grim boast in 1930 that, when he became Chancellor, a large number of Weimar "heads" would be removed to concentration camps:

Many of the political cartoons were featured in satirical magazines. The oldest of them was *Kladderadatsch* that had burst into print in 1848 with a headline, "We are traitors and king-haters. We are robbers, murderers and canaille," and a manifesto:

> The time's turned upside down!... Princes are overthrown... castles have been looted... virgins outraged... Jews persecuted... priests murdered... barricades erected... Kladderadatsch! "[2]

This radical fervor did not carry through into Weimar because after its early years of taunting kings, generals, and Junkers and fighting on behalf of constitutionalism and civil liberties, the magazine's publishers became frightened by the rise of working-class socialism, turned more conservative, and fawned on Bismarck, the "Iron Chancellor." During Weimar, though it had some doubts about Hitler, *Kladderadatsch* resolved them without a struggle and later would serve the Nazi regime docilely. Other right-wing humor journals were even more sympathetic to Hitler, jeering at the new republic and its leaders, the trade unions, Bolshevism, and the Jews.

Still, there were magazines on the other side, notably *Simplicissimus,* founded in 1896. *Simplicissimus* savaged every source of power in the system, and with the ascension of the pompous, strutting William II to the throne of the united Germany, had specialized in "Kaiserwitz," the lampooning of the king and his policies. Here, indeed, was lès majesté in its most insolent form. *Simplicissimus* did not operate with impunity. Despite the Reich Press Law, enough restrictive laws were still on the books to impose confiscations and bans on the magazine and six-month jail sentences for a caricaturist and a writer.

Yet *Simplicissimus,* using a variety of tricks to cheat the censors, survived — until the onset of the Great War, when its courageous defiance of authority ended in a whimper and *Simplicissimus* left behind its antimilitaristic, anti-nationalistic positions. The only division on the staff was whether the magazine should cease publication because satire was inappropriate at such a time (as in America after 9/11) or whether its duty (like *Punch* in World War I) was to join the war effort, which meant providing jokes to relieve the grimness of war and ridiculing the enemy nations. The decision was that "no German could stand aside" in a "defensive" war.[3]

With the war ended, however, *Simplicissimus* recovered much of its old form, speaking out for civil liberties and opposing Hitler from the beginning of the Nazi movement.

Initially the magazine treated Hitler as a buffoon, not to be taken seriously. This approach reflected the attitude of many liberal Germans at the time. It seemed inconceivable to them that the German people, so highly educated, so fortunate in their inheritance of a brilliant high culture of the arts and sciences, could be taken in by the brutal ravings of a street-corner ranter surrounded by thugs. Moreover, there seemed little reason at first to panic, for support for the Nazis was still in the single digits in 1924. Hitler, having been jailed in 1923 for taking part in an attempted coup, was banned from speaking in several of the German states in 1925 — and the Nazi Party was banned in Berlin in 1927. In any case, *Simplicissimus*'s business was satire. Hitler, with his silly little moustache, his full-arm salute, and marionette gestures was, in the eyes of any rational person, utterly absurd.

The satire turned darker toward the end of the decade as the worldwide Depression took hold in Germany and support for the Nazis shot upward. One cartoon depicted Nazism as a skeletal monster luring the German masses to their doom.[4] Even after Hitler was appointed Chancellor by Hindenburg in 1932, *Simplicissimus* included a cartoon depicting Hindenburg as a magician producing a string of chancellors from a top hat, with the caption: "So long as chancellors can be produced on the assembly line, we have nothing to worry about."[5]

In fact, they had a great deal to worry about, and *Simplicissimus*'s publisher emigrated to Switzerland. He urged Thomas Theodore Heine, a Jew and the magazine's founder and principal cartoonist, to follow his example. Heine had held on, refusing to see the grim sequence of events as anything but an absurd farce that must soon give way to reality. But the joke had a different punch line: three Nazis invaded an editorial meeting and ordered Heine to stop working, after which he left the country. *Simplicissimus* then followed the Nazis as they had followed the Kaiser into World War I.

Another stream of mockery of the Nazis came from "literary cabarets" later made famous by Christopher Isherwood's novel, *Goodbye to Berlin,* and the Broadway musical and film, *Cabaret.* Many of these revues featured nude dancing and other escapist entertainment, and those that did include political satire varied widely in their bias. Some echoed the angry resentments of the right-wing journals. Others, however, expressed liberal and left opposition to militarism, big business, and anti-Semitism. Among them was *The Wild Stage,* in which Bertolt Brecht caused a furor by performing his own "Ballad of the Dead Soldier," telling of the German army being so short of manpower that it digs up an already killed soldier and sends him back to the front.

On the far left were the communists, whose satirical *Red Revues* were intended as "agitprop" to fire up the enthusiasm of their supporters, and they primly disapproved when the audiences enjoyed them primarily as entertainment. One performer, after telling a series of jokes, scolded his audience for laughing at his jokes:

> You laugh and laugh. You even laugh at your own stupidity. Instead of banding together, going to the [reformist] trade unions and beating them to shit —you let this rubbish happen every day —and you even laugh about it.[6]

Though the Communists were hostile to the Nazis, the prime target of their diatribes and satire were the "reformist trade unions" and the moderate left Social Democrats, and this internecine warfare on the left helped open the way for Hitler.

Others on the left were less doctrinaire. Kurt Tucholsky, who wrote material for various cabarets, was a pacifist and deeply hostile to the reactionary right. Yet not all of his lyrics were radical. As an artist he was concerned about reaching his audience, and sometimes he soft-pedaled his views, even catered to their prejudices, to avoid alienating them. As he saw it:

> The harshest and most pitiless German censor does not sit in a bureaucratic office, but in the parquet . . . The middle class, the bourgeois . . . will not stand for radicalism in a variety show and will never forgive a singer for it.[7]

Something of this attitude prevailed in *Katacombe,* founded in 1929. As in most of the cabarets, its content was not solely or even primarily political. Yet *Katacombe* always included political skits and songs, some by Tucholsky. However, the cabaret's general line was cautious. There were jokes about the Nazis, yet the punches were usually pulled, as was clearly demonstrated by the fact that *Katacombe* actually continued for two years after

Hitler's ascension to power in 1933. For example, in 1935 a reviewer in a Nazi publication wrote of a performance:

> A witty program flits across the stage, in cabaret style, loosened up with the laughter of a gladly permitted fool's license ... The evening is full of happy, ingeniously honed merriment."[8]

Katacombe's survival instinct was such that, even after the Jewish members of the troupe fled the country in 1934, they were soon replaced and the show went on. Yet it is important to see *Katacombe*'s non-confrontational style in the context of the time. By the late 1920s there was always the danger of disruption by Nazi thugs. With the Nazis in power, a 1933 "law against the treacherous attacks on the state and party and for the protection of the party uniform" defined jokes about the party and its leaders as treasonous. This was no empty threat, for tellers of political jokes were among the more than 5,000 sentenced to death by a "People's Court" meeting in closed session.[9]

Directly challenging the Nazis, then, would be dangerous, even suicidal. A more ambiguous style was not merely a condition of survival, but it could be the most effective way of communicating an anti-Nazi message to a receptive and sophisticated audience. That message, if subtle, was hardly in doubt. In 1930, for example, *Katacombe* offered a comment on the German middle class that adapted docilely to the regime of the moment:

> I was a monarchist under the Kaiser, and then I was for the (Republic). And when leftist coups threatened, I was for equality all around ... And now I'm for the Third Reich.[10]

Werner Finck was *Katacombe*'s leading comedian. One admirer said of him that, even though he repeatedly risked his life:

> I don't think that happened for the sake of his convictions, but rather for the sake of his punch lines — he would have spilled his blood to defend them. He was less interested in what he said than the form in which he said it."[11]

He was not a man of the left, and some of his routines had raised the ire of Jewish organizations,[12] but he had no love of the Nazis. In 1932, when a Nazi in the audience shouted "Dirty Jew" at Finck (who was not Jewish), he responded: "I am afraid you are mistaken. I only look this intelligent." Finck was especially effective in his digs at the Nazis with a method of "indirection," such as stammering and using incomplete sentences, leaving it to the audience to fill in the gaps. The audience had no trouble doing so; and the very indirectness and subtlety of the wit was a large part of its appeal.

However oblique its references, however non-confrontational its style, sooner or later *Katacombe* was bound to become unacceptable to a movement as intolerant and humorless as Nazism. In 1935, acting on an anonymous tip, detectives sat in on the 23rd *Katacombe* revue. They found only one routine they considered offensive — a Werner Finck sketch in which Finck refuses to open his mouth for a dentist because "I don't know you."[13] But it was enough to bring detectives to the next program, the 24th, and this proved to be *Katacombe*'s downfall, for there were satirical references to Goering, control of the press, the loss of civil liberties, the danger of war, and even concentration camps.

Finck protested disingenuously that the Gestapo had misunderstood the references, but he and two other cast members were sentenced to six months hard labor in a concentration camp, then put on trial for treachery. At the trial they performed the objectionable routines, and a jury them found not guilty. The rule of law was quickly swept aside, however. The government forbade Finck to perform for a year, and in 1939 he was arrested again and placed under a permanent ban (though he performed for frontline troops during the war). It was but one minor aspect of the step-by-step closing of the system by the Nazis.

SATIRE UNDER NAZISM

Hitler was appointed Chancellor by President Hindenburg after his Nazi party received 37% of the votes cast in a multi-party election. Three months later the Nazis, having used their authority to intimidate the opposition, moved up to 44% of the total, after which Hitler pushed through an "enabling act" that gave him dictatorial powers. Thenceforth there was only one party, the labor unions were replaced by the official Labor Front, and other organizations were brought within the government's orbit. The rule of law was abandoned as millions of Jews, gypsies, dissidents, and other undesirables were summarily incarcerated in concentration camps, from which most never emerged alive.

The press was controlled, first by intimidation, then by a Reich editorial law supervised by Joseph Goebbels's Ministry of Public Enlightenment and Propaganda that held editors responsible for the appearance of any "offensive" or "subversive" material. Goebbels, anxious to prove to foreign detractors that Nazis had a sense of humor, insisted that satire be used in a number of journals as a bludgeon against detractors at home and abroad. *Simplicissimus* presented cartoons hailing Hitler as an apostle of peace, Stalin standing on a pile of corpses, Churchill and Roosevelt as diabolical exploiters and warmongers, and a Trojan Horse arriving in London spilling out Jews exiled from Germany. [14]

A *Kladderadatch* cartoon in 1939 showed Polish police attacking a German school in Poland, while British Prime Minister Neville Chamberlain tells the House of Commons: "I can only admire the remarkable calm and intelligent restraint of the Polish government."[15]

Julian Streicher's paper, *Der Sturmer*, also included heavyhanded cartoons, with a specialty of viciously mocking the Jews, while Goebbels's weekly, *Das Reich*, focused during the war on taunting Churchill, Roosevelt, and Stalin. From 1931 to 1938 the Nazis published a humor magazine, *Brennessel*, which targeted the usual culprits: enemy leaders and Jews. In a cartoon series on the theme "A Scene from the Good Old Days," the magazine pictured Jews as having controlled the German press, and a malignant Karl Marx beckoned the German workers to their destruction.

Also targeted by *Brennesel* were domestic slackers and complainers. To complain, says one commentator, "was to exhibit a lack of faith in the Führer and Fatherland. Whatever problems there were could be solved by those in authority. There was no need for meddling by the masses."[16] This was all very well as support for Goebbels's propaganda themes, but scolding the dissatisfied, rather than providing a release through humor for the dissatisfactions, was a weak formula for satire. With its circulation falling, *Brennesel* folded in 1938. Even Hitler called it "the dreariest rag imaginable."[17]

Still, no German writer during the Nazi years lacked an outlet for ferocious satire against the Jews. For example, an Austrian writing under the pen name of "Mungo" wrote "The Panic Party" in 1939, in which he jeered brutally at the fate of Jews trying to flee Germany, only to find that their ship, the Saint Louis, is turned away by country after country. Who asked them, he wanted to know, to wander through the world, trying to evoke sympathy with pitiful cries of despair and threats of suicide? And was it Germany's fault if all these countries refused to let them land?

> As far as we are concerned, they can wring their hands in their lifeboats until they look like old washer women ... Ahasver (the legendary Wandering Jew) has been moving around the world since a bit longer than 1933 without finding rest. Did we send him on his way?"[18]

This malignant satire carries an impact even today, for unfortunately it was one piece of Nazi propaganda that was not based on a lie but on a terrible reality.[19]

From 1933 to 1945 no anti-Nazi satire appeared in print in Germany. Yet the constant barrage of propaganda did not succeed in submerging all humorous thrusts at the regime. Resentment of the government sometimes surfaced in convivial gatherings in local bars after a few drinks:

> Jokes were told, songs were sung; and the leaders of the party and state from Hitler down to local functionaries, were cursed and maligned ...

Hitler was variously a dog, a swindler, a megalomaniac, an idiot, a scoundrel (ein Lausbub) and — significantly — queer or Jewish."[20]

There was always the danger that police informers or Nazi functionaries would be present, eager to report such treacherous comments. So the one widespread form of political humor was the "whispered joke," passed along from individual to individual. They had better be whispered. In 1944 a People's Court passed a death sentence on a Catholic priest for telling two members of his flock a joke about a dying German soldier who asked his chaplain: "Place a picture of Hitler on one side of me, and a picture of (Hermann) Goering on the other side. That way I can die like Jesus between two thieves."[21]

Still the jokes persisted and spread, with Goering and Goebbels as the favorite butts, though Hitler was not neglected. Sometimes the jokes were rumored to have originated with popular comedians, but usually the authors were unknown. They were not published during the Nazi era, of course, but after the war large numbers appeared in print. Among them:

Hitler falls into a lake and is saved by three passing Hitler Youths. He promises to grant each of them a wish. The first two ask to join prestigious military units. The third asks for a state funeral. Hitler asks why. "As soon as my father finds out who I've helped to rescue, he'll wring my neck."

Two men in a tramcar make strange gestures to each other, then burst out laughing. A passenger explains: "They are deaf and dumb. They are telling each other political jokes." [22]

And there were the self-deprecating Jewish jokes:

Two Jews plan to assassinate Hitler. They wait for him with guns loaded at a corner he passes every day at noon. They wait, but he hasn't arrived at 12.15. "My goodness," says one of the men. "I hope nothing's happened to him."[23]

Similar jokes were told in the countries overrun by Germany during the war. Several of them told the joke about the Nazi officer being shown around Luxembourg and being introduced to the admiralty. "But why do you need an admiralty? Luxembourg hasn't got a navy." The reply: "Isn't there a Ministry of Justice in Berlin?" The French told the story of the Nazi commandant in Paris confronting Picasso with a copy of Guernica and demanding "Did you do that?" "No," replied Picasso, "You did." [24]

There was even, in Steve Lipman's words "laughter in hell" — humor in the death camps. A Dutch Jewish teenager, who survived Auschwitz, organized vaudeville shows in the camp:

In spite of all our agony and pain we never lost our ability to laugh at ourselves and our miserable situation. We had to make jokes to survive and save ourselves from deep depression. We mimicked our top over-seers and I did impersonations about camp life, and somebody did a little tap dance, different funny, crazy things. The overseers slipped into the barracks while we weren't looking, and instead of giving us a punishment they were laughing their heads off.[25]

In Dachau in 1943 a prisoners' theater went beyond jokes about the camp's overseers to mock the Nazis and Hitler himself through an allegory in which an actor impersonated Hitler's speeches and gestures. The Nazi guards, members of the SS, sat in the front row, apparently enjoying the show — until it was closed down after a run of six weeks on orders from Berlin.[26]

HITLER IN THE WORLD OF SATIRE

Hitler had been able to suppress almost all public dissent within Germany during his 12 years of power, but he could not control what Germans were writing in exile. Neither could he control what the outside world was saying about him while he spread his domination through Europe, nor how his memory would be savaged by Germans and everyone else after his ignomini-ous demise.

Germans in exile during the Third Reich kept up a drumfire of angry sat-ire. In *The Private Life of the Master Race*,[27] Bertolt Brecht, who went into exile in 1933, shows how some Germans fearfully, others willingly, coped with life under Hitler. A physicist quotes Einstein, and then, realizing in panic that he may have been overheard, says loudly: "Yes, typical Jewish sophistry! What has that to do with physics?"[28] A judge, desperately eager to render a verdict that will please the regime, but discovering that there are disagreements among the Nazis on the case, whines:

I decide this and I decide that as they require, but at least I must know what they require. When you don't know that, there is no justice any more.[29]

A man speaks indiscreetly about the Nazis to his wife and, when his young son goes out on an errand, bursts out in terror that the boy has heard what he said, has turned informer, and has gone out to turn him in. The boy returns, shows them the candy he has bought. But, the parents wonder, is that all he did?[30]

Brecht's play, *The Resistible Rise of Arturo Ui*,[31] transposes Hitler into a Chicago racketeer who uses a protection racket to take over the vegetable trade. Brecht lampoons the tyrant's promise to protect the grocers from force and violence "with force and violence if necessary"[32] and to guarantee universal peace through more machine guns and rubber truncheons. With the extension of Ui's power to Cicero and beyond, Brecht reminds us of the insatiability of the dictator's demands for power. A few characters in the play resist, and are promptly shot. Many more are either bought off or intimidated by the gangster, or they simply go along with the tide. At the end Ui has made his deal with the established powers, The Trust.

After the war's end came an even more stark depiction of the terror of the Nazi era: *This Way for the Gas, Ladies and Gentlemen,* a collection of stories by Tadeusz Borowski, a survivor of Auschwitz and Dachau who later committed suicide by gassing himself. Borowski's book details life in the camps and takes us to the boundary between satire and horror. There is a macabre wit in the efforts of the inmates to establish normal routines in the face of the ever-present prospect of annihilation, and, as the title suggests, in the contrast between the polite language and the vicious behavior of the guards:

> "Meine Herrschaften, this way, ladies and gentlemen, try not to throw your things around please. Show some goodwill," he says courteously, his restless hands playing with the slender whip.[33]

Günter Grass's novel, *The Tin Drum,*[34] is less horrifying, for though the setting is Germany in the 1930s, the main action involves the picaresque adventures of Oskar, who decides at the age of three to stop growing and performs miraculous tricks with his tin drums and his glass-shattering voice. Yet the comedy is dark, and evil in all its banality is demonstrated by the ordinariness of the Nazi characters, including one who had "bravely" helped set fire to a synagogue on Kristallnacht but who is stricken from the party's membership lists because of his "cruelty to animals which could only impair the party's reputation."[35] Grass has derisive comments for the innumerable Germans who, at war's end, insisted they had never been Nazis — had, in fact, always been good Social Democrats.

Satirists from many other nations have joined the anti-Hitler chorus. Even as Germany launched its onslaught on Europe, Charlie Chaplin's *The Great Dictator* made Hitler the butt of international hilarity. In the dual role of Hitler and a look-alike Jewish barber who is mistakenly drafted into his shoes, Chaplin burlesqued Hitler's frenetic speeches and mocked the dictator's hunger for world conquest through a rapturous dance with an inflated world globe.

Then there are the cartoons from around the world. David Low, who had been banned in Germany before the war for his withering depictions of Hitler, showed him as an arrogant aggressor goose-stepping through one country after another. The Soviet Union's Boris Efimov drew a corrupt Nazi gang similar to that portrayed in Brecht's *Arturo Ui.* For *Punch* magazine's Bernard Partridge, Hitler was a demonic monster.

JEKYLL AND HYDE

Sir Bernard Partridge was the chief cartoonist for *Punch* from 1901 until his death in 1945. He was also a portrait painter and actor. His views were generally very conservative—hostile to unions and the women's movement. Yet he had no use for Hitler, depicting him caustically in more than 120 cartoons. This one, with Hitler as Jekyll and Hyde, is a powerful example of Partridge's approach to cartooning, as explained in a 1941 BBC interview: "I believe a cartoon needs a simple statement of theme . . . a sense of drama and of humor with powers of draughtsmanship and facility in portraiture, catching the essentials of a face in a few mocking lines." [Bernard Partridge, "Jekyll and Hyde," *Punch*, April 17, 1940.]

Theodore Geisel's style was more playful, but he went after Hitler in several cartoons in the left-wing newspaper *PM*. Later Geisel expressed his hatred of Nazism in his children's book, *Yertle The Turtle*.[36] His tyrannical turtle was, in fact, a surrogate for Hitler, and Geisel had to be persuaded not to make his anti-Nazi animus too obvious by drawing a Hitler moustache on Yertle.[37]

Among the great satirists, only George Bernard Shaw made a fool of himself on this question. In a 1933 lecture to the Fabian Society, he had found

Without Hitler, says Richard H. Minear, Theodore Geisel "might well have remained a successful commercial artist with a sideline in children's literature." But there was, indeed, Hitler; and even before Pearl Harbor Geisel was thundering in his cartoons against isolationism in general and Nazism in particular. This cartoon, the first of his lampoons of Hitler, shows the dictator as the World Dairy proprietor, consolidator of 11 defeated nations into one cow, and the hindquarter with a question mark—who's next? As for that "sideline in children's literature," Geisel never quite let go of Hitler, who was the model for Yertle the turtle. [Theodore Geisel, PM, May 19, 1941, in Richard H. Minear, *Dr. Seuss Goes to War* (New York: New Press, 1999), 81. Courtesy of ICM.]

that Hitler, though "the victim of bad biology and a bogus ethnology," was nonetheless a very remarkable and able man,[38] and that Mussolini was creating the kind of socialist society advocated by the Fabians. Shaw's 1936 comedy, *Geneva*, in which a Jew brings the fascist leaders before the International Court of Justice, makes fun of the various brands of fascism; but critics noted that Shaw gave the fascist characters wittier and more interesting speeches than he gave to the Jew.

In a 1945 preface to *Geneva*, Shaw recognized that Mussolini's state was not quite what most Fabians had in mind and that Hitler was a "mad Messiah" whose racial delusions were bound to lead to disaster. Yet in that same preface Shaw suggested that the concentration camp guards put on trial after the war were not evil but had merely been unable to cope with impossible conditions; so the mass deaths in the camps resulted from overcrowding, disease, and starvation rather than a deliberate policy of extermination.[39]

Other satirists did not follow his lead. Whatever their criticisms of democracy, they recognized the great chasm that existed between democracy and the appalling despotism imposed by Hitler and his Nazis. It is this view that pervades the continuing presence of Hitler in the world of satire.

That Hitler should be mercilessly satirized is therefore beyond question. But what kind of satire? The bitter, scouring wit of Tadeusz Borowski, Bertolt Brecht, and Günter Grass certainly fits its subject, but are Hitler and the Nazis a proper subject for broad farce?

Chaplin raised the issue. After the war he was to say: "Had I known of the actual horrors of the German concentration camps I could not have made The Great Dictator; I could not have made fun of the homicidal insanity of the Nazis."[40]

In Roberto Benigni's 1997 movie, *Life Is Beautiful,* the Italian actor-writer-director Benigni plays a Jew who is sent to a concentration camp with his young son. Using pratfalls and other clowning, he convinces the boy that it's all a game, a contest with a tank as the prize. But the farcical antics do not obscure the full horror of the camps, and though at the end the child survives, the father does not. While most reviewers found the movie's comedy painful yet poignant and touching, some were unable to accept the effort to convey the evil of the camps through a framework of farce.

A still broader, outrageous brand of farce appeared in Mel Brooks's movie and Broadway musical, *The Producers.* The plot tells of two con men who sell 25,000 percent in a prospective Broadway show in the confident expectation that it will be a flop so the investors will not expect any return on their money. But the show, "Springtime for Hitler," is so hilariously awful that it becomes a comic success, and the con men go to jail.

When the movie was released in 1968 there was some criticism from concentration camp survivors and others, and because of the sensitivities the original title for the movie, "Springtime for Hitler" (the main production number), was changed. When the Broadway show opened in 2001, however, there were few complaints. Until it closed in 2007 the capacity audiences, paying $100 or more a seat, were convulsed by comic storm troopers and chorus girls goose-stepping in swastika formation. Like most critics, the *New Yorker* gave the show a rave review.

The passage of time, it seemed, had lessened the inhibitions against laughter. In any case, Brooks himself offered a rationale for turning the evil of Nazism into musical comedy: that the one life-affirming response to horror is laughter. When he received an award for *The Producers* as the best Broadway show of the year, Brooks, putting a black comb under his nose to

imitate Hitler's moustache, thanked Hitler for being "such a funny guy."
This was a continuation of Brooks's constant attitude as a foot soldier in
Germany during World War II. He was the unit clown, singing and laughing
in the face of danger and death. It was also his way, he has said, of getting
back at the monstrous horror of Nazism.

The issue resurfaced when the Jewish Museum in New York presented an
exhibition in 2002: "Mirroring Evil: Nazi Imagery/Recent Art." It included
images of model death camps made out of Lego blocks; canisters of apparent poison gas with Chanel, Hermes, and Tiffany labels; and a photograph
of Buchenwald inmates in which the artist is digitally inserted holding a
can of Diet Coke. The curator (many of whose relatives died in the camps)
explained that the works already existed, and that the purpose of the show
was to provide a context for them in which questions could be considered
about the depiction of Nazism in the popular culture.

Still, survivors groups were outraged. Laughing at Hitler and the Nazis,
they protested, trivializes the Holocaust and the pernicious doctrines that
led to it: racial purity, worship of the Leader and the nation, and domestic
and international violence.[41]

Yet, just as the horrors of war have been the subject of farce, so Nazism
and its appalling leaders have inevitably been the targets not only of outrage
but also of ridicule. They were derided as buffoons by their opponents
before they came to power during Weimar; by their victims during their
reign of terror; and by almost everyone after the collapse of the "Thousand
Year Reich." They are properly relegated to the realms of the absurd, in
both its morbid and its ridiculous versions.

GERMANY TODAY: OPEN FOR SATIRE

Almost half a century was to pass before today's Germany could be established. In 1945, with the country divided between its rival conquerors, the
west chose democracy while the east, ironically named the German
Democratic Republic (GDR), moved from one authoritarian system to
another. The GDR was essentially a mini-version of the Soviet system, in
which dissent was suppressed by the secret police and a controlled press
and satire was mostly limited to whispered jokes.

At last the Soviet and communist edifice collapsed, and with reunification
in 1990 the entire country was brought under the democratic framework.
Laws were passed forbidding the use of Nazi symbols and paraphernalia,
and a huge Holocaust memorial was constructed in the very center of Berlin.
The memory of Nazism still had the power to destroy reputations. In 2006
Günter Grass revealed that when he was 17 he had been a member of the
SS, a fact he had failed to mention during the more than 60 years he had condemned others for their Nazi connections. Grass insisted he was drafted into
the SS and did not join it voluntarily. Nonetheless, the satirist was

relentlessly satirized. One cartoon showed him marching and drumming (as in *The Tin Drum*) under a Nazi helmet.

Nonetheless, by 2006 German humorists proved that in their country, too, it was possible to treat Hitler as an object of farce. A cartoon video appearing on the Internet and viewed by several million on YouTube and other sites, featured a manic Hitler sitting on the toilet, taking a bath with his dog, and singing: "The Luftwaffe is kaput. The Messerschmitt's a bore. The Second World War isn't fun any more." The video's popularity, according to the cabaret performer who sang Hitler's voice, proved that "the time is ripe for breaking the Hitler taboo."[42] Early in 2007 another farcical treatment appeared in a movie by Dani Levy, *Mein Führer:The Truly Truest Truth About Adolf Hitler,* in which Hitler wets his bed and gets down on all fours barking like a dog.[43]

Yet satire has also moved on from the past to the current crop of German and foreign politicians. In 2002, two months after winning an election, Chancellor Gerhard Schroeder was ridiculed in "The Tax Song," which reached the top of the charts with satirist Elmar Brandt imitating Shroeder's voice and singing to a rap beat: "I'll raise your taxes, I'll empty your pockets ... I'll get your piggy bank."[44] A year later the economy was in the doldrums, as indicated by a newspaper cartoon showing Osama bin Laden telling his followers not to bother attacking Germany because the country was already kaput. Political wit is also featured in the "Kabarettes" that are a lively feature of Berlin nightlife, and on television comedian Harald Schmidt does a late-night show of the Leno/Letterman genre on which he has mocked contemporary politicians as well as performed Hitler imitations.

Evidently, despite the popular perception of Germans as being dour and humorless, the caustic humor displayed under Wilhelm II and during Weimar is very much alive today.

chapter six

STALIN AND MAO: NO LAUGHING MATTER

Said Stalin to writers, I hereby define
Your function as serving the Socialist line.
And Chinese found subjects for poem and song
In the Little Red Book of Mao Zedong.

Karl Marx was right, and he was wrong.

He was right in predicting there would be successful communist revolutions. He was wrong in assuming they would occur in Europe's most industrialized countries. The two great communist revolutions of the era erupted in Russia and China, both of them with far more peasants than factory workers.

Again, Marx was right in predicting that a dictatorship would follow the revolutions. He was wrong in believing this would be a temporary stage, an interruption on the way to the classless society. It proved to be a long interruption. Entrenched dictatorship, under monolithic one-party rule, lasted three-quarters of a century in Russia before the Marxist scenario collapsed entirely, and it still survives in China.

Any such system would obviously be hostile to satire, and satirists have been subjected to an array of sanctions and harassments in both countries. Yet satire there has been, though much more in the Soviet Union than in the Chinese People's Republic.

THE SOVIET UNION: SATIRE DESPITE STALIN

The roster of satire in the Soviet Union is impressive.

The reason is certainly not that the Soviet regime was a tolerant one. Most of the time it was profoundly repressive, deeply hostile to any suggestion of dissent from its official doctrines, and enforced by constant surveillance and censorship.

So it had been under the Tsars. Absolute paternalism under Nicholas I was followed by some loosening under Alexander II, and his assassination

СТРАШНОЕ МЕСТО
(канцелярия)

— Сколько раз я вам говорил «приходите автра»,
а вы всегда приходит сегодня.

К. ЕЛИСЕЕВ   1925

Lenin encouraged satire and was even cited by the editors of *Korodil* as one of the magazine's founders. However, the targets were never to include Lenin himself or the Soviet regime as a whole, but most commonly foreign enemies on the one hand and bureaucracy on the other. In this cartoon, an unfortunate citizen, the Soviet common man, is being bullied by a heartless bureaucrat who tells him, "How many times have I told you: 'Come back tomorrow' and you always come today." Yeliseyev continued to produce cartoons for *Krokodil* during the Stalin era, for Stalin, too, saw satire as a useful tool again slothful bureaucracy—as long as this was not presented as an indictment of the Soviet system. ["A Bad Place," K. Yeliseyev, 1925. From the collection *Red Tape from Red Square*, Rutgers State University of New Jersey, Campus at Newark, Graduate School of Public Administration, National Center for Public Productivity.]

led to tightening under his son, Alexander III, which persisted under Nicholas II until a worker uprising in 1905 brought about once again a weakening of censorship. Altogether, however, the verdict of historians of the nineteenth century is that absolutism in Russia, with minor variations, was the rule, and the censor's grip remained tighter than in any other European country.

Yet under that same system an inheritance emerged of enormous artistic creativity. In fact, Russia in the nineteenth century generated a remarkable array of literary masterpieces, and somehow the works of Tolstoy, Dostoevsky, Turgenev, and Chekhov survived the censorship, though not without danger or sanctions.[1]

There was a flowering of satire, too. Popular plays and novels by Gogol and Saltykov-Shehedrin scoffed at the bungling and bureaucratic mindlessness of tsarist officials. There were satirical journals — over 400 in the first decade of the twentieth century. However, this number was inflated by the resurrection of banned journals under new titles. In fact, throughout the period satirists faced bans, deletions, closures, confiscations, fines, and prison sentences.

This pattern — satire persisting, but under fluctuating pressures — repeated itself during the history of the Union of Soviet Socialist Republics (USSR). It was a substantial history: three-quarters of a century, compared with the 12 years of the Third Reich, and time enough for changes in the top leadership, corresponding with changes in the rigor of the censorship. There were, in fact, five such periods under the main leaders: Lenin, Stalin, Khruschev, Brezhnev, and Gorbachev.

LENIN: SATIRE UP TO A POINT

In the aftermath of the Russian Revolution of 1917, most writers were swept along with enthusiasm for the overthrow of a hated system and with hope for the dawn of a new kind of society. Initially the only satire this generated was directed against the enemies of the regime, but in 1921 Lenin's New Economic Policy postponed the full implementation of socialism and also signaled a relaxation of ideological fervor in the arts. Consequently, from 1923 the Soviet Union experienced a brilliant era of satire featuring plays, poems, novels, essays, and feuilletons by a remarkable group of writers, including Vladimir Mayakovsky, Mikhail Bulgakov, Yevgeny Zamyatin, Ilya Ilf and Evgeni Petrov, and Mikhail Zoshchenko, as well as the cartoons and jokes of *Krokodil* and several other satirical magazines.

Lenin himself appeared to be their champion. When *Krokodil* was established in 1922, its editor-in-chief proclaimed, "We are proud that Vladimir Ilich Lenin was one of our founders. He highly valued the power of satire and often used classical images from Russian satirical literature in his own writings."[2] This gave satirists — even those who did not accept the Bolshevik ideology — scope to attack many of their traditional targets.

Yet even in this golden era, satirists were told that they had better tread carefully. The 1925 official "Instructions to Krokodil" announced that satire was to be mobilized against the class enemy; against "imperfections and ugly features" in the working class, the peasantry, and the Soviet bureaucracy; and against the world's bourgeoisie and anti-working–class parties.[3] What Lenin had in mind was that the satirist's function was to help cleanse the system of the residual bourgeois attitudes left over from Tsarist days, to "declare war on the disorganizers of the economy, pillory factories that are behind with production," and attack corruption and incompetence in state and party officials.

But there could be no ridiculing of Lenin himself or the other top party leaders. Rather, Lenin was to be pictured as a heroic leader in posters and cartoons cleansing not only Russia but the entire world of monarchs, pluto-crats, and priests.

Moreover, once satire was harnessed to a specific ideology it would be subjected to careful reviews to ensure that it adhered to the "correct" party line. As early as 1923 a debate was raging on whether or not satire was needed in a communist society. Despite Lenin's view, arguments were pro-pounded in all seriousness that, since the Revolution had abolished all social evils, there was nothing left to satirize; that only the positive should be rec-ognized to avoid giving comfort to the enemy; that satire is dangerous, even close to treason; that "Soviet satire" was a contradiction in terms, like Soviet banks and Soviet landowners; and even that "laughter was an expendable physiological action, redundant in a socialist society."[4]

These positions were too absurd to prevail even among the regime's most fawning supporters. Still, the best-known satirists of the period faced a vari-ety of sanctions. Ilf and Petrov's novel satirizing the absurdities of the NEP period, *The Twelve Chairs*,[5] was subjected to bitter attacks by the Associa-tion of Proletarian Writers (RAPP) because it described the hapless efforts of three distinctly un-Soviet characters to recover some lost diamonds, in the course of which the adventurers encounter bungling bureaucrats, venal local politicians, and compliant journalists on a scale that, in the eyes of the RAPP lackeys, went far beyond what Lenin's doctrine allowed.

After that Ilf and Petrov limited themselves to humorous feuilletons. Though most of these were noncontroversial, the pair still managed to needle RAPP with their "How the Soviet Robinson Was Written."[6] The story tells of an editor who instructs the author that some modest changes must be made: enough castaways must be found to form a local committee to collect union dues; the masses should be discovered on another part of the island; the shipwreck would have to be discarded; and, finally, Robinson Crusoe himself must be eliminated as an insufficiently Soviet character.

Yevgeny Zamyatin, too, was perennially in trouble with the authorities. Soon after the Revolution he lost his earlier fervor for Bolshevism and founded the Serapion Brethren, a group of young writers dedicated to indi-vidual expression and experimental forms. In their credo he announced:

> The Revolution does not need dogs who "sit up" in expectation of a
> handout or because they fear the whip ... It needs writers who fear

nothing... It needs writers to whom the Revolution awakens a true organic echo. And it does not matter if this echo is individual...[7]

"Individual?" In a collectivist society? This was a very incorrect line indeed! The monitors of orthodoxy attacked him for slander, vilification, and playing into the hands of the enemies of the Revolution. During the relative freedom of the postrevolutionary period, Zamyatin managed to get his stories and essays published. However, they appeared in marginal magazines rather than the official, subsidized journals. When, unable to get his satirical dystopia, *We*, published in Russia, Zamyatin arranged for its publication in England and Czechoslovakia, which infuriated RAPP's members. At a meeting in 1929 they denounced the novel's depiction of a totalitarian society providing its citizens a "mathematical faultless happiness" as a prophecy of the coming transformation of the Revolution into an all-encompassing police state. After that Zamyatin's plays were banned, and his books were withdrawn from libraries and bookstores.

Mikhail Zoshchenko's enormously popular stories and his distinguished wartime service in which he was wounded and gassed provided him with some protection against the Party's philistines. A natural rebel, however, he joined Zamyatin's Serapion Brethren, though he wrote in a vernacular style more accessible to the masses than others of the group. His themes were the everyday problems and acute shortages endured by most of the Soviet people. In "The Crisis"[8] a citizen is reduced to living in a bathroom, then has to subdivide it when he marries and his relatives move in — and all have to move into the hall whenever the other residents of the apartment take their baths. In "A Bathhouse"[9] and several other stories, Zoshchenko lampoons hopeless bureaucratic muddle and incompetence.

These works annoyed his RAPP opponents, but they were even more offended by his short novel, *What The Nightingale Sang*. It contains a speculation on the future that reads like a parody of the ultimate Marxist Utopia, when socialism is succeeded by communism and there are no more capitalist-produced scarcities:

> Perhaps people won't even have money. Everything may be free. Fur coats and scarves may be handed out gratis in department stores...
> "Here, citizen," someone will say, "take this marvelous fur coat."...
> "No, honored comrade," you will reply, "what the devil do I want with a fur coat? I have six of them already."
> ... And human relationships, what marvelous qualities they will admire! For instance, love! How luxuriantly will blossom that most delicate of emotions![10]

Mikhail Bulgakov's novel, *The White Guard*, appeared as a serial in a magazine in 1924, but it was not published as a book in Russia in his lifetime because it did not sufficiently denigrate the anti-Communist Whites, who had fought the Revolution with foreign help. *The Days of the Turbins,* his play based on *The White Guard,* though highly successful with the public, was soon banned, then accepted again, then banned again. He did get his satirical fantasy novel, *The Fatal Eggs,* published in 1925, but the novel's suggestion that something might go terribly wrong with the Soviet utopia because of bureaucratic bungling did not sit well with the true believers. By 1930 he could not get his works published at all, and he survived as a literary consultant, a dramatizer of other authors' novels, and a writer of opera librettos. Rehabilitation and publication of some of his stories and novels did not come until the 1960s.

Even the Revolution's most famous poet, Vladimir Mayakovsky, ran afoul of the censors. He had been fervently committed to the Revolution from the outset, proclaiming that writers were proletarians wielding a pen. He designed government propaganda posters, wrote commercial jingles, helped found satirical journals satirizing mainly un-Bolshevik behavior, and wrote anti-capitalist satirical verse based on his travels in Europe and the United States.

Nevertheless, he did not fit into the grey conformity demanded by the Party and the hack RAPP writers. He was a cult romantic figure, adored by the young and factory workers, who turned out in their thousands to hear his poetry readings. He used avant-garde techniques in some of his poems. He was associated with the Futurists, a defiant, essentially anarchic group of painters and writers who poured scorn on the great writers and artists of the past. He adored a Russian émigré living in Paris, and spent time with her there whenever he was allowed.

When he dedicated a poem to the lady in Paris, critics complained of his bourgeois decadence in singing the beauty of an émigré "framed in furs and beads."[11] His play, *The Bathhouse,* attacked the rigidity of the Soviet bureaucracy so harshly that it fell outside the bounds of the permissible. He was criticized for owning a car, and even for his non-proletarian Waterman pen. The official writers' groups boycotted his 20-year retrospective exhibition. Distressed by his pariah status, he alienated his friends by joining RAPP, whose members nevertheless treated him disdainfully. He was heckled at some of his poetry readings. In 1930 he committed suicide — an action condemned as un-Soviet.

AND THEN CAME STALIN

If satirists faced strenuous opposition even during the relatively relaxed time of the New Economic Policy, they had much more to fear when Stalin ascended to supreme power, for Stalin propagated and enforced an ideology that allowed few deviations, inflicting punishments on alleged defectors ranging from incarceration in the gulag to exile, torture and death.

From Lenin he inherited a system perfectly adapted to his despotic style: power concentrated at the apex of a single party; manipulated elections; a complacent judiciary willing to run show trials; the gulag; and a controlled press. As for the arts, these, too, must serve the purposes of the state.

It was not that Stalin disdained the arts. On the contrary, he read extensively in Russian and European literature, had great respect for the masters of the past, and made the novelist Maxim Gorky a close friend and confidant. According to one historian: "Stalin was the best-read ruler of Russia from Catherine the Great to Vladimir Putin, even including Lenin who was no mean intellectual himself . . ."[12] Nonetheless, Stalin sided with RAPP in its demand for the elimination of all "bourgeois" and "deviationist" writing, and its replacement by "socialist realism."

Among the first fatalities of this new rigor were all the satirical magazines created in the 1920s except *Krokodil*, which was henceforth more rigorously controlled.

To ensure that his doctrine would be enforced, Stalin designated Andre Zhdanov, who almost became his successor, as the Politburo's "culture specialist," granting him enormous power to monitor the arts and ensure their conformity with the "correct" line. In a letter reprimanding the writer Demyan Bedny, Stalin informed him that criticizing the shortcomings of everyday Soviet life was "obligatory and necessary criticism," but the writer had gone overboard with what amounted to "slander of the USSR, of its past and present."[13]

Criticizing the bureaucracy qualified as "obligatory and necessary criticism," and innumerable cartoons panned the laziness and incompetence of middle-level officials. However, for satirists to imply that their targets were not merely specific, correctable incidents or attitudes but intrinsic flaws in the Soviet system— that would be going too far; that would be slander. Even worse would be suggestions that the entire Soviet ideology was profoundly antihuman and destructive.

Most unacceptable of all was any derisive mention of Stalin himself. The poet Osip Mandelstam dared to write a lampoon of him and his henchmen in verse, in which he is described as a repulsive sadist surrounded by groveling acolytes, climbing over mountains of bodies as he "rolls the executions on his tongue like berries."[14] This could not be published, of course, but Stalin heard about it from an informer. Mandelstam was arrested and exiled to the provinces. Later he was accused of "counterrevolutionary activities," and he died on the way to the gulag.

Yet Stalin's attitude toward particular satirists was idiosyncratic. Zamyatin wrote to Stalin asking permission to leave Russia. Gorky intervened, and Zamyatin's request was granted. He went into exile in Paris, where he died in 1937. When friends of Mayakovsky sent a letter to Stalin in 1935 requesting his rehabilitation as the writer of verses that were "the strongest revolutionary weapon," Stalin bestowed his belated blessing with the comment, "Mayakovsky was and remains the most talented poet of our Soviet epoch. Indifference to his memory and words is a crime." Stalin liked Bulgakov's *The Days of the Turbins* so much he saw it 15 times. "It's easy to criticize *The Days of the Turbins,*" he told a critic. "It's easy to reject, but it's hardest to write good plays. The final impression of the play is good for Bolshevism."[15] He also enjoyed the antibureaucratic satire of Mikhail Zoshchenko, and Stalin read excerpts from his work to his two sons.

But there were severe limits to Stalin's enthusiasm. Unable to find work, Bulgakov appealed to Stalin for a visa to emigrate, and Stalin denied it in a personal phone call. Bulgakov died in 1940, soon after completing work on his masterpiece, *The Master and Margarita*. There was never any chance that it could be published in Stalin's lifetime. Imagine Zhdanov and the RAPP plodders, looking for socialist realism and finding instead this fantasy of the devil and an exotic entourage, including a talking cat, descending on Moscow in the 1920s and 1930s and wreaking havoc with black magic — all this interwoven, among other story lines, with a novel about Christ's crucifixion by Pontius Pilate. Imagine also how the inquisitors would have raged against the novel's fierce satire of Stalinist corruption, repression, and cruelty, and of the literary hacks who supported the regime. Not surprisingly, publication of *The Master and Margarita* had to wait until 1967.

As for Zoshchenko, sooner or later he would not be able to escape attacks for going beyond Stalin's "obligatory and necessary criticism." His vast popularity enabled him to continue publishing for several years without interference, though he gave up the satirical sketches that had been the basis of his popularity.[16] His autobiographical novel, *Before Sunrise,* was banned, however, because it drew on un-Soviet psychology and dream theory, and after World War II Zoshchenko was among the first targets when Stalin decided that writers must be punished if they did not play their part in a renewed dedication to the march toward Communism.

Zhdanov blasted Zoshchenko as "an unprincipled literary hoodlum" whose works were a "crude slander on Soviet life" and a poisoner of the minds of youth. Zhdanov cited the story, "The Adventures of a Monkey," which recounted the comic adventures in the city of a monkey that escaped from a zoo. The author's purpose, thundered Zhdanov, was "to make the monkey utter the foul, poisonous, anti-Soviet statement that it is better to live in a zoo than outside it, that one can breathe more freely in a cage than among Soviet people." This was a curious interpretation, for at the end of the story the monkey is adopted by a boy and lives happily with him. Zoshchenko was expelled from the Union of Soviet Writers and his works were banned, except for a few timeserving pieces compatible with Socialist Realism.

Stalin's involvement with literature, significant though it was, hardly compared with his interest in cartoons and films, for they reached the

On January 13, 1953, Pravda claimed that nine of the Kremlin's leading doctors, seven of them Jews, had murdered two of Stalin's aides, and that a plot by Western imperialists and Zionists to kill the top Soviet leadership had been uncovered. This *Krokodil* cartoon followed. It alleges that: "Organizations of government safety uncovered the terrorist group of agents of international organizations," aided by American dollars and (in the oil barrel) "American-English spies." There was to be a show trial of the doctors, but this was aborted by Stalin's death in 1953. On April 4, 1953, Pravda carried a statement by secret police chief Beria completely exonerating the doctors. [*Krokodil*, January 1953, "The Doctors' Plot."]

masses. *Krokodil* was taken over by the official daily newspaper, *Pravda,* and directed its satire mostly at the bureaucracy and at domestic and foreign enemies. In one cartoon the magazine even conveyed Stalin's paranoiac fears, in the year before he died, of a plot to poison him by Jewish doctors.

On one occasion the leading cartoonist Boris Yefimov was hauled out of a public lecture on the orders of Zhdanov, who announced that Stalin had chosen Yefimov to draw a cartoon ridiculing the U.S. military buildup in the Arctic. This seemed a dubious honor, for Yefimov was a Jew, a friend of the arch-traitor Trotsky, and the brother of a man who had been executed after Stalin gave him a similar "special assignment." Still, Stalin liked Yefimov's work, personally sketched the labels "North Pole" and "Alaska" into the cartoon, and provided the title: "Eisenhower to the Defense." Yefimov did not meet his brother's fate, and he celebrated his 100th birthday in 2000.

Stalin was even more directly involved in the cinema, seeing film as a prime medium for conveying the official ideology in the form of entertainment. He personally reviewed every film before its release. During the 1920s there had been some mildly satirical movies aimed at the bureaucracies and at everyday hardships, such as the housing shortage.[17] For Stalin, humor in the movies was acceptable — but only as long as it served to cheer people up and was consistent with the official ideology.

So, as long as Stalin and his doctrines were in control, the only kinds of satire that flourished were those directed at the deficiencies of other countries, particularly America, Britain, and France and, later, Germany; at religion; and, within careful limits, the bureaucracies.

THE KHRUSCHEV THAW

Georgi Malenkov became prime minister after Stalin's death in 1953, and he "appealed to Soviet writers to become modern Gogols and Shehedrins."[18] Yet the real power was with Secretary-General of the Communist Party, Nikita Khrushchev, who declared that he only read *Krokodil* because he was made to do so by his grandchildren, and they had to explain the jokes to him.[19] Malenkov was removed in less than two years.

Still, hopes for a more benevolent regime were raised again when word leaked out of Khrushchev's extraordinary secret speech in 1956 exposing Stalin's regime of terror. Indeed, the Khrushchev years saw the publication of Bulgakov's *The Master and Margarita;* Fazil Iskander's *The Goatibex Constellation,* a satire of the charlatan genetics of Lysenko and of Khrushchev's ineffectual agricultural policies; new editions of the novels of Ilf and Petrov; and a retrospective volume of Zoshchenko's work (with the deletion of offensive passages, such as some pro-American comments in one story).

BREZHNEV: AGAIN THE HARD LINE

When Khrushchev was ousted in 1964, Leonid Brezhnev took over, and the hard-liners were back in power.

This was bad news for Vladimir Voinovich. His writing career had enjoyed an auspicious start when Khrushchev sang Voinovich's song lyric, "Fourteen Minutes to Go," at the parade celebrating the Soviet cosmonauts return from space,[20] after which some of Voinovich's stories were published in a prestigious literary journal. However, as time passed he became more and more alienated from the system. Voinovich signed letters criticizing the arrest and imprisonment of a number of writers and demanding that they receive fair trials. He wrote satirical stories, which led to the deadly charge of being "slanderous" of the Soviet system. The Writers' Union reprimanded him, a book was withdrawn from publication, his plays and film scenarios were banned, and his works were deleted from library catalogs.

When Voinovich turned to the émigré press to get his works published, he further infuriated his critics with *The Life and Extraordinary Adventures of Private Ivan Chonkin*,[21] published in Paris. The book is a hilarious spoof on the Soviet military, secret police, and ideology, in which the bumbling Chonkin is assigned to guard a fallen plane on a deserted farm and settles down faithfully but comfortably to his assignment. He is investigated after being denounced by an informer, but he turns the tables on his accusers and routs the army, the secret police, and the entire machinery of government before a general, on the point of decorating Chonkin as a hero, arrests him instead as a traitor. Though the novel's tone is light, even slapstick, it makes vividly clear Voinovich's hostility to a regime of terror, stifling conformity, and ludicrous incompetence.

After the Writers' Union expelled him, Voinovich tried to mollify them by writing an ideologically sound novel. But he had transgressed too often, too far. During the 1970s he and his family were watched, followed, and sometimes threatened by the KGB. At last he left the country, moving between West Germany and the United States, and in 1981 he was stripped of his Soviet citizenship.

In exile his writings were even more hostile to the regime. They included a collection of essays and stories, *The Anti-Soviet Soviet Union,* and a dystopian satire depicting a totally repressive *Moscow 2042.*[22] In his satirical novel, *Monumental Propaganda,*[23] Voinovich writes of a devout Stalinist, Aglaya Stepanova Revkina, who commissions a statue of Stalin while she is a Soviet functionary and moves it into her apartment when Khrushchev takes over for fear it will be toppled. At the end, when Communism is no more, the apartment house blows up, the statue explodes onto Aglaya, she receives him "with every inch of her spreadeagled body," and dies in an orgasmic rapture.

Fazil Iskander was another novelist who had to contend with the censors during the Brezhnev era. He was forced to accept cuts of two-thirds in his collection of stories, *Sandra of Chegem,* to get the rest published. One of the excised stories includes a satirical portrayal of Stalin as a despot, musing on his paranoiac view of life:

> Power is when you must not love anyone. Because the minute you love a man you begin to trust him, but once you begin to trust, sooner or later you get a knife in the back ... But if you have to kill the ones you love, fairness demands that you make short work of the ones you don't love, the enemies of the cause."[24]

After Iskander contributed a piece to a collection of dissident works, he was not able to publish anything in the Soviet Union. Even so, he became a member of the Soviet Writer's Union in 1957, and was allowed to travel — and even publish — abroad. Moreover, 1982 saw the publication of his novel *Rabbits and Boa Constrictors*,[25] which exposed the depravity of the system more harshly and directly than any other satirical work coming out of the Soviet Union. The work is in the form of an allegory about two parallel societies, the snakes and the rabbits. The snakes are the more vicious, given to denunciations of real or imagined treachery and headed by a cruel, paranoiac, Stalinist figure, the Great Python, who enjoys describing how aberrant snakes had been punished by being forced to eat themselves.[26] But the rabbits are hardly less admirable, easily manipulated by their cunning King (a Khrushchevite figure) into accepting a meager diet of old vegetables today by the promise of an abundance of fresh cauliflower tomorrow. The rabbit culture also includes surrogates for a prime Iskander target: the timid Soviet intelligentsia, all too ready to compromise their integrity to maintain their privileges:

> At first the Poet's conscience bothered him, and he decided that the least he could do was not to write anything that directly praised the king. But something kept him from abandoning the life at court and the luxury, to which he, and most importantly his family, had grown accustomed.[27]

Why was Iskander tolerated? Primarily, it seems, because the Soviet ideology paid lip service to the folklore and traditions of the various republics, and, coming from the Republic of Abkhazia, Iskander had status as a "national writer." Moreover, he came too late for the Stalin purges. Brezhnev was a neo-Stalinist, but he was no Stalin.[28] Undoubtedly, 20 years earlier Iskander would have fared much worse.

GORBACHEV AND *GLASNOST*

After the death of Brezhnev, and of his two doddering successors, the worst of the repression at last was gone. All of Voinovich's earlier works were published in the Soviet Union, including *Ivan Chonkin*, his citizenship was reinstated, and his Moscow apartment returned. Other previously banned works of satire were published. At last, *glasnost* broke through the taboo against public lampooning of the current leader. As David Remnick tells it:

> On the stage of the Satire Theater, one of the actors starring in Vladimir Voinovich's political satire, The Tribunal, Vyacheslav Bezrukov, spun out a long and hilarious imitation of Gorbachev, complete with

his signature hand motions (karate chops, raised index finger), odd grammar, and accent.

Gorbachev's daughter, Irina, had laughed all through the show — until Bezrukov started his Gorbachev imitation. She left as soon as the curtain fell, ostentatiously failing to applaud.[29] Probably Gorbachev was no more amused than his daughter when he heard about this unanticipated impertinence. But the theater remained open, the play continued, and the actor was not punished. Under Stalin the perpetrator of any such insult would have been sent to a gulag or shot.

WHISPERED JOKES

As in Nazi Germany, the absence of printed or public ridiculing of Soviet leaders did not mean that there were no jokes about them; there were, as long as the jokes were communicated privately.

There were Lenin jokes: In heaven God asks St. Peter how Lenin's re-education program is going. "Fine, Comrade God," answers St. Peter.

There were Stalin jokes: Lenin's widow, Krupskaya, is giving Stalin a hard time. Stalin threatens her: "If you don't stop criticizing me, I'll have someone else appointed Lenin's widow!"

There were Brezhnev jokes: President Carter asks Brezhnev whether he collected jokes against himself. "I certainly do." "How many?" asks Carter. "Two camps full," says Brezhnev.

Some of the same jokes and variations on them were told in the Eastern European countries that were under Soviet domination from 1945 to 1991. One favorite, relating to the regimes of the Soviet and East European leaders, announced a competition for the best political joke. The first prize: 15 years.[30]

THE AFTERMATH

With the Soviet Union dismantled and Gorbachev gone, Yeltsin was an obvious target for the newly liberated satirists given his public bouts of drunkenness and his toleration of massive corruption, allowing the rape of the economy by a small number of predatory businessmen. He became one of the butts of a weekly television show, *Kukly,* in which puppet caricatures roasted leading politicians, many of whom vied to be portrayed on the show, for it meant they had arrived. When Yeltsin's health began to decline, his family pressured the station to ease up on him a little, but Yeltsin himself defended the show and refused to have it taken off the air. Said one journalist: "I have often thought that as long as Russia has *Kukly,* there is hope for this suffering country."[31]

Vladimir Putin saw it differently. An ex-KGB official, he was angered by criticisms of his Chechnya policy carried on the TV station by one of the media tycoons from the Yeltsin era, Vladimir Gusinsky. It was that same station that carried *Kukly,* and Putin was infuriated when he was ridiculed on the show, one week as a malevolent, czar-like figure and another week as a "punter, cruising the streets of Moscow in search of political prostitutes with whom to play election games."[32]

Pressure was brought to bear — the Putin puppet must disappear from the show. The puppet was removed, and Putin was conveyed by the thunder-claps of a wrathful god. This was not enough, however, and Gusinsky went abroad to avoid prosecution. The national gas utility company bought out the station. *Kukly* is no more.

The press, too, had to tread warily. Two Russian newspapers that carried the Danish cartoons deriding Mohammed were closed down. The regime did not want to offend its large Muslim population.

There are Putin jokes: He opens the refrigerator, a dish of jellied meat starts to tremble. He says, "Don't worry, I've only come for a beer." The Thatcher joke about her contempt for her colleagues was also told about Putin, even after he had moved from the presidency to the prime ministryship in 2008. (Putin takes President Dmitry Medvedev to a restaurant, orders steak, and when asked, "What about the vegetable?" replies, "He'll have the steak, too.") Apparently Putin enjoys jokes about how tough he is, but according to one commentator even those jokes are few in number.[33]

Thus far the Internet remains unhampered, so dissent and satire can still find at least a limited audience in Russia. One Web site by Maxim Konenenko follows the adventures of a bumbling Putin figure hopelessly misman-aging a "managed democracy."[34]

In a 2004 interview, Vladimir Voinovich argued that "the country is not ready for freedom yet:"

> I think that Russia is now turning off the road to democracy, but it will not return to the Soviet past. However, it could return to a more dis-tant past, even to a monarchy.[35]

A return to monarchy seems farfetched; but with or without the panoply of monarchy, a strong, authoritarian leadership that has little use for anti-regime satire seems likely to persist.[36]

THE COLD WIND OF MAOISM

At least in Russia, Communism is gone. Not so in China. The Chinese People's Republic, inaugurated in 1949 after Mao Zedong's army forced the Kuomintang leader, Chiang Kai-shek, into exile on Formosa (Taiwan), is still very much alive — transmuted in some significant respects from Mao's time, but still a one-party, doctrinaire Communist system.

With respect to political satire, the Chinese People's Republic has much less to offer than the Soviet Union. This was not for lack of a satirical heritage. Even though China had no internationally renowned masters of the art like Swift or Gogol or Daumier, one scholar tells us, "All the forms of Western satire appear in China, in some instances long before the West produced that kind of literature."[37] It was there in poetry, plays, short stories, novels, and village performances of "fast tales" (rhymed stories accompanied by bamboo or metal clappers). Their themes included the plight of ordinary people abused by harsh officials or savaged by war, with humor that was sad, sometimes bitter, and, despite the caution and solemnity of the Confucian heritage, often earthy and uninhibited.

Why, then, was the satirical output of the Chinese communists so meager in comparison with the Soviet products? For one thing, there was no Chinese counterpart to the explosion of political satire during the 1920s whose popularity was so great that even Stalin could not shut it off completely. And there was Mao, more Stalinist than Stalin. Later Mao was to break the alliance with the Soviet Union decisively, but he never broke from Stalin's organizational pattern, with power centered in a single party dominated by one man, fawned on and flattered by his courtiers, venerated and even worshipped by the mass of the people. He at least equaled Stalin's appetite for violence as well as his pitiless enthusiasm for vast social upheavals even if, as in the hopelessly failed Great Leap Forward, tens of millions died in the process.

Mao also matched Stalin's intolerance for any views other than his own. In fact, Mao went even further than Stalin in trying to put his stamp on the intellectual life of his country. His doctrines, captured in his speeches and his "Little Red Book," were holy writ to be parroted by party members and schoolchildren throughout the country. Everyone must also learn and declaim the deadening numerical clichés that encapsulated the current dogmas, such as the Five Red Categories, with the proletariat at the top and the intellectuals relegated to the Stinking Number Nine.

As for writers and artists, Mao's literary doctrine was unequivocal: political must take precedence over artistic criteria. Mao, like Stalin, read widely and deeply in his country's literary classics and was himself a poet and calligrapher. Yet there was to be, as under Stalin, a "correct line," and what was correct must be determined by the party. Those who followed the line could become members of the Chinese Writers' Association, with access to publication and associated privileges. All others were "rightists" to be ostracized, forced to write confessions, denounced by their own children, sent to jail, and driven in some cases to suicide.

This wouldn't leave much scope for satire. Mao himself was not entirely humorless. Often he drew on his peasant background by using crude humor to humiliate his opponents, with flatulence as his favorite theme. Of critics, he said during a period of ideological relaxation, "If they have something to fart about, let them fart! If it's out, then one can decide whether it smells good or bad,"[38]

Moreover, there was a brief moment when satirists might believe that Mao had changed his mind about free expression. Wanting to shake up the bureaucracy and promote technological advance, Mao pronounced in 1956 the slogan: "Let a Hundred Flowers Bloom, Let a Thousand Schools of Thought Contend." It seemed that everyone was to be encouraged to be creative, to express things in new ways. However, when thousands of writers and artists did precisely that, Mao took alarm. Early in 1957 the Hundred Flowers gave way to the Anti-Rightist Campaign, and those who had dared to say something new found themselves in deep trouble. Thereafter, writers were wary of periodic indications of a loosening of censorship, fearful of being caught out again.

That they had reason to be fearful was confirmed by the Cultural Revolution of 1966 to 1976, when Mao unleashed the aggressive energies of college and high school students, urging them to destroy all vestiges of élitism and privilege in Chinese society. As Red Guards they obliged by marching professors through the streets wearing dunces' caps, burning books, and smashing some of the nation's great artistic treasures, including many in Beijing, sparing the Forbidden City only because Premier Zhou Enlai ordered the gates closed and sent troops to protect the area.[39] Eventually Mao grew tired of the chaos and reined in the Red Guards, but the entire education system remained crippled for a generation.

Chinese intellectuals described the alternations of harsh restrictiveness and relative toleration as cold and warm winds.[40] Most of the time under Mao the wind was frigid, but even the warm winds were not very congenial for satirists. At the most there could be satire aimed at party cadrés and bureaucrats, and that, too, could get the author into trouble. This became apparent as early as 1942, when the Party newspaper published a satirical essay, "Wild Lily" by Wang Shiwei, which attacked the special privileges enjoyed by higher officials while the masses went hungry. At first, Mao praised the article, but then at a conference on literature and the arts Mao described Wang and his ilk as "petty bourgeois individualists . . . mere termites in the revolutionary ranks," subhumans who failed to see that the job of writers and artists was to celebrate the masses and their revolutionary struggle. Wang was expelled from the Literary Association, accused of Trotskyism, of spying for the Kuomintang, and of living mentally in a "counter-revolutionary shit-hole,"[41] tried, and executed.

The brief Hundred Flowers period produced an eruption of fresh ideas, but not much in the way of satire other than some mild exposés of bureaucratic sloth and ineptitude. At the time they were warmly praised, but in the Anti-Rightist reaction that followed the Hundred Flowers the authors were denounced.

A particularly angry furor erupted as a result of the publication between 1961 and 1965 of a series of satirical essays by three ranking officials. The essays used the Aesopean technique of describing the misdeeds of past emperors, but they were denounced indignantly in an official daily paper as a blatant attack on Mao himself. The writers stood accused of "holding poisonous sand in the mouth and spurting it at our leader;" of daring to suggest that Mao's Great Leap Forward was a failure; and of inciting "intellectuals to draw caricatures as a means of spreading discontent over current social conditions."

No such caricatures were published during Mao's reign. Of the three authors of the essays, says one account of the affair, "none has been heard of since May 1966."[42]

Given the circumstances, then, it is not surprising that the Mao era yields little in the way of published political satire. Inevitably, though, there was a crop of whispered jokes. These included salacious stories, current even among the Red Guards, of how "army entertainment groups were turned into procurement agencies" to satisfy Mao's sexual needs.[43] In a specially built lounge adjoining a dance hall, "Mao would take one or several girls into it to engage in sexual play or orgies."[44]

AFTER MAO

Following Mao's death and the defeat of his ferocious widow and the "Gang of Four," the winds turned warmer under Deng Xiaoping. Satire flourished in short stories, plays, comedians' sketches, "fast tales," and cartoonists' posters on walls in the cities. One fast tale depicts a section leader who responds to every request with "We'll think it over" or "We'll talk about it."[45] Tyrannical behavior by local party leaders is featured in a comedian's jabs at the party secretary, whose idea of the official doctrine of democratic centralism is "you do your democratizing, and I'll do my centralizing."[46] Another sketch laughs at both the tyrants and their obsequious staffs by describing the writing down of everything said by a director, including all the "ahs" and "tsks," because "these might be of inestimable value to all the subordinates in their efforts to puzzle out and comprehend the great man's thinking."[47]

Even so, the old pattern of restriction alternating with toleration had not ended. Periodically writers and performers were pulled up short. A Democracy Wall in Beijing on which even subversive ideas could be posted was closed down. Deng spoke out against "bourgeois liberalism." Though capitalism might be allowed to invade the economic sector, writers and artists must follow the "Four Upholds:" socialism, the dictatorship of the proletariat, Communist party leadership, and Marxism-Leninism-Maoism. Moreover:

> It is absolutely forbidden for a Party member to peddle notions like freedom of speech, freedom of the press, or freedom of assembly if these are extended to counterrevolutionaries.[48]

If they tried to ignore these injunctions, satirists could be excluded from the Chinese Writers' Association, the key to making a living. If the State Publication Administration didn't like your ideas, they could simply cut your allocation of paper — a drastic matter during periods when paper was in short supply. In 1989 the Tiananmen Square massacre came as a brutal reminder of the limits to dissent set by the hard-liners in the regime.

Tiananmen Square, it is true, was the extreme case of suppression during the Deng era, and most of the time punishments of dissidents were less draconian than they had been under Mao. As elsewhere, Chinese writers learned how to get around the censors. They took advantage of the huge size of the country and its population, publishing in areas remote from the centers of power and more tolerant of unorthodox views. They used Aesopian techniques to make their dissenting views less obvious. Even so, most of the satire after Mao's death was relatively mild and cautious. For example, *What If It Really Were* by Sha Yexin, Li Shoucheng, and Yao Mingde, is a satire inspired by Gogol's *The Inspector General* on nepotism, bureaucracy, and corruption. The play's antihero is mistaken for the son of a high-ranking party leader and privileges are showered upon him — until his alleged father pays a visit.[49]

Still, the play ends with the imposter facing a criminal trial after a resounding defense of the regime by an incorruptible party elder. Possibly the authors' reluctance to go further resulted from their commitment to the Communist Party's goals. But there was also a concern that the wind might have turned uncomfortably cool. The concern was justified. *What If It Really Were* was sharply criticized in party journals, most of its performances were for restricted audiences, and it was never published in China except for editions limited to party cadres.

Under Deng's successors, Jiang Zemin and Hu Jintao, the winds have continued to blow somewhat warmer. With private entrepreneurship expanding and China emerging as a world economic power, there is talk of more responsiveness to the masses and the extension of elections at the local level. Expectations that these developments will lead to a more open system are fuelled by the rapidly increasing access of the Chinese population to the technologies of mass communication: cell phones, the Internet, and satellite TV.

These changes make the system ripe for satire: a Communist regime inviting businesspeople to join the Communist Party, the unceasing creation of new millionaires amidst widespread peasant poverty, and the fascination of the masses with pop stars rather than political doctrines.

Moreover, things have become somewhat easier for satirists. Writers and performers are given more leeway. In fact, for the first time since the inauguration of the People's Republic, a comedian in 2000 made fun of the current top Communist Party leader in public. The comedian-musician was Xuan Ke, who had met Jiang when he attended an Ancient Music concert. The barbs were fairly mild, but they were not without a certain edge. Xuan had been jailed during the 1957 Anti-Rightist campaign, and Jiang had told him that he should thank Deng Xiaoping for his release. Xuan used this in his routine to appreciative laughs, for his audience knew that Deng had also been in charge of the Anti-Rightist campaign. [50]

The year 2002 saw another notable appearance of a satirical work in China. It was a new version by director Shang Chengjun of *Animal Farm*, performed at the Central Academy of Drama's Experimental Theater in Beijing. Shang's adaptation focused less on the rulers (the tyrannical pigs) than on the apathetic, intolerant, and lazy masses (the horses, sheep, and chickens), and this might have made it more acceptable to the censors. Yet the audiences appeared to have little difficulty in making the connections between Orwell's fable about the Soviet Union and Chinese communist history.[51] Moreover, anti-party jokes were making the rounds, such as: "If we don't root out corruption, the country will perish; if we do root out corruption, the Party will perish".[52] The rebelliousness of the young, no longer unleashed into the destructive fury of the Cultural Revolution, found expression in a popular culture (at least among the well-to-do urban classes) similar in many ways to that of the West; and a popular cartoon series, *Bad Girl*, by Song Yang, captured the new spirit of defiant, misbehaving youth.

Yet there is still centralized power; and if no leader has the personal charisma of Mao or Deng, a small group at the head of the Communist Party still makes the key decisions. Satirists know that the censors are watching. No anti-regime cartoons appear in any newspaper. Song's *Bad Girl* cartoon has not been censored because he avoids the "obvious hot buttons: pornography, violence, or overt criticism of the government."[53] Every play must receive official approval before it can be presented. Criteria for movie censorship, reaffirmed in 2008, include explicit sex; "excessively terrifying scenes;" and anything that "distorts the civilization and history of China and other nations" or that tarnishes "the image of revolutionary leaders, heroes, important historic characters, members of the armed forces, police, and judicial bodies."[54]

Party leaders continue to pound numbers into the heads of party members and the public. For Jiang Zemin it was the "Three Represents," which included the idea of allowing capitalists to join the Communist Party and which produced a crop of jokes, unpublished but easily communicated by the rapidly increasing number of cell phones. For example: How would various leaders catch Osama Bin Laden? Bush would launch missiles at him, Putin would seduce him with Russian girls, and Jian would annoy him to death with the "Three Represents."

So with the number of Internet users in China increasing at an extraordinary rate,[55] the government blocked Web sites that contained views that criticized or mocked the Chinese leadership, closed down a number of Internet cafes, and required all Web sites and Web logs to be registered with the government. In the run-up to the 2008 Olympics in China the controls were strengthened still further, aimed especially at videos with unacceptable political or sexual content.

As a condition of doing business in China (and competing with the indigenous Chinese Baidu system), Microsoft and its Chinese partner agreed to attach a warning to "forbidden language" on their Web sites, including "democracy," "liberty," "human rights," and "capitalism." Google and Yahoo! have also cooperated with the Chinese government in censoring or blocking online content, and in 2006 Google decided to bypass the problem by offering its search engine in China without e-mail or blogging.[56] This did not lead to it being criticized within China, of course, but cartoonists in the West jumped on the issue, one showing representatives of Google, Microsoft, and Yahoo! marching in step with Red Army soldiers and saluting a giant portrait of Mao.

International news services, including Reuters, Dow Jones, and Bloomberg, have been warned that they are subject to censorship of anything likely to run counter to Chinese government policies. Nor is television likely to provide a forum for anti-regime satire. Rupert Murdoch, who had trumpeted the power of satellite TV to open up authoritarian systems everywhere, dropped the BBC from his Star TV north Asian schedule as a condition of being able to reach the Chinese mainland market.

Of course, Internet pirates and bloggers continue to find ways to evade the government's efforts at control. And the cell phone, a natural communicator of whispered jokes, remains largely beyond the censor's reach.

All in all, the atmosphere is now more relaxed than it was earlier. Yet open criticism of the fundamentals of the system is rare, and it is still the case that, as the great Chinese writer, Lu Xun, said in 1933, "To be a satirist is dangerous."

Consequently, the most cutting satire about the Chinese Communist system comes from outside the mainland. Some comes from Taiwan and Hong Kong, where there is still an ebullient satirical scene, including revues, stand-up comedians, radio programs, and an annual exhibit: Hong Kong in Caricature: Lampooning the Leadership.[57]

Then there are the exiles who have moved to the West. Ha Jin, who came to the United States, wrote a series of novels in English about life in the Chinese People's Republic, including *In the Pond,* featuring an artist who is

Google, Microsoft, and Yahoo have been faced with an embarrassing dilemma in their efforts to do business in China. On the one hand, China, with more than 100 million Internet users, is an irresistible market; and the Internet is often cited as an instrument for undermining despotic governments. On the other hand, the People's Republic of China imposes antidemocratic restrictions on the Internet, and the American companies have, after protesting, accepted the limits. Patrick Chappatte, a Lebanese-Swiss cartoonist whose work appears in European and American newspapers and magazines, leaves no doubt where he stands on this issue, as representatives of the corporations genuflect in lockstep with Chinese troops before a portrait of Mao. [Patrick Chappatte, *International Herald Tribune*, © Patrick Chappatte. Used by permission.]

bitterly attacked for circulating satirical cartoons that expose party corruption,[58] and *War Trash*.[59]

Dai Sijie settled in France. His novel[60] and film, *Balzac and the Little Chinese Seamstress,* tells of two music students sent by Mao to be reeducated by the peasants. They bring their violin, an instrument never before seen by the peasants, who threaten to burn it as a "bourgeois toy." When they are asked to listen to a Mozart sonata, they are puzzled and infuriated still more — until they are reassured by the information that its title is "Mozart Is Thinking of Chairman Mao".

Evidently the paucity of political satire inside China today does not stem from any inherent lack of satirical talent. Nor does it suggest a universal failure to see anything ridiculous in the regime and its utterances.

chapter seven

IMPERIAL IRONIES:
INDIA AND THE RAJ

On India, Britain is often commended:
Democracy came when the Empire was ended.
However, next door, keep your voice to a murmur
If you want to make fun of the rulers of Burma.

The Raj, the British imperial occupation of India for almost two centuries, was at once a remarkable accomplishment and an absurdity crying out for satire.

The accomplishment consisted in the conquest of a subcontinent by agents of a small island thousands of miles away; the creation of a sense of nationhood out of a number of separate principalities and fiefdoms; the establishment of an efficient system of administration and courts; the building of roads, railways, dams, and factories; the suppression of suttee (the immolation of widows), and thugee (the ritual murder of groups of travelers by bandit gangs); and finally, the transition to complete independence from British control.

Yet, as British as well as Indian satirists were to observe in newspapers, comic journals, plays, poems, and cartoons, the situation was absurd. Taking control of a vast distant domain with a rich array of cultures totally alien to the colonial power was, at least in a twenty-first century perspective, breathtakingly presumptuous. The British, of course, were not alone in such overseas adventures, but it was the most successful of the several European colonial powers, building a vast empire on which the sun never set. And the crown jewel in the imperial diadem was India.

At first came naked plunder. The merchants of the East India Company, operating under a royal charter and backed by military force, imposed their own laws, collected onerous taxes, and governed with little concern for anything but making themselves and the Company's shareholders rich.

This was exposed by satire which, in the 1780s, came in the pages of the *Bengal Gazette,* popularly known as "Hickey's Gazette" after its publisher, James Augustus Hickey. Despite its tiny circulation, the paper's disclosures of the Company's gross venality and its rude comments on top British administrators led to the first example of censorship in the British Raj.[1] Hickey was charged with defamation, sentenced to a year in jail, and the *Gazette* was closed down.

However, Hickey was not the only Briton to find the conduct of the East India Company intolerable. There was a barrage of criticism in the British Parliament. The playwright-politician Richard Brinsely Sheridan called the British governor general "a man holding in one hand a bloody scepter, while with the other he was picking pockets"; and Parliament abolished the authority of the East India Company, replacing it with a new breed of honest, efficient administrators.

Purging corruption did not bring an end to dissent and satire. On the contrary, it was to make starkly clear the irreconcilable contradictions at the heart of the Raj. By replacing unbridled commercialism with the full authority of government, the claim of legitimacy had to be asserted. This claim took the form, put forward by many British leaders, that their country's mission was to bring civilization in place of obscurantism, education in place of ignorance, the rule of law in place of anarchy and ethnic violence. Eventually, in fact, the Indian people might be lifted up to the point at which they could govern themselves — within the framework of the Empire. Yet this role of tutelage, however benign in intent, was basically authoritarian — ostentatiously so, for the British gloried in imperial pomp and circumstance, New Delhi being "the setting for the grandest living on earth, with more bowing and curtseying, more precedence and protocol, than anywhere else in the empire, London included."[2] On the other hand, Britain itself by the late nineteenth century was on the way to becoming a full-fledged democracy, with competitive elections, an expanding electorate, a lively, uncensored press, and an aristocracy in decline. No doubt, in the minds of British reformers these were to be the goals for Indians, too, but the devil was in the details implied by the word "eventually."

Meantime, what was to be done about the growing impatience of an increasing number of Indians, some of them bringing back radical ideas from an education in England? There were negotiations after negotiations, but the British were cautious, reluctant to cede enough power to take the edge off the increasingly clamorous Indian demands. Periodically Indian hostility erupted into violence, and each time the response was the kind of repression typical of authoritarian regimes everywhere. Police and the military used force, some of it brutally disproportionate to the provocation.

The response in London and New Delhi to these confrontations was of two kinds. On the one side were the hard-liners, the irreconcilables. The most formidable of these was Winston Churchill, described by one British historian as "the villain in the long saga of the end of British rule in India."[3] Both before and during his prime ministership Churchill did everything he could to undermine the periodic negotiations with Indian leaders. His vaunted wit turned into pomposity. He had not, he proclaimed, "become His Majesty's First Minister to preside over the dissolution of the British Empire." (Transcribed later by *Private Eye* into "I have not become the Tory's First Rebel to watch over the liquidation of the British Empah.") In judging Gandhi he could produce only a racist cry of outrage at "the nauseating and humiliating spectacle of this one-time Inner Temple lawyer, now turned seditious fakir, striding half-naked up the steps of the Viceroy's palace . . . to parley on equal terms with the representative of the King Emperor."

On Nazi Germany Churchill was a doughty, eloquent warrior. On India he was Colonel Blimp.

Arrayed against the hard-liners were the reformers, dismayed by the use of repression. Yet, since they were not quite ready to surrender their colonial power, the taint of hypocrisy could not be avoided. As Robert Darnton observes, "Liberal imperialism was the greatest contradiction of them all."[4] A contradiction so blatant was an obvious invitation to satire, with the consequent struggle, inescapable in an authoritarian society, between the satirist and the censor.

Initially the censorship consisted of little more than a bureaucratic compilation of summaries of printed materials.[5] As the Indian drive for independence gathered force, more draconian press laws led to bans on books, journals, and newspaper articles, raids on bookshops, fines and jail sentences, even "the use of secret agents to report on what was said in meetings and what was read in schools."[6]

In India, as elsewhere, sexual references upset the censors. The erotic frankness of Hindu mythological tales provoked such comments as: "a description of the first amorous dalliances of Radha and Krishna, altogether a filthy book." But a Bengali novel raised a more serious question:

> The story of love is mixed with another story, the object of which seems to be to excite in the native mind a strong hatred for British rule and the English character. There are passages in which the author's language becomes almost seditious.[7]

Proof of sedition was often elusive, however, for Indian poets and novelists used Aesopian techniques, leaving their readers to draw contemporary analogies from ancient myths and folktales of oppression and corruption in high places. The result was interminable wrangling by lawyers during sedition trials, the prosecution seeing sinister references to imminent revolution, and the defense finding only innocent celebrations of ancient cultures.

However, the British censors were less worried about the novels and poetry read by the educated elite than about the media that reached the masses. Newspapers and pamphlets were not only for the literate; they were read aloud to eager audiences in the villages. Performances that included drama and songs were immensely popular. One self-proclaimed Swami was sentenced to seven years transportation for writing and performing a seditious song book. In an 1876 case the police banned a play because it contained a song that "ridiculed a law-abiding subject of the King." When, in defiance of the ban, the play was performed under a different name, the author and theater manager were arrested, charged with "the propagation of Indian nationalism and anti-British feeling," and sentenced to a month's imprisonment. The sentence was overturned on appeal, so the government introduced new laws banning controversial plays. Thereafter the Bengali theater was limited mostly to "innocent, insipid and lighthearted plays."[8]

There were cartoons. As one Indian cartoonist tells it, "Cartooning, like cricket, came to India with the British" and "Indian journalism and Indian cartooning subsequently became, as British rule turned intolerable, vehicles of protest, agitation, and peaceful revolution."[9] Inevitably such cartoons invited censorship. A Bengali newspaper ran afoul of the censors with a cartoon in the 1870s suggesting that the authorities covered up instances of Indians being fatally attacked by Europeans by arranging for a verdict of death by an "enlarged spleen." The cartoon depicted a dead coolie being given a perfunctory postmortem by a European doctor while the perpetrator stands by smoking his cigar. This and other allegedly seditious pieces led to a censorship clampdown in 1878. Twenty years later another satirist revived the issue:

It is deeply to be deplored that Indians should have maliciously . . . developed such big spleens, which are ruptured at the slightest touch of a human animal's boots . . . In order to save kickers . . . trouble and expense in the future . . . we have invented the Spleen protector."[10]

Along with newspapers, a major outlet for social and political cartoons in the latter part of the nineteenth century was the proliferation of comic journals, many of them inspired by the British *Punch* magazine. Several of the *Punch* spin-offs were owned and run by British expatriates in India, but some — *Hindi Punch,* for example — were run by Indians, and though far from radical they stung the British with unflattering caricatures of British administrators.

The great Indian master of political caricature was Gaganendranath Tagore, whose lithographs have been compared to those of Daumier. One of his cartoons depicts a Nationalist Party member selling out his party to accept a position as a minister in the British-controlled government. Another pictures a brutal British Governor of Bengal lashing out at nationalist rebels in 1917.

Indian satirists were frustrated by the fact that Britain could not have held on to power in India for so long without the cooperation, indeed the massive participation, of Indians. In the police and the army they were indispensable

THE TERRIBLY SYMPATHETIC

Gaganendranath Tagore (1867–1938), was an influential painter, art connoisseur, and actor, but he was best known for his cartoons commenting on Indian life and politics. In an introduction to this book of Tagore's cartoons, Professor O. C. Gangoly suggests that "there is no bite in his humours and no malice in his jokes . . . his hits never wound or hurt the feelings of his targets." Yet this cartoon leaves no doubt of the intensity of Tagore's anger at British colonial repression. Here we see the huge figure of the British Governor of Bengal terrorizing the fleeing members of the Bengal Nationalists' Freedom movement in 1917. [Gaganendranath Tagore, "The Terribly Sympathetic," The Humorous Art of Gaganendranath Tagore (Calcutta: The Birla Academy of Art and Culture), Plate 24.]

not only for maintaining order but for fighting Britain's wars abroad: a million Indians fought for Britain in World War I, and two million fought in World War II.

Furthermore, the entire British administrative, legal, and commercial structure required staffing by great numbers of educated Indians, some of them appointed to high positions in the Indian Civil Service. These members of a professional middle class were known disparagingly as "baboos," and

Indian satirists expressed derision at Indian professionals who rejected Indian culture and snobbishly adopted British dress, manners, and attitudes. In the newspaper *Comrade*, Wilyat Ali, writing as "Bambooque," mocked "The English Returned Barrister" desperately aping the sahibs in manners and speech and pretending to have forgotten his native tongue during his brief stay in England."[11] Tagore made the point wittily in a cartoon: "Find the Indian: A Puzzle for the Younger Generation," in which all but one of the figures is dressed in western clothing.

IMPERIAL SATIRE

Back in Britain satire took a very different form. Cartoons in *Punch* and the *Daily Express* conveyed contempt for Gandhi and for reformist British ministers, and the Russian Revolution added a conspiratorial note to the barrage of attacks. A cartoon in the *Daily Express* showed a malevolent Soviet figure instructing Gandhi to twist the tail of the British lion.

The "baboos" were mercilessly jeered at in *Punch* as pathetic social climbers, ridiculous imitators of their British overlords. On the other hand, the many Indians who fought in Britain's wars were showered with praise. A *Punch* cartoon in 1914 celebrated the Indian contribution with a glowing depiction of Indian warriors over the caption "India for the King," and the Indian sepoy was already firmly established in the affections of the British public by Rudyard Kipling.

Yet the British satire on India was not all so self-righteous. In fact, George Orwell dissented fiercely. As the young Eric Blair he came to Burma, then a province of India, as assistant superintendent of police in the Indian Imperial Police. When he arrived he held many of the conventional beliefs of his self-described "lower-upper-middle-class" background. After five years, he left with the profoundly anti-imperialist view that was to permeate his novel *Burmese Days*.[12]

In this novel, Orwell offered satirical studies of the various types who were caught up in this tyranny. The ranting racist Ellis bitterly protests the moves toward equality. The expatriate wife, Mrs. Lackersteen, complains that the servants are getting almost as lazy as the lower classes back home. There is Westerfield who has no prejudice against Orientals and finds them charming — as long as they are given no freedom. But Flory, who speaks for Orwell, tells of "the lie that we're here to uplift our black brothers, instead of to rob them ... it corrupts us in ways you can't imagine."[13]

It corrupts the Burmese, too, as we see from the consternation of Flory's Burmese friend, Dr. Veraswami, when Flory abuses his fellow pucka sahibs. Veraswami lauds the English gentlemen as "the salt of the earth." He admires their "glorious loyalty to one another! The public school spirit! Even those whose manner is unfortunate — some Englishmen are arrogant,

I concede — have the great, sterling qualities that we Orientals lack. Beneath their rough exterior, their hearts are of gold."[14]

At the end of the novel a despairing Flory commits suicide. Orwell's own solution was less drastic. He resigned and went home to England, confirmed in his belief that imperialism was "an unjustifiable tyranny."[15]

AFTER THE RAJ: TOWARDS DEMOCRACY

The Raj ended with a precipitous British withdrawal, followed by a cataclysmic bloodbath. Yet even as the riots raged, satirists urged the case for humor.

When the humor journal, *Shankar's Weekly,* made its debut in May 1948, the editor complained that, "Years ago we lost our gift of laughter and gained an unhealthy seriousness ... we seem to think it is vulgar to laugh and we never laugh at ourselves."[16] No doubt this was an overstatement given our examples of Indian satire before independence, but this earlier record pales in comparison to the burst of satire that followed independence. Until it ceased publication in 1975, *Shankar's Weekly* delivered on

Abu (Abu Abraham) (1924–2002) worked as a cartoonist for several Indian and British newspapers and magazines, and he published a number of books. From 1972 to 1978 he was a member of the upper house of the Indian Parliament. Initially a supporter of Indira Gandhi, he became disenchanted when she declared a State of Emergency in 1975, suspending most constitutional rights. This cartoon, showing Gandhi leading a reluctant India toward her idea of a revolution, is one of a number that Abu drew during the Emergency. A few were censored but most were published at the time in the Indian Express and the Sunday Standard. In his foreword he explains: "I have not bothered to investigate why I was allowed to carry on so freely. And I am not interested in finding out." [Abu Abraham, *The Games of Emergency* (New Delhi: Bell Books, 1977), courtesy of Bell Books.]

its promise "to laugh with a purpose, to expose the ridiculous part of our pompous selves."

So did a panoply of cartoonists, including Shankar himself, Abu Abraham, and several others in Shankar's and other journals as well as R. K. Laxman in the *Times of India*[17] and Sudhir Dar in the *Delhi Times*. Much of their work was relatively mild, but some of the satire was scathing. After Prime Minister Indira Gandhi declared a state of emergency from 1975 to 1977, suspending many constitutional rights and press freedoms, cartoonists persisted in lampooning her even more trenchantly than the British were to mock Thatcher. They drew the prime minister cowing her opposition with a rolling pin, knocking them about with cudgels, and locking democracy in a birdcage with the caption: "P.M. has refuted the charge of forsaking Democracy. It is safe and sound."[18] Abu Abraham did manage to get most of his cartoons published during the emergency, and subsequently he produced a book of his work during that period.[19]

Several Indian novels — Arundhati Roy's *The God of Small Things*, Amitav Ghosh's *The Glass Palace*, and the works of the Indian expatriate, Salman Rushdie — have included satirical comment on political themes. Shashi Tharoor's *The Great Indian Novel* [20] uses the format of the great Indian classic, the *Mahabharata*, to provide a satirical history of India during the Raj and after independence. As Tharoor tells it, the British had learned nothing from their experience with the American colonies, actually imposing a tax on a previously free good, the mango. "Why the pink blackguards bothered to tax Indians I will never understand, for they had successfully stolen everything they needed for centuries."[21] But in the novel Tharoor's wit spares nobody, not even his heroes Gandhi and Nehru.

To essayist and publisher Rukun Advani (Arundhati Roy's husband), these novels provided the truest insight into the state of his country. India, he said, "is frequently a parody of itself, and . . . Indian life is therefore more truly represented by satiric fiction than the hollow piety of news magazines."[22]

The Internet age brought political satire through a number of Web sites. *Jaal* jeers at both government ministers and left radicals. *Noise of India* aims at "putting the mock back in democracy" and promises to "take utmost care in providing its readers with the most inaccurate information possible (though) given the fact that weird stuff does happen, there is a real danger that some accuracies may creep in."

Some Indian satire has reflected the lingering legacy of the British. There are still jibes at the "baboo culture," for among the middle and upper classes some still favor English manners and affectations, such as including thinly sliced cucumber sandwiches in their high tea entertainments.

Yes Minister came to Indian TV in Hindi as a BBC Worldwide project. As the actor who played the counterpart of Sir Humphrey pointed out:

All the long convoluted sentences Sir Humphrey used to speak work beautifully in Hindi. The series adapts very well because the systems of democracy and the bureaucracies in Britain and India are pretty much the same.[23]

Nonetheless, as *Shankar's* inaugural number pointed out, "The situation has changed; it is entirely Indian now. Instead of the English saheb we have the Indian saheb."

The British had been accused of a policy of "divide and rule." In the immediate aftermath of independence, as Pakistan broke off from India and as Hindus and Muslims launched murderous attacks on each other, the carnage might be blamed partly, but no longer solely, on the legacy of the British. The caste system might have been encouraged and intensified by the class-conscious British, but it was an indigenously Indian invention. Now where there was corruption, it was Indian corruption. The massive poverty and the throngs of homeless in the cities had all been there under the British, but now they were India's problems.

Now where there was censorship it was imposed by Indians. Portrayals of anything suggestive of sex, despite the tradition of the Kama Sutra and explicit temple engravings, were subject to severe prohibitions. Dissenting political views, too, were placed under pressure from a variety of sources. The pressure was at its most intense during the state of emergency declared by Indira Gandhi from 1975 to 1977, but limitations on free speech and press have become a continuing part of the Indian political landscape.

Given the intensity of the ethnic and religious hostilities that erupt periodically, it is not surprising that newspapers and magazines have been caught in the crossfire. Conflict between Hindu nationalists and Moslem fundamentalists has led to physical attacks on editors and reporters. Sikh priests have excommunicated the editor of a Sikh newspaper. Courts have banned reporters from covering politically sensitive trials.

Satirists have not been exempted. In 1987 the editor of a popular weekly in the southern Indian state of Tamil Nadu was sentenced to three months in prison for publishing a cartoon lampooning a state legislature, though the state's chief minister ordered his release after 48 hours. In 1994 a group of ethnic activists vandalized an exhibition of "Cartoons Against Communalism."[24]

Accordingly, the 2005 annual report of Reporters Without Borders, an organization that assesses the degree of press freedom around the world, expressed deep concern about several examples of censorship in India. Even so, the report commented approvingly of "a broadcast and written media that is more and more independent and vigilant about defending the rights it has carved out over recent decades. Indian journalists are always ready to mobilize when their freedoms come under threat." Though divided by an array of tensions far more intense than those caught up in America's "culture wars," India is commonly recognized as among the world's democracies in most contemporary classifications, with an impressive, if imperfect, record of vigorous criticism of authority, including the insolent jabs of the satirists.

INDIA'S NEIGHBORS: POST-COLONIAL DISAPPOINTMENTS

In July 2005, the Indian prime minister told an Oxford University audience of several "beneficial consequences" of British rule, including constitutional government, an efficient civil service, the rule of law, and a free press; and a Delhi newspaper opined that the British had been "the best colonial administrators in the world."

If this was true of India, it was much less so of other countries that were once part of the British domain. Colonialism under the British is also part of the historical experience of six of India's neighboring countries: Pakistan, Bangladesh, Singapore, Malaysia, Sri Lanka, and Burma (Myanmar). None have advanced as far toward democracy as India. Though all adopted multiparty, parliamentary systems after independence, intense ethnic and factional struggles have led to mostly authoritarian government, with a strong role for the military and frequent attacks on press freedom.[25] Political satire exists in all these countries, but everywhere it is subject to severe limits, as seen in the following examples.

Malaysia has tolerated Web sites parodying politicians and cartoons poking fun at corruption and the military. There is even a best-selling 1999 novel, *Shit,* by the National Laureate Shahnon Ahmad, in which the action takes place inside a large intestine, and the country's politicians are depicted as lumps of excrement. (The title is in English, though the book is written in Bahasa Malaysia.) The scatological humor, as the author makes clear in his preface, is aimed at the general quality of Malaysian politics: "If politics is foul and can foul other things, then I as a writer will present the foulness and elements that are fouling other things in my own way." Moreover, the long-established one-party domination has begun to erode. Nevertheless, critics of the government in Malaysia must be constantly aware of the 1970 Internal Security Act, which severely limits free speech and press and allows imprisonment without trial.

Singapore, which joined with Malaysia after independence from Britain before becoming a separate nation in 1965, has a parliamentary system but a reputation for being a "nanny state," imposing the government's moral standards on the private behavior of its citizens. Domination of the political system by the People's Action Party and tight control of the media by the government have taken the edge off most satire. "The tradition of political cartoons in Singapore ... is that of consensus-shaping in the context of the political process of nation-building."[26] A cartoonist says that "almost anything can be banned if, in the government's eyes, it affects the development of Singapore," including jabs at other countries friendly to Singapore. Another alleges: "There are so many things to satirize, but at the newspapers the editors shoot them down; even in the schools, the teachers say 'don't satirize the leaders' ." Editors tell satirists: "Don't criticize the government; it rules well, thus, there is not much to criticize . . . "[27] Yet there was something to criticize, in particular the censorship. After the Singapore Board of Film Censors imposed 27 cuts on *15,* a film by Royston Tan about violent teenage gangs, he retaliated by making *Cut,* a 12-minute musical spoof of the censors. *Cut* won an international award and a reproof from a government minister for attempting to undermine the standing of the Board of Film Censors.[28]

Sri Lanka (formerly Ceylon) saw a resurgence of political satire in the 1990s, despite the fact that the country was plunged into the carnage of civil war between the central government, paramilitary troops, and separatist forces. A State Drama Festival of 1988 drew large and appreciative audiences that could "laugh at the pretensions and (transient) powers of petty politicians and people in authority."[29] But this was an exception in a country where democracy had given way to military rule in the 1980s, and the tolerance for theater contrasted sharply with rigid censorship of the press. Thus, in 2005 cartoonist Jiffry Younoos was "badly beaten by the palace 'Goon Squad' " after the publication of a series of cartoons on the president, including one asking why the president was hiding rather than attending the funeral of a man whose assassination many believed was arranged by the president.[30]

Pakistan, nominally a federal democratic republic with a president, prime minister, and bicameral legislature, has three times undergone military takeovers since independence, the latest in 1999. In newspaper columns and on radio and TV, satirists feasted on charges of the corruption and incompetence of party leaders during periods of civilian government, nor have they given up during the military regimes. Indeed, under President and (until January 2008) Army Chief Pervez Musharraf, there was a substantial expansion of TV comedy programs that included irreverent political quips. Among them was *The Late Show with Begum Nawazich Ali,*, a vehicle for the cross-dressing comedian Ali Saleem. Until the assassination of Benazir Bhutto in December 2007, Saleem specialized in impersonating her; he mocked Bush's view of Islam as paranoiac, and he used his bisexuality to challenge one of his country's deepest taboos.[31] More satire came from Fasi Zaka, a TV and radio host, music critic, and columnist whose TV show, *News, Views, and Confused,* is based on the BBC's panel show *Have I Got News For You.* The privately owned GEO TV also offered a show in which Musharraf was ridiculed as a loudmouthed buffoon.

In December 2007, however, Musharraf declared a state of emergency under which new curbs were placed on the electronic media. One of Fasi Zaka's episodes was banned, and he saw the program's future as "extremely mild, not worth doing."[32] GEO TV, whose president was satirical playwright and journalist Imran Aslam, had its cable transmission blocked. With the emergency lifted in January 2008, GEO was back on cable, and the defeat of Musharraf's party in elections later that year and his resignation in August 2008 again improved the prospects for dissenters. Yet the country's past experience and uncertain political future made most commentators wary of predicting the emergence of a truly open society.

Whatever the constraints on free expression in other countries in the region, *Myanmar*'s depth of despotism places it in a separate, dismal category. Even during the Raj, Burma had enjoyed a considerable tradition of biting political satire, especially in cartoons, and it continued after the British left in 1948. Then came a military coup in 1962, after which the government closed down the cartoonists' association. For 26 years political cartoons survived only in the most pallid, disguised form, and even those could land a cartoonist in jail.

In 1988 political satire came back furiously during an intercession from military government known as the "democracy movement." It lasted one summer until it was crushed in another military coup. An election in 1990 was overturned, the leader of the winning party was imprisoned, press laws were tightened, and newspapers were banned and replaced by an official press. Cartoonists were arrested, including one sentenced to life imprisonment who died in jail. Others went into exile in Bangkok. Though a few critical cartoons did manage to slip by the censor, most did not. A cartoon depicting a chessboard in which a solitary opposition pawn is arrayed against the massed might of the government was banned. So was another that featured a teacher's advice to a student — tell the truth, and "when you've said it, we run away!"[33] As one cartoonist put it in 1993, "We are free now to draw what we like except political satire."[34]

The government also made it clear that comedians had better not tell jokes at its expense. Two members of a long-established comedy troupe, the Moustache Brothers, were sentenced to seven years in 1996 for performing a satirical skit at the home of opposition leader, Aung San Suu Kyi. (A favorite joke of the troupe's leader, Par Par Lay, echoed Werner Finck's dentist joke about the Nazis. Asked why he went to India to have a tooth pulled instead of seeing a Myanmar dentist, Par Par Lay explained that "in Myanmar, we are not allowed to open our mouths.") Though a campaign by Amnesty International led to the comedians' release after six years, their troupe was allowed to perform for small groups of foreigners only, and Par Par Lay was jailed for another five weeks in 2007.[35]

In June 2008, another popular comedian, Zarganar, was arrested and charged with causing public unrest for giving interviews to foreign media criticizing the government's slow response to the devastation cyclone that caused massive havoc in May.

In 2005 an American journalist published an account of her saga retracing Orwell's footsteps in Burma.[36] She found a military government which, under the Orwellian title "The State Peace and Development Council," presided over a system of secret police and citizen informers, with a rigid censorship of ideas labeled (like those in communist states) as "incorrect." The suppression of political satire is but one indication that Myanmar's indigenous despotism is even more oppressive than was Burma's under colonial rule.

Clearly Myanmar is the worst of these cases, a painful reminder on a smaller scale that the appalling dictatorships of the twentieth century can still inspire imitators. Malaysia, Sri Lanka, Pakistan, and Singapore all provide some openings in their systems for determined dissidents. However, their political systems fall well short of demonstrating the "beneficial consequences" of colonial rule that some have claimed for India.

chapter eight

THE MIDDLE EAST: RAGING AGAINST CARTOONS

> The Danish cartoons started cultural clashes—
> Riots and embassies burned down to ashes.
> Still there is hope in the dissident voices
> Who see beyond *jihad* more civilized choices.

Humor has always been an important element in Arab culture. From the earliest recorded Arab history, the lonely, constantly moving life in the desert placed a high value on verbal communication, generating a rich tradition of poetry. Arab poets, drawing on the range and flexibility of the language, made extensive use of a variety of devices of verbal wit. In doing so they could draw on the authority of Mohammed, who is said to be the only prophet known to have enjoyed a joke, even a joke on himself.[1]

Yet, most Arab humor was not about politics:

> This is understandable in view of the despotic style of the medieval government and the fact that most writers were attached to this or that prince who enjoyed, in the Muslim world, religious as well as secular authority.[2]

That medieval despotic style still holds. There are no democracies today among the Middle Eastern Muslim countries.[3]

Still, from time to time in Arab history there have been examples of satirical anger leveled at the corruption and incompetence of the rulers. Village jesters made a living by telling jokes and derisory anecdotes about rapacious local governors and judges, and poets unleashed their scorn at sultans and caliphs.[4] Wider audiences were reached as newspapers spread throughout the Arab world, and the early twentieth century saw the emergence of several humorous and satirical magazines. With a few lively exceptions, however, the scope for political satire was sharply limited by the ruling groups' historical hostility to dissent, a hostility that has continued to the present time.

EGYPT

Egypt in the 1920s was one of the exceptions, for political satire flourished in poetry, the theater, and magazines. The leading magazine was *Rose Al-Youssef,* named after its publisher and featuring a number of highly popular writers and cartoonists.

A principal cause taken up by the satirists was the struggle for national independence. Since the seventh century Egypt had been part of the Ottoman empire. Then came the French, who built the Suez Canal, followed by the British, who, after concluding the canal couldn't be built, purchased 44 percent of the canal's shares. Between them the British and the French controlled the Egyptian ruler, the Khedive. In 1882 a British fleet suppressed nationalist riots and installed a Consul General, Sir Evelyn Baring (whose style was recognized in his nickname "over-Baring"). When Turkey, still the nominal sovereign in Egypt, joined the war on the losing side in 1914, Britain declared Egypt to be a British "protectorate" — in effect, part of the British Empire.

It remained so until 1922, when furious nationalist opposition forced Britain to declare that the protectorate was officially over. However, the British retained bases in Egypt and installed Fu'ad as king, whom the Egyptian poet, Bayram al-Tunisi, mocked ("Where can they find a fool and a rogue the like of you?"). He was beaten repeatedly for his insolence.[5]

In 1936 the British negotiated a treaty that confirmed the fact that "Egypt was not sovereign at all, but a princely state on the Indian model."[6] So now there were two prime satirical targets, the Egyptian government and the British. *Rose Al-Youssef* set the pace. When the government's Ministry of Education engaged in a heavyhanded move to close the Institute of Drama for allegedly encouraging immorality, *Rose Al-Youssef* renamed the Ministry of Education the "Ministry of Tradition;" the Ministry of Health was dubbed the "Ministry for the Eradication of Illness by Putting Down Ill People;" and the Ministry of Communications became the "Ministry Cursed by Travelers Both Ways of the Journey."

Attacking ministries was one thing; criticizing the monarchy was another. Unable to print anything unflattering about King Fu'ad, the magazine used the Aesopean technique of publishing numerous articles on previous awful monarchs. Then *Rose Al-Youssef* went after the British high commissioner, whose visit occasioned a great deal of ceremonial deference from the Egyptian government. In 1928 the government struck back, warning the magazine that it had "established a disgraceful precedent harming the honor of the press and degrading ethics and morality" and that it must stop carrying "obnoxious material, wicked stories, and indulgence in lies and fabrications." Furthermore, the magazine must publish the warning in its next issue.

The magazine duly published the warning, with the sarcastic comment:

> We accept that we have established a disgraceful precedent ... But do
> we not have the right to ask our beloved ministry ... to instruct the
> Publications Department to issue a list of the lies ... which we must
> then avoid and spare the much aggrieved honor of the press from the
> disgraceful precedent which we so unfairly established.[7]

The government did not oblige by printing a list of unacceptable lies, but
in 1933 it issued a new restrictive press law. The magazine was prosecuted
and suspended several times, yet it continued to harass the government and
the British. Its example led to the creation of other magazines that joined
in the assault — until the inauguration of much stricter censorship on the
outbreak of World War II and the invasion of Egypt by German and Italian
forces.

Nationalist resistance, fuelled by Britain's harsh suppression of riots,
intensified after the war, and in 1952 a group of army officers under the
leadership of Gamal Abdel Nasser took over the government, expelled
Fu'ad's successor, Farouk, and negotiated the withdrawal of all British
troops from the canal zone. When this was followed by the nationalization
of the Suez Canal and the collapse of the British-French-Israeli plan to
invade Egypt and take over the canal, the Egyptians were at last in charge
of their own destinies.

Yet independent Egypt did not move in the direction of democracy.
Instead there was military rule, sanctioned by Nasser's being elected with
99% of the vote. At first this did not inhibit satire. Nasser was said to have
"insisted on a daily brief of the latest current jokes about him and his
regime"[8] and to have enjoyed jokes about his claims to omnipotence — such
as one suggesting that God did not rise to greet Nasser when he reached
heaven for fear that he would take his place on the throne.

Even so, the press came under stringent government control during the
regime of Nasser and his successors, Anwar Sadat and Hosni Mubarak.
Since 1952 all media publications must obtain a license from the Supreme
Press Council. The Egyptian constitution bans censorship except during a
state of emergency — which has been in force ever since 1981. An
opposition press survives, but under stultifying conditions: a 1995 press
law could require editorial writers, columnists, and cartoonists to prove
the accuracy of any criticism of public officials.

Rose Al-Youssef is still alive, but now it is owned by the state. The Egypt
State Information Service proudly proclaims that it is "one of the most
popular and widely circulated weeklies in Egypt and the Arab world,"[9]
and it has not forsworn humor. Its cartoonist, George Bahgory, has been
described as "a latter-day, more politically conscious James Thurber,"[10]

poking fun at the absurdities of daily life in Egypt. Yet the magazine has become "Egypt's all-in-one answer to the *National Inquirer, Private Eye* and *Punch*,"[11] and though it has frequently been the target of libel suits, there is little left of its earlier tradition of lampooning the Egyptian government.

There are other outlets for dissenting views — as long as they don't go too far. For example, the government has tolerated editorial cartoonist Ahmed Hijazi, despite the fact that his work expresses hostility to imperialism, international business, and "the cult of personality and the worship of the state, even in the guise of the nation."[12] But his cartoons don't feature the president, and his left-wing attitudes, though very clear, are expressed mostly in his popular comic strips for children.

Cartoonist Salah Jaheen found that he had a good deal of leeway under Sadat with his antiestablishment jibes. Yet his newspaper pulled one of his cartoons that scoffed at promises made by Nixon and Kissinger when they visited the Middle East, and another was vetoed because it supported student riots protesting Sadat's Israel policy. After that, "he knows the limits, which he cannot pass in criticizing the Americans with his pen."[13] When he made fun of Islamic conservatives for opposing a law to improve the status of women, he was denounced in sermons and received death threats.

In a weekly column in *Al-Ahram,* a government-owned newspaper, el-Ramly regularly joked about the government's propaganda claims. As he noted, however, there were four taboo subjects: "sex, the president, religion, and social values." He added that, though you can't write directly about them, "you can touch on them in satire."[14] Evidently, very delicately.

The government insists that its hard line is driven by its need to protect against the growth of religious fundamentalism and periodic eruptions of terrorism. Yet this does not explain why a number of journalists have been sent to jail for accusing government ministers of corruption, and even for criticizing America's invasion of Iraq (U.S. aid being vital to the Egyptian economy). Nor does the containment of terrorism have anything to do with the sentencing to prison in 2000 of cartoonist Essam Hanaft on a charge of libeling the deputy prime minister, leaving Hanaft unable to attend the ceremony at which he received the Cartoonists Rights Network annual award for "Courage in Editorial Cartooning."[15]

To some extent the role of publishing opposition views was taken over by the *Cyprus Press* — media published in Cyprus and other countries neighboring Egypt — for Egyptian censorship of imported publications was much milder than its domestic products. The Egyptian government finally clamped down on the *Cyprus Press,* but the importers looked for loopholes in the law and played the kind of cat-and-mouse game with the censors common to authoritarian systems.

SYRIA

During the era of French control, one satirical magazine existed on and off for 36 years from 1929, with periodic suspensions by the authorities. After Syria won its independence from France in 1946, a lively independent press emerged and a 12-member League of Satirists was formed. However, censorship was imposed as military governments took over. All independent papers were banned in 1963, and in the 1970s a popular writer of satirical short stories was forced into exile in London, where he joined a number of other expatriate Arab intellectuals.

In February 2001, under the new Syrian president, Bashar al-Assad, the first independent newspaper since 1963, *The Lamplighter,* appeared and sold out immediately. The paper, published by cartoonist Ali Farzat, was a satiric weekly that skewered repressive government, the dismal economy, bureaucracy, and corruption.[16] Occasionally the paper would target a venal official, but its criticisms were mostly of a general nature rather than directed at particular countries or individuals. Still, any autocratic regime was likely to be alarmed by a cartoon showing starving men begging for food and being given medals by the military instead, or another depicting a man being tortured while his torturer is moved to tears by a mushy television show, or one showing a man being beaten for insisting, against the official line, that 1+1=2.

Within a year Syrian government officials were expressing irritation with *The Lamplighter,* and in June 2002 Farzat was ordered to delete two articles from an issue, along with a cartoon allegedly defaming the prime minister. Said Farzat, "We had obtained permission for a satirical newspaper and suddenly we are forbidden from criticizing." There was worse to come. "When I finally went too far for them, the government issued a resolution, and within one hour they had closed my newspaper and my office, and taken away my printing license," Farzat said.[17] He also aroused the wrath of one of his regular targets, Saddam Hussein, who barred him from Iraq and threatened to kill him.[18]

JORDAN

For a time, more political satire was tolerated in Jordan than in any of its Arab neighbors. According to the comedy team of Nabil and Hisham, the breakthrough for satire came when Jordan was besieged during the first Gulf War:

There was a harmony to our collective agonizing. Internal reins were loosened. In our fight for survival satire finally became an accepted weapon. It's as if a whole country got together and said, "hell, at least we can be funny."[19]

Ali Farzat is one of the most widely admired and enjoyed cartoonists in the Middle East, despite (or because of) his periodic clashes with the authorities. Thus, when a new Syrian president allowed him to publish a satirical magazine in 2001, it sold out immediately. However, within a year the magazine was being censored, and it later was closed down. A book of his work published in the United States is organized around his perennial targets: tyrants, terror, torture, presidents, bureaucrats, the rich, opportunists, war, and so on. This cartoon in a section of the book on civil liberties drives home the point made by Kafka and many other opponents of tyranny —the necessity of insisting, in the face of official lies, that 1+1=2. [*Ali Farzat, A Pen of Damascus Steel: Political Cartoons of an Arab Master* (Seattle: Cune Press, 2005).]

In 2001 Nabil and Hisham performed on television and in a theater, spoofing everyone, including then King Hussein. Nabil explained:

> The moment the censor was put aside, we took off like racehorses. Artists are usually social critics, latent politicians, sensitive to the events around them … Yes, we are political — *Shakespearean*, Brechtian, improvisational. We do what we feel like doing, whatever suits us.[20]

After Hussein's death Nabil and his troupe continued their political lampooning of the government and even of King Abdullah II (though not by name). However, the involvement of Nabil and Hisham in the Palestinian-Israeli peace movement alienated some of their supporters. The Jordanian government also made it clear to critics that some subjects remained out of bounds. Despite the official abolition of prior censorship, an issue of an independent weekly that carried an article about torture in Jordan was banned, and a cartoon in another issue critical of the prime minister had to be replaced by a cartoon on a less controversial topic.

SAUDI ARABIA

In a country still tightly controlled by a monarchy and with laws based on the Islamic religious code, there would not seem to be much room for disrespectful satire. In 1993 two Indian editors working for the *Arab News* were sentenced to two years in prison and 500 lashes for printing an American comic strip, "B.C.," by Johnny Hart, which the authorities interpreted as questioning the existence of God. Only intense international pressure produced a royal pardon. In 2003 Jamal Khashoggi, the editor of a provincial newspaper, *Al-Watan,* was fired by order of the Information Ministry because he had attacked Islamic radicals and "published caricatures linking Islamists with terrorists."[21]

Yet every Ramadan since 1993 Saudi television has carried a comedy series, *Tash Ma Tash,*[22] that has lampooned not only problems of everyday Saudi life but also discrimination against women, bureaucratic incompetence and corruption, bungling by intelligence agencies, and even religious extremism in public schools. The program, which began as an effort to boost the declining ratings of state television, became enormously popular.

Is this, then, an indication that the system is becoming more open? Hardly. One sociologist suggests that the program "is tolerated because it is light and funny . . . the program doesn't challenge the system; we are dealing with a social critique within the existing social framework."[23] Even so, the program ran up against fierce criticism. After an episode that criticized discrimination against women in restaurants, the press was full of angry condemnation by religious conservatives. A sequence accusing judges, all of them sheikhs, of working only two or three hours a day, provoked a *fatwa,* or religious edict, by senior sheikhs declaring that it was a sin to watch the program.[24] And an episode ridiculing terrorist groups within the Kingdom led to death threats against the actors.[25]

IRAQ

Under Saddam Hussein Iraq was the most secular but the most repressive of all the Arab states of the Middle East, with only four tightly controlled newspapers. After Saddam was ousted in 2003 there were close to 100 newspapers and magazines, and uncensored news flooded in via satellite television and Internet cafés.

And, yes, there was satire. Editorial cartoonists were back in form. In Saddam's time they had to tread very carefully. Now they could go after their own leaders, the inefficiency of their police force, the insurgents, and the Americans. Cartoonist Khudair Hemiyar drew a U.S. tank thrusting a microphone on the end of a gun turret at an Iraqi with the question: "How does it feel to be living in a democracy?"[26]

On television, *Caricature* was a hit comedy show, with sketches lampooning government incompetence, energy outages, gas shortages, and Iraq and U.S. officials. Other TV programs mocked George W. Bush and Iraqi leaders. When an Iraqi minister was ridiculed, he complained to the station, only to provoke the offending comedian into saying, "Of course, that made us want to do it even more. So after that, we stepped up the pressure."[27]

Unfortunately, the comedian's ardor was likely to be dimmed by the news that Walid Hassan, a regular performer on *Caricature,* was shot down in Baghdad in November 2006.[28] He had committed the unpardonable sin of satirizing not only the U.S. forces and Iraqi politicians but also the Shiite and Sunni militias.

There was evidence of press manipulation in the revelation in December 2005 that a Pentagon contractor had secretly paid Iraqi newspapers to publish positive stories about the war. This led former *National Lampoon* editor, Henry Beard, to invent a program that paid humorists like himself to insert ponderous jokes in Arab publications. ("Like everything else this administration does, it's a total joke.")[29]

So, despite some opening up of the system, Iraq is still listed in the bottom third of international press freedom ratings.

IRAN

There had been a long tradition of political satire in Iran until the regime's hostility to dissent[30] compelled a number of satirical performers to leave for Britain and the United States, where they perform in comedy clubs and beam their lampooning of the mullahs into Iran via satellite TV. Ebrahim Nabavi, a columnist and author of several books of satire, left Iran for Belgium after being jailed twice. Now he writes for BBC News in Persian and broadcasts from Holland.

Ardeshir Mohasses had left Iran for New York in the 1970's after his satirical art had led to warnings from the Shah's secret police. He had hoped to return, but the 1979 Iranian revolution led to his decision to settle in New York, where his works were featured in a major show in 2008.

A 2005 movie by Maryam Khakipour, *The Joy Makers,* told the story of a troupe of actors in Tehran who performed improvised skits poking fun at Iranian life and politics until they were closed down by the authorities. This was not surprising, an Iranian scholar explained in an article: "The Iranian Republic did not ignore theater, but considered it a valid tool for promoting the ideology of the Islamic revolution and educating the public on the orientation of the regime."[31]

In 2006 a cartoon by Mana Neyestani provoked riots among the Azeri population, which believed that the cartoon demeaned their language and culture.[32] The cartoonist and his editor were fired and thrown in jail.

The Internet, despite close monitoring by the regime, provided some opportunities for dissent within Iran. For example, a number of young Iranians discovered an American book lovers' Web site[33] that they used as a forum to express criticism of their president and his policies. After they discussed Orwell's *Animal Farm,* one participant said: "I hope our ending does not turn out like this."[34]

However, the regime was not about to concede that it was afraid of satire. In December 2007 Iranian satirists were invited to compete for a Satirical Book of the Year award, and 276 entries were submitted. The event's secretary "lamented the fact that Iranian officials neglect satirical books," and he "expressed hope that the event would raise the status of satire in Iran."[35] It was doubtful this would produce any anti-regime satire rather than the kind promoted by President Mahmoud Ahmadinejad when he sponsored a cartoon show mocking the Holocaust.[36] Moreover, in 2007 "Iran's only cartoon magazine with an international flavor," *Kayhan Caricature,* was forced to close, the management citing financial constraints and asserting that "publishing a cartoon magazine is not important under the circumstances."[37]

THE ARABS AND ISRAEL

These examples are sufficient to show that, though there is political satire in the Arab world, it is still severely constrained.

However, we should remind ourselves that our focus to this point has been mainly on internal dissent and wit directed at one's own regime. It is a very different story if we include ridicule aimed at other countries. In cartoons, TV shows, and newspaper articles, the Arab world teems with furious derision of Israel as well as of its protector and guarantor, the United States.

Thus the Jordanian Nihad Awartani drew an Israel staggering under the weight of bags of U.S. dollars, with the caption, "Poor Israel . . . Under Enormous U.S. Pressure."[38] A Kuwait newspaper carried a cartoon of a handcuffed Palestinian facing Israeli tanks and forsaken by the world.[39] These were mild examples of the anti-Israel fusillades fired by Arab cartoonists at Israel. Palestinian cartoonist Oomaya Joha, whose husband was killed in a shoot-out with Israeli forces, drew Ariel Sharon washing his hands in blood in a basin manufactured by the United States and standing on a UN rug.[40] Other Arab cartoonists portray Israel as a Nazi state, waging war on its peace-loving Arab neighbors. A Jordanian newspaper printed a cartoon of the railroad to the death camp at Auschwitz — carrying Israeli flags.[41] From Qatar came a cartoon showing Sharon masterminding the 9/11 attack on the Twin Towers.[42] Jews are depicted as vampires and octopuses, an insidious force corrupting and controlling the world.[43] Repeatedly there is the theme drawing on the anti-Semitic "blood libel" — Jews murdering Christian babies for their blood to be used in Passover services, as in a cartoon posted on the Web site of the Palestinian Authority's Information Center showing Sharon as a butcher carving up a Palestinian baby.[44]

An Arab TV program offered the same theme, with Sharon proposing the launching of a new cola drink based on Arab blood and named "Dra-cola."

On their side, Israeli satirists generate a constant supply of political wit. This is not surprising. Israel is the one Middle Eastern country listed as a democracy in international rankings. Moreover, Israelis are the inheritors of a famous tradition of Jewish humor. It is humor derived from centuries of marginality and oppression that used laughter to protect against the otherwise intolerable. Much of it turns inward, using self-deprecation to mock the foibles and pretensions of their own culture. So it was natural that, settled at last in their own country, they would take aim at the follies of their compatriots.

Ephraim Kishon was among the writers who laughed at bureaucrats and politicians. On television a weekly mock-news show, *Eretz Nehederet,* derides politicians far more savagely than did the gentler Kishon. In fact, the program, with its "combination of biting sarcasm, travesty, savage mimicry and carnivalesque mayhem," is said to make Jon Stewart's *The Daily Show* appear "like a benign dose of verbal humor." One *Eretz Nehederet* show in 2004 included a skit in which an elderly couple, worried about security dangers in a holiday trip abroad, are sent by their travel agent to Auschwitz, where they are delighted "by the security offered by the barbed wire fences and watch towers."[45] Editorial cartoonists are carried in newspapers and magazines, leveling their fire at every prime minister from Ben-Gurion to Sharon and Olmert. Amos Biderman, of the liberal *Haaretz* newspaper, says of his fellow cartoonists, "This generation has a conscience but no problem criticizing the government, the leaders, the state," and see it as their job to be critical. Biderman himself prefers not to satirize Arabs: "I need to criticize my own society. That is my satire."[46]

However, Biderman's reluctance to target Arabs has not been shared by most Israeli cartoonists. During the intifada, their prime target was the Palestinian's Yasir Arafat. The leading cartoonist Ze'ev (Yaacov Farkas) drew Arafat with his ever-present sunglasses in the shape of two bombs until the Oslo accords in 1993. Then Ze'ev showed him throwing away his bomb-glasses — until, with the intifada, the bomb-glasses were back. While Yaakov Kirchen's popular *Dry Bones* strip in the *Jerusalem Post* lampooned corrupt Israeli politicians and the rigidity of Orthodox rabbis, it frequently featured the intransigence of Arafat.

Moreover, Israel's democratic status is inevitably affected by limits on free speech and assembly in the West Bank. A survey by Israeli scholar Meron Benvenisti concluded that during the period of direct Israeli rule of the West Bank and Gaza, Israeli censorship banned a large number of publications — and not all of them by Palestinians, for at one point they actually proscribed Orwell's *1984*. Benvenisti's conclusion was that the censorship was basically futile in face of the ability of Arab radio and TV to reach the general population.[47]

Another study by two scholars, an Israeli and an Arab, showed that during the period of direct control, the Palestinian media clearly fit the authoritarian model, with military censors repeatedly intervening to try to limit the expressions of fierce hostility to Israel.[48] Even when, under the Oslo accords, the Palestinian Authority in 1993 took over responsibility for media policy, newspapers required a license from the Israeli military in order to publish. And the 2004 Reporters Without Borders annual report detailed harassment and intimidation of Palestinian journalists by the Israeli army.

Yet it was not only the Israelis who were inhibiting free expression after 1993. Though the Palestinian Authority abolished official censorship, the Palestinian Liberation Organization applied pressures that produced "self-censorship or covert censorship,"[49] and the same Reporters Without Borders report that had criticized the Israelis also accused the Palestinian Authority of intolerance to critics. Consequently, Palestinian satirists get it from both sides. Cartoonist Bahaa Al Boukahari complained he was "immensely frustrated with Israeli authorities," but it was the Palestinian chief of police who threatened to retaliate physically after being skewered in one of Bahaa's cartoons in 1996.[50]

Bahaa had reason for concern. Another Palestinian cartoonist, Naji Salim al-Ali, was a bitter opponent of Israel, but his cartoons infuriated the Palestinian leaders by accusing them of being too ready to compromise. Expelled from the Arab Nationalist Movement for lack of party discipline and jailed in Lebanon for political reasons, he moved between Arab countries and then to England. In 1987 he was gunned down in a London street.[51]

THOSE DANISH CARTOONS

Throughout the Middle East, even more draconian than censorship protecting the political leaders has been the banning of any comment that raised the specter of blasphemy.

The Saudi condemnation of an allegedly blasphemous comic strip in 1993 was repeated in Kuwait, one of the most open of the Arab states. When Kuwait's *Arab Times* in 1996 carried a *Hagar the Horrible* strip that made a mild joke addressed to God, furious fundamentalists chased the editor out of his office at gunpoint, and the newspaper apologized for the strip. Even in Morocco, enjoying a new era of openness when Mohammed VI came to the throne in 1999, the weekly magazine *Nichane* was banned for publishing an article in 2006 on "How Moroccans Laugh at Religion, Sex, and Politics," and the editor and the article's author were indicted for damaging the public morality and defaming Islam.[52]

The explosive potential of these attitudes had already been made clear by the *fatwa* calling for the death of novelist Salman Rushdie after the publication in 1988 of his novel *The Satanic Verses*.. The book was banned and burned in several Muslim countries, and there were violent riots leading to several deaths.

Then in September 2005 a Danish publisher complained that he couldn't find illustrators to draw images of Mohammed for a children's book to contribute to intercultural understanding. He had been turned down by several artists, said the publisher, because they were afraid of reprisals by Muslims insisting their religion forbade visual representations of the Prophet.[53] Eventually, the book did appear with 10 respectful pictures of Mohammed and became an immediate best seller.

In the meantime, however, the Copenhagen *Jyllands-Posten,* as a protest against the publisher's problem, commissioned and published 12 cartoons about Mohammed.[54] Not all of the cartoons were disrespectful of Mohammed. Three, in fact, were critical of *Jyllands-Posten* or of the author of the children's book.[55] But most were clearly derisive of the prophet. One showed him telling Muslim martyrs arriving in heaven that they have run out of the promised 72 virgins. Another depicted Mohammed with devil horns. The cartoon that aroused more controversy than any other, however, was one by Kurt Westergaard that depicted Mohammed with a bomb in his turban.

As Westergaard saw it, "I wanted to show that terrorists get their spiritual ammunition from Islam . . . that does not mean that all Muslims are responsible for terror."[56] The newspaper's cultural editor later explained the rationale for commissioning the cartoons:

> Those images in no way exceeded the bounds of taste, satire and humor to which I would subject any other Dane, whether the queen, the head of the church or the prime minister. By treating a Muslim figure the same way I would a Christian or Jewish icon, I was sending an important message: You are not strangers, you are here to stay, and we accept you as an integrated part of our life, And we will satirize you, too. It was an act of inclusion, not exclusion: an act of respect and recognition.[57]

Danish Muslims were unimpressed by the paper's rationale and demanded an apology. A Danish imam set out on a tour of the Middle East with the 12 cartoons, to which he added others, much more gross, that the paper had not published. A summit meeting of the Organization of Islamic States condemned the cartoons. Saudi Arabia withdrew its Ambassador to Denmark. Danish goods were boycotted in several Muslim countries. (Iran renamed Danish pastries "Roses of the Prophet Mohammed."[58]) The UN appointed two experts on racism to investigate the matter.

In September 2005, the Danish newspaper, *Jyllands-Posten*, protesting against alleged censorship by Muslims, published 12 cartoons featuring the prophet Mohammed. Muslim leaders in Denmark and abroad reacted angrily. However, it was not until other European newspapers reprinted the cartoons in solidarity with *Jyllands-Posten* in February 2006 that the resentment exploded into riots in a number of Muslim countries. All 12 cartoonists have subsequently had to seek police protection. But it was this cartoon by Kurt Westergaard, depicting the prophet as a suicidal terrorist with a bomb and a lit fuse and inscribed with the shahada Islamic creed in his turban, that aroused the deepest anger, resulting in numerous threats and plots against his life and his having to move among safe houses under the protection of the Danish secret service. In March 2008, insisting that he was against terrorists, not Muslims, Westergaard sued the Dutch right-wing politician Geert Wilders for using the cartoon inappropriately and without permission as the opening image of his anti-Qur'anic short film, Fitna. [Kurt Westergaard, "Bomb in the Turban", Copenhagen, September 30, 2005, © Kurt Westergaard, Used with permission.]

When newspapers in France, Germany, Italy, and Spain reprinted the cartoons in February 2006 in solidarity with *Jyllands-Posten,* thousands of Muslims demonstrated in several countries, and riots erupted in the Middle East and Asia in which several rioters were killed and Danish embassies torched. In northern Nigeria, between 100 and 200 people died in the rioting as Muslims outraged by the cartoons attacked Christians, leading to retaliation by machete-wielding Christian mobs. In Libya 11 people were killed in riots protesting the decision of an Italian cabinet minister to wear a tee-shirt imprinted with copies of the cartoon. What had begun as a local religious controversy had suddenly become an international political confrontation, and political satire was the lead story in newspapers and on television all over the world.

There was a strong whiff of hypocrisy in the Arab countries' expressions of righteous indignation. They had never complained of the frequent appearance in several Arab countries of the anti-Semitic, "blood libel" cartoons. That Muslims would be offended and organize protest demonstrations was as natural as when Christian groups were outraged by the treatment of Jesus in *Jerry Springer: The Opera* or Jewish organizations by anti-Semitic cartoons. But riots and embassy burnings are another matter. As Maureen Dowd put it, "It used to take an Israeli incursion to inflame the Arab world. Now all it takes is a cartoon in Denmark."[59]

The only consistent element in the demands made by Muslim leaders was their call for new laws against defamation of their religion. This, after all, was the policy in Muslim countries throughout the Middle East. Newspaper editors in Yemen and Jordan were arrested for publishing some of the cartoons, even though they did so to make clear to their readers just how heinous was the Danish offense. Similarly, an editor in Indonesia was charged with blasphemy, and a Malaysian newspaper was shut down.

It was not only Muslims who criticized *Jyllands-Posten,* however, especially after it was revealed that the paper had previously rejected some cartoons on Jesus. An editor explained, "I don't think our readers will enjoy the drawings . . . I think they will provoke an outcry. Therefore I will not use them."[60] Cynics therefore wondered: Was the paper concerned solely with the principle of free expression — which could have been demonstrated perfectly well by publishing some simple, non-satiric drawings of Mohammed instead of the deliberately provocative cartoons? Or was the real motivation the anti-immigrant animus that was currently widespread in Denmark?

That same anti-immigrant sentiment was present in some of the other European countries — France, Germany, and the Netherlands,[61] for example — where newspapers had reprinted the Danish cartoons.

As shown in earlier chapters, most American and British newspapers did not follow the European example. Still, many editorials in both countries defended *Jyllands-Posten*'s right to publish the cartoons, and a resolution passed by the European Parliament summed up a widespread European sentiment. The resolution regretted the hostility toward immigrants then prevalent in Denmark and expressed sympathy to those offended by the cartoons, yet insisted that *Jyllands-Posten* and its cartoonists had a right to express their ideas, however crass and offensive: "The freedom of expression and the independence of the press as universal rights cannot be undermined by any group that feels offended by what is being said or written."[62]

For a time the controversy seemed to die down. Not for the Danish cartoonists, however, who still lived under police protection; Kurt Westergaard, in fact, was moved from safe house to safe house.[63] The issue erupted again in February 2008, when three men were arrested on suspicion of plotting to kill Westergaard,[64] and several Danish newspapers reprinted the Westergaard cartoon to demonstrate "they will not be intimidated by fanatics." This provoked several days of riots by young Danish Muslim men, protests in Gaza and Pakistan, and a denunciation by the Organization of the Islamic Conference. Next came an audio message, purportedly from Osama bin Laden, in which he declared that the printing of "these insulting drawings" was an even worse offense against Islam than the bombing of villages, and warned Europeans of a strong reaction.[65]

In June 2008, a Danish court rejected a suit against *Jyllands-Posten* for publishing the cartoons: "It is a known fact that acts of terror have been carried out in the name of Islam and it is not illegal to make satire out of this relationship." This decision, said the Organization of the Islamic Conference, would provoke Islamophobia.

To many analysts in the West, the furious insistence of Muslim leaders that their religion must be immune from ridicule, and that anyone who transgresses against this view should be punished, revealed a clear cultural divide, an apt illustration of Samuel Huntington's thesis of a "clash of civilizations." Even those who saw the cartoons as unnecessarily provocative were repelled by the retaliatory riots and bombings.

No doubt the reaction to the Danish cartoons is an extreme example of the sensitivities of the Muslim countries of the Middle East. Even so, the general conclusion from the material in this chapter is that throughout the region there is a profound intolerance to dissenting opinions, including those expressed in satirical form.

However, whatever the merits of Huntington's argument about a clash *between* cultures, we have noted some significant examples of a clash *within* cultures. Though that clash is still kept under rigorous control, a number of news stories have told of Internet bloggers continuing to find ways around government intervention in, for example, Egypt, Syria, and Bahrain. As we've seen, there are skillful satirists throughout the region who, in face of persistent hostility and repression, have the courage to mock their leaders and their policies.[66]

CONCLUSION:
STILL MORE SATIRE—
AND WHY WE NEED IT

Wherever there's power, there's satire to mock it.
Wherever there's satire, the censors will block it.
And where there are censors, satirists fight 'em,
The battle continues, ad infinitum.

Where do we stand today on the conflict between political satirists and those who would shut them down?

The several countries discussed so far can provide only a partial answer to that question. They contain a substantial proportion of the world's population and a great diversity of political systems, yet they comprise only a minority of the current total of more than 190 nations. In addition to citing some brief examples from still more countries, this final chapter focuses on some major political trends of the past century.

Two of these trends seem to tip the balance in favor of the satirists.

The first is a major shift from authoritarian regimes to the relatively open, pluralistic systems we call democracies.[1] These are systems that allow, even encourage, political satire. Though there have been superb examples of satire under authoritarian rule, and satirists in democracies are by no means free from the censor, in general satirists have a much easier time of it when they're not subject to the whims of even the most benign of autocrats.

This being so, the twentieth century, despite all its horrors and disasters, finally brought good news for satirists. As the century began America and Britain had been joined in the democratic camp only by several countries in Western Europe, Scandinavia, and the former white settler British colonies. Though the number of democracies grew after World War I, the gains were nullified as fascism, Nazism, and then communism took control of most of Europe. But from around mid-century, more solid democratic gains began.

First the defeat of the Axis powers in World War II opened the way to democracy not only in Germany, Italy, and Japan but (with the subsequent end of authoritarian rule in Spain and Portugal) in all of Western Europe.

France, for example, has continued its great satirical traditions into the twentieth century, beginning with Anatole France's mock history of France, *Penguin Island*,[2] and continuing with the satirical magazines *Le Canard Enchainé*[3] and *Charlie Hebdo*, a brilliant array of newspaper cartoonists, and the television puppet "fake news" show, *Les Guignols de l'info*.

Next came the collapse of western colonialism, bringing India, with its population now exceeding a billion, into the democratic camp and opening the way for a great burst of satire in cartoons, novels, and other media.

Later in the century came three more momentous advances for democracy. There was the collapse of military rule in most of Latin America, so there are now robust satirical scenes in cartoons and on television in, for example, Argentina and Mexico.

The 1990s saw the end of communist rule throughout Eastern Europe. Henceforth, no European satirist was likely to suffer the bans and imprisonment imposed on Václav Havel for his plays satirizing the country's post-World War II communist state.[4]

Finally, the 1990s also brought to a close apartheid, or official segregation, in South Africa. The authorities, anxious not to exacerbate international hostility to their racist policies, had allowed a good deal of leeway for the satirical barbs of playwright and solo performer, Pieter-Dirk Uys.[5] Even so, he had been careful not to upset his audiences too much: "Forty-nine percent anger versus 51 percent entertainment has always been the sacred remedy. So there has to be more tickles than punches."[6] When apartheid and white rule ended in 1990, Uys was free to launch punches rather than tickles at, for example, the government's tardiness in launching a campaign against the AIDS epidemic (a campaign in which he was joined by the cartoonist Zapiro).

Taken together with the emergence of still more countries from authoritarianism — South Korea, Indonesia,[7] and Ukraine, among others — these changes mean that almost half of the world's nations today can reasonably be classified as democracies.

A second trend that greatly increases the spread of disrespectful anti-regime humor has already been noted: the vast expansion of opportunities opened up by the new communication technologies. In the last two decades of the twentieth century, television in several countries was carrying impudent portrayals of political leaders to appreciative audiences. By century's end the Internet spread subversive wit through e-mails and Web sites. Though authoritarian regimes closed down Internet cafes and blocked Web sites, the more enterprising of their youthful populations delighted in finding ways to outwit the censors in the Middle East, in Russia, even in Myanmar. Now cell phones provide an even less vulnerable device for expressing unofficial and anti-official ideas.

On the face of it, this combination of worldwide political and technological trends ought to herald the ultimate golden age of political satire.

Unfortunately there is also plenty of bad news for satirists. The censor has not disappeared from today's world. As we've seen, this is the case even in well-established democracies like America and Britain.

France is another case in point. Though the repeal of the censorship laws in the late nineteenth century means the end of the kind of retribution inflicted on Daumier and Phillipon, satirists have not been entirely freed from harassment, both official and unofficial. Wartime brought its inevitable constraints: during World War I many of the articles in *Le Canard Enchainé* were deleted or published with white spaces in place of offending statements; and after the fall of France in 1940, *Le Canard* avoided being controlled by the collaborationist Vichy regime only by ceasing to publish until war's end.

Even in peacetime, there could be problems for satirists. Issues of a French satirical journal, *Hari-Kiri Hebdo,* were banned twice by the French government during the 1960s, then closed down permanently by the government in 1970 after it carried a mocking title on the death of President Charles de Gaulle.[8] The magazine's successor, *Charlie Hebdo,* was sued in 2007 by Islamic organizations for insulting their religion by publishing the Danish cartoons, the charge carrying a potential six-month jail sentence and a heavy fine. However, the court ruled in favor of the magazine.[9]

Italy provides even more examples of the problems faced by satirists in democracies. When fascism collapsed as World War II ended, satire surged forth with an abundance of new targets. Popular comedian Beppo Grillo, for example, specialized in jokes about the deep-rooted corruption in government and business, but Grillo was soon to come up against the limits of what would be tolerated. When he scoffed at the ethical transgressions of Socialist prime minister Bettino Graxi during a program on state television, the program's host walked off the set and Beppo was banned from TV.[10]

There was no chance the ban would be lifted when Silvio Berlusconi was elected prime minister for a second term in 2001, this time with a fairly secure majority. His country's richest man, Berlusconi owns newspapers, magazines, publishing houses, advertising agencies, and Mediaset, the operating company of three television networks; and as prime minister he was in a position to apply pressure on state television. He was able to influence 90 percent of Italian TV, and he did not hesitate to use that influence to advance his political agenda, protect himself against lawsuits, and force the cancellation of satirical programs. When one series was cancelled after the first episode, the RAI director explained: "I love satire . . . but . . . I said 'satire' and not political campaigning."[11]

Satirists had a brief reprieve after Berlusconi's narrow defeat in the 2006 election; but reelected by a still larger majority in 2008, Berlusconi exemplifies in extreme form the danger to free expression represented by concentrated media ownership. Evidently, some of the same new media that have contributed to the expansion of satire can also be used to repress satire.

Yet another limitation on satire in democracies — the power of taboos—
is especially evident in Japan. Since its World War II defeat, Japan, with a
U.S.-designed constitutional structure, has qualified as a political democracy. But the irreverence of satire doesn't fit easily into the nation's deferential culture, and members of the Japanese royal family are still safe from the
kind of ridicule heaped on the British royals. (Politicians, however, are not
immune. One was a leading member of the Japanese Wind Party; and his
party had been made to look foolish by a newspaper cartoon that, with a
single missing stroke of a character, had changed the word "wind" to "lice."
The mortified politician "stood up in the middle of a meeting with newspaper executives, said the traditional Japanese pre-suicide words for honor,
bowed in the direction of the Imperial Palace, and shot himself with a pair
of pistols."[12])

There is also the problem that, in several of the countries that have gradu-
ated from authoritarianism in recent years, the transition to democracy is
still fragile. This was true of India. It is also evident in much of Latin
America. Argentina today does not face the prospect of having satirical magazines closed down, as was the case in the 1960s when the military banned
the popular humor magazine, *Tia Vicenta,* edited by the cartoonist,
"Landru." Nor do Argentine satirists fear a repetition of the kidnapping
and murder in the 1970s of political cartoonist Hector Oesterfeld and his
two daughters after he portrayed members of the Argentine junta as extra-
terrestrials.[13] Even so, decades after the end of military rule in Argentina,
the past still haunts the work of cartoonist "Quino":

> When I started, I made jokes about prisoners . . . But when people were
> imprisoned on political grounds in Argentina, I stopped handling the
> subject, and I still couldn't deal with it today. I think it's counterpro-
> ductive to tackle issues as tragic as prisons and torture through humor,
> and though I've been criticized for it, I couldn't bring myself to join in
> Amnesty International's campaigns. I still find it very hard to get out of
> the habit of self-censorship.[14]

Colombia, despite its lively press and periodic elections, has been torn
apart for years by the armed conflict between the government, the paramilitary, and the Revolutionary Armed Forces of Colombia. In 1999, Jaime
Garzun, Colombia's most popular television humorist, lambasted all sides
in this civil war, then tried to act as unofficial peacemaker between the con-
tending parties. He was shot dead in his jeep by two men on a motorbike.

In Venezuela, too, democracy is anything but firmly established despite
the move from military government to multiparty elections in 1958. This
became clear when the elected president, populist Hugo Chavez, was ousted
in a coup in April 2002 (apparently approved by the U.S. government), then
reinstated in a counter-coup 48 hours later. (Political satirists called Pedro

Carmona, the in-and-out president, "Pedro the Brief.") Chavez was able to use Venezuela's oil wealth for political advantage in Latin America and even in the United States, for the joke was on the Bush administration in 2005 when Chavez provided consignments of heating oil at a discount to the poor in New York, Boston, and Chicago. When Chavez tried to change the constitution to increase and perpetuate his power, however, he ran into strong opposition, including that of many of the country's leading comedians and satirists, who participated in an anti-Chavez rally in December 2002.

Among them was the painter and cartoonist, León Zapata, long a man of the left. In 2000 a Zapata cartoon skewered Chavez as a militarist. Chavez hit back in his weekly TV program, wanting to know if Zapata really believed this or drew it for the money. This vastly increased the interest in the Zapata cartoon, so he replied with another cartoon asking Chavez how much he was paid to promote the cartoon. Though his paintings are admired internationally, for Zapata this was a time in Venezuela when it made more sense to be a cartoonist than a painter. "For me, cartoons are the perfect form for expressing fully all that happens to me inside as a consequence of what is going on outside."[15]

So there are resistances to political satire even in those countries that, securely or somewhat precariously, can claim to be democracies.

The resistances are stronger among the several nations that have made some progress toward openness but still remain outside the democratic orbit,[16] such as those noted in the discussion of India's neighbors. Another is Nigeria, whose leading playwright, Wole Soyinka, was awarded the Nobel Prize for Literature for his plays deriding dictators and dictator-worship. Soyinka served 22 months as a political prisoner in 1967 because he appealed for a cease-fire during a period of civil war. Later Nigeria turned to civilian government, but it endured a number of military coups and counter-coups.

Still more deeply entrenched in authoritarian government are nations containing well over one-third of total world population,[17] including most of the Middle Eastern countries. China, though allowing the winds to blow more warmly than during Mao's time, is still a one-party communist state in which no one can hope to earn a living with anti-regime satire. The same is true of Cuba; though dissident groups are sometimes heard from, published anti-Castro satire has come mostly out of Miami, with a consequent right-wing tinge contrasting with the left-of-center tendency of Latin American satire today.

Much of post-colonial Africa, too, has failed to produce stable democracies. Among the worst has been the vicious and blundering regime of Robert Mugabe, which, after a heady period of liberation from colonial rule, imposed a steadily increasing state of repression, including a law against insulting the president. Dissenting voices have persisted in Zimbabwe, published in the few remaining independent newspapers and magazines and in a flourishing satirical theater scene, but they have operated in defiance of unremitting hostile pressure.

Silvanos Muzvova, a playwright, director, and actor, made it his business to insult the regime and Mugabe in his plays, but one of them was closed in mid-performance in Harare and Muzvova and two of his colleagues were arrested. Muzvova used various devices to evade the censorship on other plays. He performed for private audiences only; he sponsored "Invisible Theater," in which actors planted themselves in bars and on trains and engaged in improvised conversations; and he organized groups that did "hit-an-run" street performances in poor neighborhoods, making fast entrances and exits to evade the police.[18] Mugabe was also mocked by comedian Edgar Langeveld, performing a drag act in a small Harare theater. In 2000 he was threatened and beaten by thugs. He went into exile saying, "I don't want to die for comedy," then returned and courageously resumed his act, but after receiving a favorable newspaper review of one of his performances he felt compelled to write the paper, asking: "Are you trying to get me killed?" He begged the paper not to use him as a tool of any of the anti-Mugabe groups.[19]

Even more repressive than Zimbabwe, even more than Myanmar, is North Korea, where, as far as we know, the possibility of publicly ridiculing the leaders has been completely expunged, to be replaced by fawning adulation.

This catalog of infringements on political satire provides evidence that, despite the impressive gains toward openness since the mid-twentieth century, a large part of the globe remains obstinately authoritarian. Perhaps in time the bastions of tyranny will fall. Optimists can point to the possibility that Medvedev will be more accommodating than Putin; that the Chinese leaders will gradually allow more democratic responsiveness, as may Cuba after Castro; that the defeat of Musharraf's supporters in a 2008 election will open the Pakistani system; that Mugabe's reign of intimidation and terror may be coming to an end. But for every optimistic assessment of continued progress toward openness around the world, there is at least one gloomier analysis.[20] So it remains a reasonable assumption that for political satirists, despite a long-term shift in their favor, the battle with the censors in most countries is likely to continue well into the twenty-first century.

Still, there will be satire in most countries, for there will always be people with the urge and the skills to ridicule the powerful. They do so in part because it is their nature to be irreverent, but also because they believe that, to some degree at least, what they do can make a difference. But does it?

DOES POLITICAL SATIRE MATTER?

Absolutely! says the Italian anarchist playwright, Dario Fo. In *Mister Buffo,* Fo describes the jester's role: make fun of the powerful, reveal them for what they are, pull out the plug, and "pssss ... they deflate."[21]

Unfortunately, when *Simplicissimus* with its "Kaiserwitz" pulled the plug on Wilhelm II he didn't deflate, but plunged his nation into war. The vast amount of ridicule heaped on Hitler at home and abroad in the 1920s failed to slow the Nazis' march toward power. *Kukly* and its demise did not put a dent in Putin's popularity. George W. Bush was reelected in 2004 in face of a prodigious outpouring of anti-Bush satire. Anti-war satire didn't prevent the invasion of Iraq or weaken Bush's and Tony Blair's enthusiasm for it.

There is even the possibility that political satirists hinder rather than help their cause. Freud's analysis of jokes[22] suggests that satire serves as a safety valve, venting tensions that might otherwise be expressed in political action. The authorities in Sri Lanka and Malaysia, for example, are said to have tolerated a certain amount of satire as an alternative to more dangerous forms of dissent. Better laughter than riots![23]

In democracies it may be that political satire discourages political involvement by increasing the level of cynicism about politics and politicians. Many late-night comedy shows encourage a frivolous view of politics, focusing on the personal foibles of politicians rather than substantive policy issues.

Political satire can even be counterproductive by provoking action among hostile segments of the population. One of the factors that brought conservatives flooding into the 2004 presidential campaign was their fury at Michael Moore's *Fahrenheit 9/11* movie. Maureen Dowd, a fierce opponent of the war, ruefully quoted her conservative brother thanking Moore, along with Bill Maher, Al Franken, Jon Stewart, and various Hollywood liberals, for having "energized the (conservative) base."

Liberal fears that satire could energize the conservative base were aroused again by a *New Yorker* cover on July 21, 2008, depicting Barack Obama in traditional Muslim garb, "fist-bumping" with his wife, Michelle, who is drawn as a machine gun-toting terrorist. They're in the Oval Office, with a portrait of Osama bin Laden on the wall and an American flag burning in the fireplace. Though this was obviously a spoof by a liberal magazine on right-wing anti-Obama themes, it raised fears that, in the context of a particularly fraught campaign, the cartoon might be use against Obama. An Obama spokesperson called the cartoon "tasteless and offensive." Obama himself said it didn't bother him personally, but it was an insult to Muslims.[24]

On the other hand, a *Private Eye* editor has suggested that the satirists' caricatures of Mrs. Thatcher may actually have helped her because

> the perceived vision of her as an extremely strong, arrogant, aggressive woman, was exactly the image she wanted to project . . . She didn't mind the caricature: it was part of what she was.[25]

So we are well advised not to make excessive claims for satire's political achievements. By themselves the jibes of satirists don't topple thrones, or overthrow tyrants, or decide elections. Yet this doesn't mean that political satire is totally ineffectual. Wherever a repressive regime is being buffeted by forces for change and reform, satire is likely to constitute one of those forces, and probably intensifies the threat to the regime.

In democracies, satirist attacks on particular policies may bear fruit when a substantial body of public opinion is moving in the same direction. The satirists' rage against the Vietnam War played its part in the shift of public sentiment against the war that forced its end. If Michael Moore energized the conservative base in the 2004 election, he may also have brought large numbers of young Democratic voters to the polls. If late-night satirists increase the cynicism of some by focusing on politicians's personalities rather than their policies, the character of political candidates is not irrelevant to their qualifications for office. Moreover, some studies suggest that Stewart, Colbert, and the rest, by attracting an audience that is otherwise apathetic about or repelled by politics, actually increase the level of political awareness and involvement.[26]

As for the concern that political satire may serve as a safe outlet for hostility to the regime, most tyrants would rather not take the chance and prefer to suppress it in case it encourages more direct forms of opposition.[27]

In any event, the case for political satire rests less on its pragmatic effects than on its core values. The first is that it gives us pleasure, entertains us. We surely don't need to question the value of any activity that provides so much amusing, provocative, and informative pleasure.

Next, political satire is therapeutic. Every day we are confronted in the newspapers and TV with accounts of the carnage of war, the blundering and arrogance of leaders, the never-ending examples of greed and corruption. To pay attention to all this as dutiful citizens is extremely depressing. Satirists transmute these continuing tales of human depredation and folly into ridicule so that we may find solace in laughter.

As Byron put it:

And if I laugh at any mortal thing
'Tis that I may not weep.

The final case for political satire is even more important. It is an expression of free speech, of peaceful dissent, and thus a bellwether of the extent of openness in a society. Among the several tests by which we measure the extent of individual freedom, the right to ridicule must be included.

BUT ARE THERE NO LIMITS?

Political satire, then, must be protected as a derivative of the principle of free speech. More than that. Free speech faces limits in law and ethics when it is accused of malicious distortion and exaggeration, but satire, as a condition of its existence, distorts and exaggerates, and is usually malicious — all of which are justifiable on the grounds that the intent is humorous. As the very conservative Chief Justice William Rehnquist declared in the *Hustler* case discussed in Chapter 2, "a lampoon could not be factually false." But does this mean that for political satire anything goes?

One answer is that this is already an inescapable fact. No matter what inhibitions are imposed by the mainstream media, the Internet provides a well-nigh unlimited opportunity for anyone to reach an audience with humor related to politics, sex, religion, race, or ethnicity, no matter how gross or grotesque. So absolute censorship in democracies, and even to an extent in autocracies, has become impossible.

Still, the larger part of public communication still takes place in the mainstream media, and since everything can't be included, editorial decisions on what goes in or out are inevitable.

Joe Szabo makes the point. Szabo has unimpeachable credentials as a fighter for free expression since his International Cartoon Center publishes banned cartoons from around the world. On the cover of one collection of these cartoons, Szabo chose a Portuguese artist's depiction of "Boris Yeltsin with a soft, bent missile in place of his penis" (which, said Szabo, made a "successful statement about Russia's declining military power at the time"). Even so, Szabo insists he won't accept some proposed cartoons on the grounds that "What some people call censorship is nothing else than sound editorial judgment" based on "the difference between sophistication and boorishness. Or taste, if you will." For example, he would reject a cartoon showing "the Pope holding a cross made out of penises or a woman pictured as making love to a pig."[28]

No doubt this raises as many questions as it answers since political satire is, by its nature, constantly subject to the charge of tastelessness. For example, Sacha Baron Cohen is always deliberately tasteless, and his movie *Borat* offended the proprieties with gross toilet and sexual humor. But this was tame stuff by current cinematic standards. Still, some critics raised a different objection: should there be limits to a satirist's use of manipulative techniques, such as *Borat's* "reality" interviews with people who did not realize their anti-Semitic and racist views were going to feature in a hit movie?[29]

Or go back to the Danish cartoons controversy and the decision of most American and British newspapers not to publish the Danish cartoons after the controversy had erupted and become international news. The philosopher, Ronald Dworkin, defended their decision.[30] Even though, said Dworkin, "in a democracy no one, however powerful or impotent, can have a right not to be offended or insulted," he did not believe the public has a right "to read or see whatever it wants no matter what the cost." In this context the cost would include inflicting great pain on Muslims and the possibility of provoking more riots.[31] In any case, he noted, the cartoons were available to anyone online. After carefully weighing all the arguments on both sides, he concluded that the decision not to publish was, "on balance," right. Others, myself included, might see the balance tilting the other way, arguing that unless there are to be restrictions on satirizing every religion, race, ethnicity, gender, or political orientation whose members protest against perceived slurs, it is difficult to see why one group alone should be protected. Still, the arguments of so distinguished an advocate of civil liberties as Dworkin can hardly be ignored.

In fact, most of us, open-minded and tolerant though we may be, are likely to draw the line somewhere, will prefer that some things be kept out of the public dialog. Most commonly this is when the satire is directed downward, against those at the bottom of the status and power scale. Even there, however, we have noted the dangers involved in too much political correctness, and we had better keep our exclusions to extreme cases.

And the exclusions should be fewer still when the satirizing is directed at those who hold key positions of power. For power, though necessary to the functioning of any society, is always potentially dangerous and needs to be checked by dissent, of which satire is a lively component.

Thus the thrust of this book suggests that in almost all circumstances the urge to censor should be resisted, in open as well as in despotic regimes. No matter who is offended, satirists should not be subjected to intimidation and certainly should not have to fear being fined, or imprisoned, or exiled, or worse.

The quality of satire varies, of course. Much of it is trite, crude, unfunny. Yet as this volume has demonstrated, political satirists have provided us in profusion with a buoyant, often brilliant, art that, by debunking pomposity and hypocrisy with the irreverent power of wit, provides a vital counterbalance to the arrogance of power and the tyranny of unquestioned authority.

NOTES

INTRODUCTION: SATIRISTS AND CENSORS

1. *The Incomparable Max* (London: Heinemann, 1962), 345.

2. *Prejudices, Third Series* (New York: Alfred A. Knopf, 1958), 102.

3. In some cultures in antiquity satire was used literally as a deadly weapon: ancient Arab poets projected their satires at the enemy on the battlefield, and poets in Old Irish literature brought down death and disgrace on their victims with lethal satire. See Robert Elliot, *The Power of Satire: Magic, Ritual, Art* (Princeton: Princeton University Press, 1960), 18.

4. Robert R. Provine, *Laughter: A Scientific Investigation* (New York: Viking, 2000), 28; and Willow Lawson, "Humor's Sexual Side," *Psychology Today,* (September/October 2005), 17–18.

5. Sigmund Freud, *Wit and Its Relation to the Unconscious,* A. A. Brill, trans., (New York: Dover Publications, 1993), 150.

6. Lionel Feinberg, *The Satirist* (New York: Citadel Press, 1965), 216.

7. Art Buchwald, *Leaving Home* (New York: Putnam, 1993), 13.

8. "Before Sunrise," in *Nervous People and Other Satires*, Hugh McLean, trans., (Bloomington: Indiana University Press, 1963), 332, 338–339.

9. "Such, Such Were the Joys," in *A Collection of Essays by George Orwell,* (New York: Harcourt Paper Library), 1–47.

10. Stephen Hess and Sandy Northrop, *Drawn and Quartered: The History of American Political Cartoons* (Montgomery, AL: Elliott & Clark, 1996), 10.

11. Jonathan Swift, *A Modest Proposal and Other Satirical Works* (Toronto: Dover Thrift Editions), 1996, 52–59.

12. Bernard Crick, *George Orwell: A Life* (Middlesex, England: Penguin, 1982), 64–65.

13. Paul Lewis, *Cracking Up: American Humor in a Time of Conflict* (Chicago: University of Chicago Press, 2006), 157.

14. Al Franken ran as the Democratic candidate for the U.S. Senate from Minnesota in 2008.

15. Here we use the contemporary American definition of liberalism. It differs from the nineteenth century European definition emphasizing free-market capitalism. Some on the left complain that the liberals are not radical enough. However, all in this category attack the same targets, and their consistent antiauthoritarianism sets them apart from the communists, who oppose authority only until they gain power.

16. These broad areas of agreement do not prevent bitter disagreements on the left. For example, Jon Stewart has been accused in a Canadian journal of the left (*Seven Oaks Magazine*, January 20, 2006) as doing a good job of merely "*acting* like a voice for meaningful change" and toadying to the antiprogressive forces by mocking Venezuela's Hugo Chavez.

17. And also some, like H. L. Menken, who, as we'll see, defy categorization.

18. The wide range of conservative positions includes libertarians, who oppose not only the economic interventionism of the left but also the social interventionism of most mainstream conservatives.

19. This and similar quotes has led conservatives to claim Orwell as one of their own. However, he always called himself a socialist.

20. Christopher Buckley, himself a conservative satirist, conceded that: "As objects of fun Republicans just make better targets than Democrats; likewise conservatives over liberals." But this was from his introduction to a *New Yorker* collection of political cartoons, in which he noted that five times as many of the cartoons lampooned Republicans than Democrats — hardly surprising given the fact that the *New Yorker* was the source. See Robert Mankoff, ed., *The New Yorker Book of Political Cartoons* (Dobbs Ferry, NY: Bloomberg: 2000).

21. Dolf Zillman and Joanne R. Cantor, "A Disposition Theory of Humor and Mirth," in Anthony J. Chapman and Hugh C Foot, eds., *Humor and Laughter: Theory, Research, and Applications* (New York: Wiley, 1976), 100–101.

22. See Jonah Goldberg, *Liberal Fascism* (New York: Doubleday, 2008). The book's cover shows a liberal smiley face with a Hitler moustache.

23. In Paris there was the song parody through which people wrote verses, often lewd, about current events and set them to popular tunes, leading Parisians to describe their system of government as "an absolute monarchy tempered by songs." See Robert Darnton, "Paris: The Early Internet," *The New York Review of Books,* June 20, 2000, 44–45.

24. The most famous cartoon of the century was produced by Philipon depicting King Louis-Philippe as a pear, which was particularly insulting not only because the king's head looked somewhat like a pear but also because "poire" means a fool as well as a fruit. The pear motif became an antigovernment contagion, appearing in a giant statue in the Place de la Concorde and featured in graffiti all over the country. See Robert Justin Goldstein, *Censorship of Political Caricature in Nineteenth Century France* (Kent, Ohio: Kent State University Press, 1989), 128–132.

25. Tad Friend, "Is It Funny Yet?," *The New Yorker*, February 11, 2005, 28.

CHAPTER 1. PUNCTURING THE IMPERIAL PRESIDENCY: FDR TO GEORGE W. BUSH

1. A British import, *That Was The Week That Was,* ran for two seasons in 1963 and 1964 but was not easily transplanted from the BBC to the American commercial arena.

2. Cartoonists joined the Internet with animated cartoons, some political.

3. Arthur P. Dudden, *The Assault of Laughter: A Treasury of American Political Humor* (New York: A. S. Barnes-Thomas Yoseloff, 1962), 34.

4. Hunter S. Thompson, *Fear and Loathing on the Campaign Trail, 72* (New York, Popular Library, 1973).

5. H L. Mencken, *Prejudices: Third Series* (New York: Alfred A. Knopf, 1958), 26, 28–29.

6. Fred Hobson, *Mencken: A Life,* (Baltimore: Johns Hopkins University Press, 1994), 385.

7. Jon Stewart et al., *America (The Book): A Citizen's Guide to Democracy Inaction,* (New York: Warner, 2004), 45.

8. Edward S. Corwin, *The President: Office and Powers* (New York: New York University Press, 1948), 38.

9. Gerald Gardner, *The Mocking of the President* (Detroit: Wayne State University Press, 1988), 228.

10. A rating of the first 41 presidents by 58 historians, commissioned by C-Span in 2002, listed Lincoln, Franklin Roosevelt, and Washington as the top-three presidents. Others mentioned in this book were rated as follows: Theodore Roosevelt (4), Truman (5), Kennedy (8), Eisenhower (9), Johnson (10), Reagan (11), Jackson (13), George H. W. Bush (20), Clinton (21), Carter (22), Ford (23), Nixon (25), Harding (38).

11. Westbrook Pegler, *The Dissenting Opinions of Mister Westbrook Pegler* (New York: Charles Scribner's Sons, 1938), 39–40.

12. Ibid., 79.

13. Norman Mailer, *Miami and the Siege of Chicago* (New American Library, 1968), 44–46.

14. Gore Vidal, *Empire* (New York: Random House, 1987), 38.

15. Art Buchwald, *I Am Not A Crook* (New York: G. P.Putnam's Sons, 1973, 1974), 52.

16. Ibid., Author's Note.

17. Mark Green and Gail MacColl, *Ronald Reagan's Reign of Error* (New York: Pantheon Books), 103. From a radio address, November 1978.

18. Lou Cannon, *President Reagan: The Role of a Lifetime* (New York: Simon and Schuster, 1991), 486–489.

19. Art Buchwald, *While Reagan Slept* (New York: CP Putnam, 1983), 26–28.

20. Robert Dallek, *An Unfinished Life* (Boston: Little, Brown, 2003), 475–476).

21. Paul Krassners's *Realist* magazine told of rumors of young models being on call to fit into Kennedy's busy schedule; and there were hints in *Esquire*. See Stephen E. Kerchner, *Revel With A Cause: Liberal Satire in Postwar America* (Chicago: University of Chicago Press, 2006), 393.

22. Dallek, *An Unfinished Life.*

23. The jokes continued to reverberate into the 2008 primary campaign. When New York governor Eliot Spitzer resigned over a sex scandal, David Letterman quipped: "I thought Bill Clinton legalized this years ago."

24. Editors of the *New Republic*, *Bushisms* (New York: Workman Publishing, 1992).

25. Ibid., 21, 76, 78. All from press conferences.

26. Jacob Weisberg, *The Deluxe Election-Edition Bushisms* (New York: Fireside, 2004). See also Mark Crispin Miller, *The Bush Dyslexicon: Observations on a National Disorder* (New York: W. W. Norton, 2001).

27. www.nationallampoon.com/MoDstyles/wwwaste/Pstate/Pstate.asp.

28. *The New Yorker,* September 19, 2005.

29. "Letter to the US," urbanlegends.about.com, January 28, 2005. Attributed initially to John Cleese. However, several Web sites have claimed that others have contributed.

30. Aaron McGruder's *Boondocks,* appearing in *Los Angeles Times,* January 20, 2005.

31. Molly Ivins, "I Love Enron," *The Progressive,* March 2002, 46.

32. Molly Ivins and Lou Dubose, *Bushwacked* (New York: Random House, 2003), 184–203.

33. Maureen Dowd, *New York Times,* January 28, 2002.

34. Art Buchwald, "The Art of Darkness," *Washington Post,* January 3, 2006.

35. "Mike's Words," June 26, 2003, http://michaelmoore.com/words/message/index.php

36. Cartoon appeared in *The Economist,* January 5, 2007, 7.

37. http://thedailyhowler.com, October 27, 2003.

38. http://theonion.com, October 2, 2002.

39. When Trudeau, in August 2001, drew a strip quoting a Lovenstein Institute study claiming that George W. Bush had the lowest IQ of all presidents in the past 50 years (91, with his father at 98, Reagan at 105, and Clinton at 182), the joke was on Trudeau. There is no Lovenstein Institute. The report, as Trudeau later conceded, was an Internet hoax (though he implied that 91 was an overestimate).

CHAPTER 2. CENSORSHIP, AMERICAN STYLE

1. *New York Times* columnist, Maureen Dowd, was not able to get her White House press pass renewed when George W. Bush became president.

2. In 2008 a triple digital image of Colbert was put on display for a six-week run at Washington's National Portrait Gallery.

3. Mort Sahl, *Heartland* (New York: Harcourt Brace Jovanovich, 1976), 92. Later he alleged that his anti-Johnson quips resulted in the cancellation of his TV talk show (though others have pointed out that he did great damage to his career by turning off his audiences by focusing his routines on an obsessive onslaught on the Warren Commission report on the Kennedy assassination).

4. Chris Lamb, *Drawn to Extremes* (New York: Columbia University Press, 2004), 177.

5. U.S. television networks maintain "standards" departments for this purpose and allow representatives of the advertisers to review some programs before they air.

6. Samuel Eliot Morison, Frederick Merk, and Frank Feidel, *Dissent in Three American Wars* (Cambridge, MA: Harvard University Press, 1970), 87.

7. Jim Zwick, ed., *Mark Twain's Weapon of Satire: Anti-Imperialist Writings on the Philippine-American War* (Syracuse, NY: Syracuse University Press, 1992).

8. Lotos Club speech, March 23, 1901, cited in *Dissent in Three American Wars,* p. 95.

9. Janet Smith, *On the Damned Human Race* (New York: Hill and Wang, 1962), 64–67.

10. *Bulletin for Cartoonists,* August 31, 1918, cited in Hess and Northrop, *Drawn and Quartered* (Montgomery, AL: Elliott and Clark, 1996), 82.

11. "Pro-German List Bared by Army Sleuth," *The Nation,* March 15, 1919.

12. See The Palmer Raids, http:/chnm.gmu.edu/courses/hist409/red.html

13. Joseph Heller, *Catch 22* (New York: Everyman, 1995), 91.

14. Ibid., 316.

15. Quoted in Hess and Northrop, 103.

16. Tom Lehrer, *Too Many Songs by Tom Lehrer* (New York: Pantheon Books, 1981), 153.

17. The idea had wide currency among nuclear strategists at the time. See Herman Kahn, *On Thermo-Nuclear War* (Princeton, NJ: Princeton University Press, 1960).

18. James H. Wittebols, *Watching M*A*S*H, Watching America* (Jefferson, North Carolina: McFarland, 1998), 34.

19. Larry Gelbert, *Laughing Matters* (New York: Random House, 1998), 44.

20. John H. Dower, *War Without Mercy* (New York: Pantheon, 1986), 9.

21. Doug Hill and Jeff Weingrad, *Saturday Night* (New York: Beech Tree Books, 1986), 23.

22. Mike Luckovich, *Washington Post,* September 27, 2001.

23. Jason Zengerle, "The State of the George W. Bush Joke," *The New York Times,* August 22, 2004.

24. *Modern Humorist,* September 23, 2001

25. solidarity.com/hkcartoons/artshow/marland.html, March 9, 2002.

26. Dorian Lynskey, "Crude Missile," a review of the film *The Aristocrats* in *The Guardian,* August 21, 2005.

27. *The Onion,* September 26, 2001

28. Steve O'Donnell quoted in *Los Angeles Times*, March 4, 2002.

29. Aaron McGruder, *A Right to Be Hostile* (New York: Three Rivers Press, 2003), Introduction.

30. Roz Chast, *The New Yorker,* October 15, 2001.

31. Initially there was strong opposition to going to war with Iraq over its invasion of Kuwait. But the war ended so quickly that there was little time for much satire to develop.

32. In one of the great ironies of the era, a Ramirez cartoon in the *Los Angeles Times* defending Bush by showing a man labeled "politics" aiming a gun at Bush (an echo of a 1968 photo of a South Vietnamese general executing a Vietcong officer), was misinterpreted by many readers as a call for the assassination of Bush. The consequence was that a Secret Service agent tried to interview Ramirez for this alleged "threat against the president." The paper denied the agent access to Ramirez.

33. The Ramirez cartoon appeared in *Los Angeles Times,* May 30, 2004.

34. Elain Dutra, "Dems, Foes of 9/11 Gearing Up," *Los Angeles Times,* June 18, 2004. A conservative group, Citizens United, asked the Federal Election Commission (FEC) to prevent the movie being advertised during the run-up to the presidential election, but the FEC dismissed the complaint when Moore indicated he wouldn't run the ads during the campaign period.

35. The sexual content of comic books, too, came under censorship. After the Senate conducted hearings, the comics industry created the Comic Code Authority to administer a censorship system to ensure the triumph of good over evil and law enforcement over crime, " the value of the home and the sanctity of marriage," and the prohibition of nudity and illicit sex relations. See Steef Davidson, *The Penguin Book of Political Comics* (New York: Penguin, 1982), 18–19.

36. Gerald Gardner, *The Censorship Papers* (New York: Dodd, Mead, 1987).

37. Anthony Lewis, *Freedom for the Thought We Hate: A Biography of the First Amendment* (New York: Basic Books, 2007), 139–140.

38. The conviction was confirmed on appeal, but Bruce died while out on bail. In 2003 New York's Republican governor, George Pataki, granted him a posthumous pardon. See Kercher, *Revel With a Cause,* 397–424.

39. Richard Zoglin, *Comedy at the Edge* (New York: Bloomsbury, 2008),

40. The comic book code, too, was abandoned.

41. The 5-4 ruling left unclear questions of context, such as when the offending words are blurted out unscripted, or whether children might be listening. These were questions left for later review by the Supreme Court.

42. Jon Stewart bleeps out the f-word on his cable show *The Daily Show,* at which the audience always laughs. The word is cheerfully used, unbleeped, in his *America (The Book)* (New York: Warner Books, 2004).

43. Hunter Thompson, *Fear and Loathing on the Campaign Trail,'72* (New York: Warner Books, 1973), 380.

44. David Rees, *Get Your War On* (New York: Soft Skull Press, 2002)

45. See David Wallis, ed., *Killed Cartoons* (New York: W. W. Norton, 2007), 29, 51.

46. Pew Research Center, Press Release, "Reading the Polls on Evolution and Creationism," September 28, 2005.

47. "Mitt's No J. F. K.," *New York Times,* December 9, 2007.

48. Chris Lamb, *Drawn to Extremes: The Use and Abuse of Editorial Cartoons,* (New York: Columbia University Press, 2004),156–158.

49. Ibid., 126–127.

50. Steinberg's routine included a mock sermon about Jonah and the whale, in which he said that skeptical New Testament scholars "literally grab the Jews by the Old Testament — indicating with a hand gesture the particular scroll he was referring to." See Zoglin, *Comedy at the Edge,* 70.

51. Doug Hill and Jeff Weingrad, *Saturday Night* (New York: Beech Tree Books, 1986), 168

52. http://theonion.com, December 29, 2005.

53. Racial and other minorities have always retaliated via aggressive jokes directed at the majority. See Joseph Boskin, *Humor and Social Change in Twentieth Century America* (Boston: National Endowment for the Humanities Learning Library Program, Boston Public Library, 1979), 45–60.

54. Ben McGrath, "The Radical," *The New Yorker,* April 19 and 26, 2004, 155.

55. Justin Kaplan, *Born to Trouble: One Hundred Years of Huckleberry Finn* (Washington: Library of Congress, 1985), 11.

56. John H. Wallace, "The Case Against *Huck Finn*" in James S Leonard et al., eds., *Satire or Evasion: Black Perspectives on Huckleberry Finn* (Durham, NC: Duke University Press, 1992), 16–17.

57. Charles H. Nichols, "A True Book — With Some Stretchers," in James S. Leonard et al., 213.

58. Hess and Northrop, *Drawn and Quartered,* 147.

59. Barry Humphries' alter ego, Dame Edna, *Vanity Fair,* February 2003.

60. It was an especially difficult time for comedians of Middle Eastern background. As time passed and the tension eased, however, a group of them formed

the Axis of Evil Comedy Tour, which appeared on TV's Comedy Central in 2007. See Ashrap Khalil, "An Axis of Laughter," *Los Angeles Times,* March 25, 2007.

61. *Philadelphia Inquirer,* February 6, 2006.

62. *The Los Angeles Times,* February 3, 2006.

63. Scott Collins, "Viewers Didn't See the Humor," *Los Angeles Times,* April 15, 2006.

64. Bruce Tinsley cartoon, King Features Syndicate, 2006.

65. Mallard Fillmore cartoon, King Features Syndicate, 2004.

66. Conservatives accuse *Wikipedia* of having a leftist bias and have responded with Conservapedia, which aims to set the record straight on homosexuality, evolution, religion, foreign policy, and so forth.

67. Sinclair Lewis, *Babbit* (Mineola, NY: Dover, 2003), 143.

68. Al Franken, *Lies and the Lying Liars Who Tell Them: A Fair and Balanced Look at the Right* (New York: Dutton, 2003).

69. The increasing consolidation of newspapers in recent years has contributed to a sharp reduction in the number of full-time political cartoonists to about 100 today. See Dan Gilgoff, "Political Cartoonists Impact Presidential Races," *U.S, News and World Report,* March 4, 2008.

70. Cited in Hess and Northrop, 21.

CHAPTER 3. BRITAIN: FROM BULLDOGS TO POODLES

1. Gary Trudeau's *Doonsebury* is carried by *The Guardian.* When the paper went to a smaller format in 2005, *Doonesbury* was dropped — and quickly reinstated after a barrage of complaints from outraged readers.

2. *Punch* closed down in 1992, was resurrected by Mohammed Al Fayed, the owner of Harrod's, in 1996, but closed down again in 2002.

3. Vincent Cable, acting Liberal Democrat leader, during Prime Minister's Questions, November 29, 2007.

4. Jonathan Lynn and Anthony Jay, eds., *Yes, Minister* (London: British Broadcasting Corporation, 1982), 29.

5. Usually depicted as wearing only a towel because he was inspired by Low's overhearing two military types in a Turkish bath insisting that, if tanks were to replace cavalry, troops ought to have the right to wear spurs inside their tanks.

6. Steve Bell, *The Guardian,* October 1, 2002.

7. There have been allegations of a plot by elements in MI5 and the army, supported by a press lord and others, to overthrow the Wilson government in a coup. The rumors were denied in an official 1987 report, but they surfaced again in a BBC melodrama, *The Plot Against Harold Wilson,* in 2006. See Jonathan Freedland, "Enough of this Cover-Up: The Wilson Plot Was Our Watergate," *The Guardian,* March 18, 2008. If so, like Watergate, it belongs in the annals of farcically bungled plots.

8. Geoffrey Grigson, ed, *The Oxford Book of Satirical Verse* (Oxford: Oxford University Press, 1980), 387.

9. Legislation in 1999 reduced the number of hereditary members from about 700 to 92 (until the next stage of reform). All the other members are appointed.

10. Macmillan, it seemed, had learned nothing from his humiliation when John Profumo, his war minister, was forced to resign after lying to Macmillan and

Parliament about the fact he was sleeping with a woman who was also sleeping with an aide in the Soviet Embassy. Initially Macmillan had believed his denial. An English gentleman would not lie to his prime minister and to the House of Commons. It simply wasn't done!

11. However, in 2008 Conservative Boris Johnson, an Eton-educated, upper-class "toff," was elected mayor of London, ousting Labour's two-term mayor, the leftist and working class Ken Livingston.

12. Unlike a U.S. president, a prime minister is not elected directly by the nation as a whole, but simply as a Member of Parliament who, however, happens to be the leader of the majority in the House of Commons. This means there is no American-style separation of powers, which is a basic source of prime ministerial power.

13. When Gordon Brown's poll ratings plummeted in 2008, his authority was clearly weakened. Yet even with ratings similar to George W. Bush, he still maintained more legislative leverage than did Bush.

14. In the post-World War II Labour government Bevan was to preside over the creation of the National Health Service.

15. "Aesop Revisited," *Private Eye,* February 8, 1963, 16. Churchill headed the government ministry ultimately in charge of the World War 1 disaster at Gallipoli, though he was exonerated by a subsequent official review.

16. Clement Attlee, though personally much less impressive than Churchill, Thatcher, or Blair, chaired the wartime cabinet whenever Churchill was away, then presided effectively over the most talented British Cabinet in modern history.

17. Des MacHale, *The World's Best Maggie Thatcher Jokes* (London: Angus and Robertson, 1989).

18. Matthew Parris, *Chance Witness: An Outsider's Life in Politics* (London, Penguin, 2003), 212.

19. Simon Hoggart, *House of Ill Fame* (London: Robson Books, 1985), 70.

20. "Wurgggh churrgh gok! Freddie's back," *The Guardian,* September 11, 2003.

21. "Labour Conference Special," October 30, 2002, 6, 16.

22. Accusations of receiving illegal campaign donations were later to be leveled at members of Prime Minister Gordon Brown's government.

23. John O'Farrell, *I Blame the Scapegoats* (London: Doubleday, 2003), 14.

24. Ian Hislop, ed., *The Private Eye Annual 2003* (London, Pressdam, 2003), 63.

25. British Film Institute, www.screenonline.org

26. "Supermac," *Evening Standard,* November 6, 1958.

27. Roger Wilmut, *From Fringe to Flying Circus* (London: Methuen, 1980), 19.

28. Vicky, *Evening Standard,* December 6, 1962.

29. Dimbleby, BBC1 interview with Willam Bundy, cited in David Dimbleby and David Reynolds *An Ocean Apart* (New York, Random House, 1988), 270.

30. Cover of *Private Eye,* May, 2, 1986.

31. Ian Hislop, ed., *The Private Eye Annual 2003* (London: Pressdam, 2003), 11.

32. Max Beerbohm, *The Incomparable Max* (London: Heinemann, 1962), 70–73.

33. Alan Bennett, *The Madness of King George* (New York: Random House), 1985, 12.

34. Humphrey Carpenter, *That Was the Satire That Was* (London: Victor Gollancz, 2000), 251.

35. Favorable publicity also followed the request of Prince Harry, a Household cavalry officer, that he serve in Iraq, as his uncle, Prince Andrew, had fought in the Falklands war. Harry's request was rejected, but he served briefly in Afghanistan until a news blackout on his posting broke down and he was recalled.

36. John O'Farrell, *I Blame the Scapegoats* (London: Doubleday, 2003), 35

37. Max Beerbohm, *The Incomparable Max* (London: Heinemann, 1962), 70–73.

CHAPTER 4. CENSORSHIP, BRITISH STYLE

1. "Impartiality" regulations governing British TV also apply to Murdoch's Sky Television.

2. Roger Wilmut, *From Fringe to Flying Circus* (London: Methuen, 1980), 70.

3. Ibid.

4. http://writewords.org.uk/news/381.asp

5. The magazine won its first ever libel victory in 2001. See Jessica Hodgson, "Hislop savors first libel victory," *The Guardian,* November 7, 2001.

6. In November 2007, after Blair had resigned, he and his wife, Cherie, won substantial damages from the *Daily Mail* for invading their privacy while they were on holiday in Barbados.

7. Dominic Shellard and Steve Nicholson, *The Lord Chamberlain Regrets*(London: British Library, 2005), 162–163.

8. Cover of *Private Eye,* September 19, 2001. The royals, too, can have recourse to libel suits, as when Prince Charles successfully sued a newspaper in 2006 to stop it printing further excerpts from his private diaries. The royal family can also look to the law for protection against illegal invasion of their privacy. In January 2007 the royals editor of the *News Of The World* was sentenced to four months in jail for tapping into Prince Williams's phone. Moreover, the royals are not limited to a defensive posture. The Queen has launched The Royal Channel on YouTube.

9. Punch, *Mr. Punch's History of the Great War* (New York: Frederick A. Stokes, 1920), xv–xvi.

10. George Bernard Shaw, *Plays Pleasant and Unpleasant* (Middlesex, England: Penguin, 1946), 29.

11. Letter by George Bernard Shaw, "Shaw Objects to Hard Labour for Pacifists, *The Guardian,* June 12, 1917.

12. Joan Littlewood, ed., *Oh! What a Lovely War* (London: Methuen, 1965). The show ran for 11 years in an East London theater from 1963, moved to the West End of London and Broadway, was made into a film in 1969, and was revived by the Royal National Theatre in 1998.

13. Ibid., 41–47.

14. Ibid., 74.

15. Similarly, the bitter irony of novelist Pat Barker's trilogy of novels on World War I, *The Regeneration Trilogy* (London:Viking, 1996), worked well in the 1990s. From 1914 to 1918 it would have produced outrage.

16. George Orwell, *Orwell: The War Broadcasts* (London: Duckworth: The British Broadcasting Corp., 1985), Appendix A: "Censorship at the BBC in Wartime," 283.

17. Bernard Crick, *George Orwell: A Life* (Harmondsworth, Middlesex, England: Penguin, 1982), 452–463.

18. The Campaign for Nuclear Disarmament took a new lease on life, supported by cartoons in the *Guardian,* when the Blair government announced in 2006 its intention to replace the aging Trident nuclear submarine system.

19. But not for Tony Blair, who said in March 2007 that he would have done the same thing as Thatcher, for it was "the right thing to do."

20. William Pfaff, "A Lesson for America in Iraq," *International Herald Tribune,* October 2, 2005.

21. *Private Eye,* May 21, 1982, p.13. See also Robert Harris, *Gotcha! The Media, the Government and the Falklands Crisis* (London: Faber and Faber, 1983), 48.

22. *Private Eye,* June 18, 1982, 11.

23. *Paradise Postponed* (New York: Penguin, 1986), 311.

24. In *Steven Berkhoff: Plays One* (London: Faber and Faber. 1996).

25. Tim Binding, *The Anthem* (Basingstoke and Oxford: Picador, 2003), 163.

26. Rodolfo Fogwill, an Argentine sociologist, wrote a short novel depicting the absurdity and misery of the war from the perspective of 24 Argentine soldiers who desert and hide in an underground cave: *Malvinas Requiem: Visions of an Underground War,* transl. Nick Caister and Amanda Hopkinson. (London: Serpent's Tail, 2007).

27. Martin Rowson, *The Guardian,* September 20, 2001.

28. Later she used the same line in appearances in America, producing similar reactions. Except for one man in the audience who buried his head in his hands: his sister had died in the World Trade Center. (Interview with Ed Bradley, *60 Minutes,* May 2, 2004.)

29. However, the number was reduced step by step, until only a few thousand were left in Iraq when Gordon Brown, who was clearly not enthusiastic about the British involvement, became prime minister in 2007.

30. Steve Bell, "Drawing Fire," *The Guardian,* April 10, 2003. Actually, as Bell informed me in an e-mail: "I was engaging in absurd speculation in that piece — there's never been a ghost of a chance of me becoming embedded in the military."

31. Ibid.

32. John Trevelyan, *What the Censor Saw* (London: Michael Joseph, 1973), 41–42.

33. Humphrey Carpenter, *That Was Satire, That Was: The Satire Boom of the 1960s* (London, Phoenix, 2002), 100.

34. Dominic Shellard and Steve Nicholson with Miriam Handley, *The Lord Chamberlain Regrets: A History of British Theater Censorship* (London: The British Library, 2004).

35. Carpenter, *That Was the Satire That Was,* 205.

36. "Transatlantic Cleavage: The Press (Janet Jackson's Breast)," *The Economist,* February 7, 2004.

37. Trevelyan, *What the Censor Saw* (London: Michael Joseph, 1973), 40.

38. Shellard and Nicholson, *The Lord Chamberlain Regrets,* 170.

39. "Vicar Innocent—It's Official!!!"*Private Eye,* March 4, 2004

40. Blair's aides were relieved that his conversion to Catholicism came after he resigned as prime minister.

41. Carpenter, *That Was Satire That Was,* 142.

42. In 2007 the high court rejected a private prosecution of the BBC for screening *Jerry Springer*. The suit claimed an infringement of the common law offense of blasphemy, protecting Christianity from "scurrilous vilification." The House of Lords voted to repeal the law.

43. Other than French Huguenots, who fled to Britain to avoid persecution in the seventeenth century, and Jews, who escaped from pogroms in Russia and East Europe from the late nineteenth century.

44. Paul McCartney briefly tried his hand at satire with a verse about Pakistanis that was intended to mock Powell's "Rivers of Blood" speech. However, the verse did not appear in the final cut of the Beatles "Get Back" and was available only in bootleg versions of a rehearsal session.

45. David Blunkett, "Religious Hatred Is No Laughing Matter," *The Guardian,* December 12, 2004. Further government efforts to combat terrorism came when Gordon Brown's government proposed, in the face of strong civil libertarian objections, to increase the time suspects could be held before being charged from 28 to 42 days.

46. The law gave Muslims the same kind of protection against stirring up religious hatred already provided Jews and Sikhs, but it limited the defined offense to a clear intent to stir up hatred, and against words and behavior that were "threatening" rather than merely abusive or insulting.

47. One rationalization for the special sensitivity toward the Muslim religion in the British and American media came from Stewart Lee, the author of the farce featuring a gay Jesus, *Jerry Springer: The Opera*. According to Lee, Jesus is fair game and Mohammed is not because Christians have always used representations of Jesus, whereas Muslims have been more "conscientious about protecting the brand." Quoted by Daniel Wolf, "Censorship Wasn't All Bad", www.spectator.co.uk /article_pfv.php?id=7281.

48. *Wikipedia* explained that, for copyright reasons, its reproduction of the cartoons was blurred and unclear.

49. Leader: "Insults and Injuries," editorial, *Guardian,* February 4, 2006.

50. Editorial in the *Independent,* February 3, 2006. However, the same editorial expressed uneasiness about the firing of the *France Soir* editor for publishing the cartoons.

CHAPTER 5. WHAT'S FUNNY ABOUT HITLER?

1. Heinrich Mann, Der Untertan (The Loyal Subject), Helmut Peitsch, ed. (New York: Continuum, 1998), 42. Though it was written in 1914, it was not published until after the war.

2. Ann Taylor Allen, *Satire and Society in Wilhemine Germany* (Lexington, KY: The University Press of Kentucky, 1984), 14, 16.

3. Ibid., 135.

4. The cartoon, by Paul Weber, was published in 1932, the year before Hitler came to power. It illustrated a widely read booklet by radical publisher Ernst Niekisch. See Zbynek Zeman, *Heckling Hitler: Cartoons of the Third Reich* (London: Orbis, 1984), 29.

5. Ibid., 218.

6. Peter Jelavich, *Berlin Cabaret* (Cambridge, MA: Harvard University Press, 1993), 224.

7. Alan Lareau, *The Wild Stage: Literary Cabarets of the Weimar Republic* (Columbia, SC: Camden House, 1995), 135.

8. Ibid., 163.

9. Steve Lipman, *Laughter in Hell: The Use of Humor During the Holocaust* (Northvale, NJ: Jason Aronson, 1993), 34.

10. Lareau, *The Wild Stage: Literary Cabarets of the Weimar Republic,* 144.

11. Ibid., 165–166.

12. Jelavich, *Berlin Cabaret,* 236.

13. Ibid., 239.

14. W. A. Coupe, "Cartoons of the Third Reich,"*History Today,* September 1998.

15. The *Kladderadatch cartoon* appeared on August 20, 1939. See Ernst Herbert Lehman, "With Poison Pen: Current History in Caricature," http://www.calvin.edu/academic/cas/gpa/lehmann.htm.

16. Randall L. Bytwerk, *Bending Spines* (East Lansing, MI: University of Michigan Press, 2004), 122.

17. Albert Speer, *Inside the Third Reich,* Richard Winston and Clara Winston, trans., (New York: Macmillian, 1970), 125. Cited in Bytwerk, *Bending Spines,* 127.

18. "Mungo" and "Die Panic Party," in *Die Marsbewohner sind da! Politische Satiren* (Berlin: Carl Stephenson Verlag, 1939), 50–62.

19. The satire exaggerated the reality somewhat. The *St. Louis* was turned away from its destination, Cuba, and the United States made no effort to allow it to dock in Miami. But Holland, Belgium, France, and Britain did accept most of the passengers between them (several later finishing up in the death camps).

20. Tim Kirk, "The Policing of Popular Opinion in Nazi Germany" in Dermot Cavanaugh and Tim Kirk's, *Subversion and Scurrility: Popular Discourse in Europe from 1500 to the Present* (Aldershot, England: Ashgate, 2000), 182.

21. Lipman, *Laughter in Hell: The Use of Humor During the Holocaust,* 34.

22. Egan Larsen, *Wit as a Weapon: The Political Joke in History* (London: Frederick Muller, 1980), 48–49.

23. Lipman, *Laughter in Hell: The Use of Humor During the Holocaust,* 16, 196.

24. Larsen, *Wit as a Weapon: The Political Joke in History,* 51.

25. Sylvia Rothschild, ed., *Voices from the Holocaust* (New York: New American Library, 1982), 409.

26. Lipman, *Laughter in Hell: The Use of Humor During the Holocaust,* 73.

27. Bertolt Brecht, *The Private Life of the Master Race,* trans., Eric Russell Bentley (London: Victor Gollancz, 1948), 30–31.

28. Ibid., 37.

29. Ibid., 55.

30. Ibid., 64.

31. Bertolt Brecht, *The Resistible Rise of Arturo Ui* (London: Eyre Methuen, 1976).

32. Ibid., 39.

33. Tadeusz Borowski, *This Way for the Gas, Ladies and Gentlemen* (New York: Penguin Books, 1976), 38. No less harrowing an account of Jewish torment under

the Nazis was *Maus,* by Art Spiegelbaum (New York: Pantheon, 1973), with the Jews as mice and the Nazis as cats.

34. Günter Grass, *The Tin Drum,* trans., Ralph Manheim (New York: Pantheon, 1961).

35. Ibid., 201.

36. Theodore Geisel's Dr. Seuss, *Yertle the Turtle and Other Stories* (New York: Random House, 1950).

37. Richard H. Minear, *Dr. Seuss Goes to War* (New York: New Press, 1999), 81.

38. Cited by Bernard Crick, "Shaw As Political Thinker" in T. F. Evans, ed., *Shaw and Politics* (Philadelphia: The Pennsylvania State University Press, 1991), 25.

39. In the 1933 Fabian Society speech Shaw also spoke approvingly of Stalin as an "interesting gentleman whose personal acquaintance I have had the pleasure of making" and who had no interest in making revolutions beyond his own country.

40. David Robinson, *Chaplin: His Life and Art* (New York: McGraw Hill, 1985), 485.

41. Many were made uncomfortable by Tovar Reich's satiric novel, *My Holocaust* (New York: Harper Collins, 2007), which mocks those who have turned the horror of the Holocaust into a profit-making industry. Tovar Reich's husband, Walter, is a former director of the United States Holocaust Memorial Museum.

42. Thomas Pigor, quoted in Jeffrey Fleishman, "A Farcical Attack on Hitler Taboos," *Los Angeles Times,* December 17, 2006.

43. However, the reviews were mostly negative, and even the comedian who played Hitler didn't think the movie was funny. Mark Landler, "In Germany, a Comedy Goes Over with a Thud," *New York Times,* January 11, 2007.

44. Jeffrey Fleishman, "German Leader Gets a Thumping as Anti-Tax Tune Tops the Charts." *Los Angeles Times,* November 26, 2002.

CHAPTER 6. STALIN AND MAO: NO LAUGHING MATTER

1. Dostoevsky narrowly escaped the death penalty, and was sentenced to four years hard labor in Siberia. Turgenev was sentenced by the tsar to a month's incarceration and exile to his estate for publishing a eulogy of Gogol.

2. Aleksey Pynanov, *Soviet Humor: The Best of Krokodil* (Kansas City: Universal Press, 1989), Foreword.

3. Peter Henry, ed., Vol. 1, *Classics of Soviet Satire* (London: Collet's, 1972), xxi.

4. Ibid., xi–xii.

5. Ilya Ilf and Evgeny Petrov, *The Twelve Chairs,* trans., John H. Richardson (Evanston, IL: Northwestern University Press, 1997}.

6. Mirra Ginsberg, *The Fatal Eggs and Other Soviet Satire* (New York: Grove Press, 1964), 221–227.

7. Mirra Ginsburg, "Introduction to Yevgeny Zamyatin," *We* (New York: HarperCollins, 1972), xi.

8. Mikhail Zoshchenko, *Nervous People and Other Satires* (Bloomington: Indiana University Press, 1963), 137–140.

9. Mikhail Zoschenko, *The Galosh and Other Stories* (Woodstock, NY: Overlook, 2006), 79–81.

10. Ibid., 3–4

11. Francine du Plessix Gray, "Mayakovsky's Last Loves," *The New Yorker,* January 7, 2002, 47.

12. Simon Sebag Montefiore, *Stalin: The Court of the Red Tsar* (New York: Alfred A. Knopf, 2004), 97.

13. Peter Henry, ed., Vol. 1, *Classics of Soviet Satire,* xi.

14. From Carolyn Forché, ed., W. S. Merwin and Clarence Brown, trans., *Against Forgetting* (New York: W. W. Norton, 1989).

15. Montefiore, *Stalin: The Court of the Red Tsar,* 98.

16. Richard L. Chapple, *Soviet Satire of the Twenties* (Gainsville, FL: University of Florida, 1980), 131.

17. Andrew Horton, ed., *Inside Soviet Film Satire* (Cambridge: Cambridge University Press, 1993).

18. Michael Friedberg, "Introduction to Ilf and Petrov," *The Twelve Chairs* (New York: Random House, 1961), vii.

19. Reported by Harold Macmillan in George Hutchinson, *The Last Edwardian at No. 10* (London: Quartet Books, 1980), 96.

20. Karen L. Ryan-Hayes, *Contemporary Russian Satire* (Cambridge: Cambridge University Press, 1995), 194.

21. Vladimir Voinovich, *The Life and Extraordinary Adventures of Private Ivan Chonkin,* Richard Lurie, trans. (New York:Bantam, 1979).

22. Vladimir Voinovich, *Moscow 2042* (New York: Harcourt Brace Jovanovich, 1986).

23. Vladimir Voinovich, *Monumental Propaganda* (New York: Alfred A. Knopf, 2004).

24. "Belshazzar's Feast'" in *Sandra of Chegem,* Susan Brownsbeger, trans. (London: Jonathan Cape, 1983), 196.

25. Fazil Iskander, *Rabbits and Boa Constrictors* (Ann Arbor, MI: Ardis, 1989).

26. Ibid., 16.

27. Ibid., 65.

28. Deming Brown, *The Last Years of Soviet Literature: Prose Fiction 1974–1991* (Cambridge: Cambridge University Press, 1993). Brown argues that despite the repressiveness of the Brezhnev era, Soviet literature "was vastly freer, more genuine, and original than it had been in the Stalin years"though, except for Iskander and a few others, there was not much satire.

29. David Remnick, *Lenin's Tomb: The Last Days of the Soviet Empire* (New York: Vintage, 1993–1994), 148.

30. C. Banc and A.Dundes, *First Prize: Fifteen Years!* (Cranbury, NJ: Associated University Presses, 1986).

31. Faces and Voices: "Puppeteers Keep Some of the Humor Intact," *Moscow Times,* March 18, 2000.

32. Ibid.

33. Lynn Berry, "Did You Hear the One About Putin and the Jellied Meat?" *Los Angeles Times,* July 16, 2006. Berry is the former editor of *Moscow Times.*

34. Gary Shieyngart, "Adventures of a True Believer," *New York Review of Books,* May 26, 2005.

35. Ilya Milstein, Vladimir Voinovich, "Russia Has Been Unable to Cope with Freedom," *New Times,* September 2004.

36. Early in 2008, Russia closed down some of the offices of the British Council and arrested Stephen Kinnock, the son of the former leader of the British Labour Party, Neil Kinnock, who opined, "Orwell appears to be meeting Gogol."

37. Leonard Feinberg, ed., *Asian Laughter* (New York: Weatherhill, 1971), 20.

38. Philip Short, *Mao: A Life* (New York: Henry Holt), 453, 458.

39. Roderick MacFarquhar and Michael Schoenhals, *Mao's Last Revolution* (Cambridge, MA: Harvard University Press, 2006), 118–119.

40. Perry Link, ed., *Stubborn Weeds* (Bloomington, IN: Indiana University Press, 1983), 9

41. Ibid., 285–287.

42. Feinberg, *Asian Laughter,* 231–237

43. Jun Chang with Jon Halliday, *Mao* (New York: Alfred A. Knopf, 2005), 333, 449.

44. Ibid., 440. See also Andrew J. Nathan, "Foreword" to Liu-Zhisui, *The Private Life of Chairman Mao* (New York: Random House, 1994), ix.

45. Link, *Stubborn Weeds,* 285.

46. Ibid., 268.

47. Perry Link, *The Uses of Literature* (Princeton, NJ: Princeton University Press, 2000), 69.

48. Link, *Stubborn Weeds,* 17.

49. Ibid., 198–250.

50. Kevin Platt, "Can China's Leadership Take a Joke?" *Christian Science Monitor,* February 24, 2000.

51. Henry Chu, "Beijing Theater Marks Orwell's Year of the Pig," *Los Angeles Times,* December 1, 2002.

52. Perry Link, "China: The Anaconda in the Chandelier," *New York Review of Books,* April 11, 2002, 67.

53. Evelyn Iritani, "A Cartoon for China's New Generation," *Los Angeles Times,* March 18, 2007.

54. CHINA.ORG.CN, March 10, 2008, http://www.china.org.cn?english/NM-e/ 155786.htm.

55. According to the Chinese government, it reached 210 million in 2007.

56. Google issued a disclaimer: "Because of local rules and policies, some results weren't displayed."

57. For examples of dissident writing from Hong Kong and Taiwan, see Henry Y. H. Zhao and John Cayley, *Under-Sky Ground: Chinese Writing Today* (London: The Wellsweep Press, 1994), and Geremic Barme and John Minford, eds., *Seeds of Fire* (Hong Kong: Far Eastern Economic Review, 1986).

58. Ha Jin, *In the Pond* (New York: Vintage, 2000).

59. Ha Jin, *War Trash* (New York: Vintage International, 2005). The novel tells of a Chinese soldier captured during the Korean War, whose American captors tattooed "FUCK COMMUNISM" on his belly, and who has some of the letters removed before he returns to mainland China so the tattoo reads a politically correct: "FUCK...U...S..."

60. Dai Sijie, Ina Rilke, trans., *Balzac and the Little Chinese Seamstress* (New York: Knopf, 2001).

CHAPTER 7. IMPERIAL IRONIES: INDIA AND THE RAJ

1. Roshni Johar, "220 Years Old and Still Going Strong," *Sunday Tribune*, January 30, 2000.

2. David Cannadine, *Ornamentalism: How the British Saw Their Empire* (Oxford: Oxford University Press, 2001), 56.

3. Brian Lapping, *End of Empire* (New York: St. Martin's Press, 1985), 96.

4. Robert Darnton, "Literary Surveillance in the British Raj: The Contradictions of Liberal Imperialism," in (*Book History*, Volume 4, 2001), 168.

5. N. Gerald Barrier, *Banned: Controversial Literature and Political Control in British India, 1907–1947* (Columbia, MO.: University of Missouri Press, 1974).

6. Darnton, (*Book History*, Volume 4, 2001), 153.

7. Ibid,, 139–140

8. Hiranmoy Bhattacharya, *Raj and Literature: Banned Bengali Books* (Calcutta: Firma KLM, 1989), 50–51.

9. Abu Abraham, ed., *The Penguin Book of Indian Cartoons* (New Delhi: Penguin, 1988), xv.

10. Partha Mitter, "Cartoons of the Raj," *History Today*, September 1997.

11. "Political Satire in Modern India," *The Hindu*, April 6, 2003.

12. George Orwell, *Burmese Days* (New York: Harcourt, 1934).

13. Ibid., 39.

14. Ibid., 37

15. George Orwell, *The Road to Wigan Pier* (New York and London: Harvest/ HBJ, 1958), 144.

16. *Shankar's Weekly*, May 23, 1948.

17. R. K. Laxman has complained of the decline in the art of cartooning in the Indian press. There is much "India shining" and "India whining," and "neither in the shining bit or the whining bit is there much room for satire and irony." Henry Chu, "Sharp Cartoons Reflect India's Foibles," *Los Angeles Times*, August 17, 2008.

18. *Shankar's Weekly Souvenir Number*, September 1975, 109–110.

19. The clampdown on the press included pre-censorship. However, the pre-censorship was lifted for cartoons after the first three months of the Emergency. See Abu Abraham, *The Penguin Book of Indian Cartoons* (New Delhi: Penguin Books), xiii.

20. Shashi Tharoor, *The Great Indian Novel* (New Delhi: Penguin Books, 1989).

21. Ibid., 116. The mango tax, says Tharoor, gave Gandhi the issue for his first nonviolent protest campaign, which resulted in the first of his several incarcerations.

22. Rukun Advani, "The State of India," *The Hindu*, May 25, 2003.

23. Luke Harding, "Sir Humphrey Moves to India in a BBC First," *The Guardian*, April 20, 2001.

24. www.wittyworld.com.

25. In its annual report for 2007, Freedom House gave India a "Free" rating; Singapore, Malaysia, Bangladesh, and Sri Lanka (formerly Ceylon) were listed in the "Partly Free" category; and Pakistan and Myanmar were included in the "Not Free" category.

Freedom House, whose ratings are cited in this and subsequent chapters, receives most of its money from the U.S. government and has been criticized by Noam Chomsky and others on the left for being an instrument of the political right. However, at various times its reports have criticized South African apartheid, Pinochet's Chile, Saudi Arabia, and the U.S. government's recent detention and interrogation techniques. By and large the rankings referred to in this book seem to make sense, though there is obvious room for debate in the margins between Freedom House's three categories of "free," "partly free," and "not free." For other democratic-authoritarian assessments, see Ted Robert Gurr and Keith Jaggers, *Polity III: Regime Change and Political Authority, 1800–1994,* http://webapp.xml.umich.edu/cocoon/ICPSR-STUDY/06695.lepsr, and Robert A. Dahl, *On Democracy* (New Haven: Yale University Press, 1998).

26. Lim Cheng Tju, "Singapore Political Cartooning," *Southeast Asian Journal of Social Science,* Vol. 25, no. 1, 1997, 143.

27. John A. Lent, "Political Adversaries and Agents of Change: Editorial Cartoonists in Southeast Asia," *Asian Thought and Society,* Vol. 19, No. 56, May–August 1994), 109–110.

28. Wong Kim Hoh,"Singapore: New Film Makes Fun of Singapore Censors," *The Straits Times,* March 7, 2004.

29. Ranjini Obeyesekere, *Sri Lankan Theater in a Time of Terror* (Walnut Creek: AltaMira Press, 1999), 150

30. Robert Russell, *Cartoonists Rights Network,* http://www.cartoon-crn.com/.

31. Sohena Rahen, "I Get to Have the Best of Both Worlds," *Newsline,* January 2006; and Bruce Wallace, "The Sassy Voice and Face of Pakistan," *Los Angeles Times,* January 22, 2008.

32. "Musharraf's Detractors Knock Double Posts:" Renee Montague interview with Fasi Zajka, National Public Radio, "Morning Edition," December 14, 2007.

33. Jennifer Leehey, "Message in a Bottle: A Gallery of Social/Political Cartoons from Burma," *Southeast Asian Journal of Social Science,* Vol.25, Number 1, 1997), 157, 163.

34. Lent, "Political Adversaries and Agents of Change: Editorial Cartoonists in Southeast Asia," 114.

35. Choe Sang-Hun, "Sober Times for Myanmar's Comics," *International Herald Tribune,* October 28, 2007; Aye Lee, "A Visit with the Moustache Brothers," *Tne Irrawady,* January 9, 2008.

36. Emma Larkin, *Finding George Orwell in Burma* (London: Penguin, 2005).

CHAPTER 8. THE MIDDLE EAST: RAGING AGAINST CARTOONS

1. Khalid Kishtainy, *Arab Political Humor* (London: Quartet Books, 1985), 18.

2. Ibid., 37.

3. According to Freedom House, Jordan, Kuwait, and Bahrain were listed in the organization's "Partly Free" category; the rest of the Arab Middle East nations languishing in the "Unfree" group.

4. Kishtainy, *Arab Political Humor,* 57–58

5. Ibid., 184-185

6. Brian Lapping, *End of Empire* (New York: St. Martin's Press, 1985), 240.

7. Kishtainy, *Arab Political Humor,* 83–85.

8. Ibid., 147.

9. Egypt State Information Service, "Rose Al Youssef, Pioneer of Art and Press (1898–1958)," April 10, 2005. The Mubarak government has also started a daily newspaper with the same name.

10. Joseph Fitchett, "Sharper then the Sword," *Saudi Aramco World*, March/April, 1976.

11. Samir Raafat, "Gagging Egypt's Vocal Chords," *Jordan Star*, April 30, 1998.

12. Allen Douglas and Fedwa Malti-Douglas, *Arab Comic Strips: Politics of an Emerging Mass Culture* (Bloomington: Indiana University Press, 1994), 62.

13. Trudy Rubin, "An Egyptian Political Cartoonist Looks at the Conflict," *Christian Science Monitor* and The Alicia Patterson Foundation, 1974. http://www.aliciapatterson.org/APFOO1974/Rubin/Rubin05/Rubin06/Rubin07.jpg.

14. Zvi Bar'el, "Anything But Sex, Religion, and the President," *Haaretz*, August 9, 2005.

15. Subsequently Hanaft was released, but forced to pay a fine.

16. In 1988 Farzat had entered a cartoon showing a general distributing medals from a stew pot to a starving man into an exhibit in Paris. Iraq threatened to withdraw funding for the show; the cartoon was withdrawn, then reinstated after other cartoonists threatened to withdraw. See Barry Rubin, *The Long War For Freedom: The Arab Struggle for Democracy in the Middle East* (New Jersey: John Wiley, 2006), 28–29.

17. *BBC News*, March 25, 2005.

18. Ali Farzat, *A Pen of Damascus Steel* (Seattle: Cune Press, 2005), editors' note, 17.

19. Lisa Fliegel, "A Comedy Team that Keeps Jordan Happy," *The New Middle East Magazine*, June 2001, 2.

20. Ibid.

21. Barry Rubin, *The Long War For Freedom: The Arab Struggle for Democracy in the Middle East*, 74. Khashoggi had been friendly to Osama bin Laden, but he rejected terrorism, so bin Laden supporters parodied *Al-Watan's* (The Homeland) logo as *Al-Wathan* (the pagan idol).

22. Roughly translated as "either you get it, or you don't."

23. Pascal Ménoret, "Saudi TV's dangerous hit," *Le Monde diplomatique*, September 2004.

24. "Tash Ma Tash: A Barometer of Self-Criticism," *Arab News*, November 3, 2004

25. "Tash Ma Tash Actors Receive Death Threats," *Arab News*, October 27, 2004.

26. Khudair Hemiyar cartoon appearing in the *Los Angeles Times*, January 29, 2006.

27. Edmund Sanders, "Cameras on a Roll in Iraq," *Los Angeles Times*, May 9, 2005.

28. Thirty Iraqi journalists were killed in 2007.

29. Henry Beard, "Secrets of the Bagdad Giggle Sheets," *Los Angeles Times*, December 4, 2005.

30. A certain amount of dissent is allowed through periodic national and local elections, though candidates outside the mainstream are commonly disqualified and the dominant groups are theocratic.

31. Dr. Mohamed Al-Saeed Abdul Mo'men, "Iranian Theater Propagates Shiism," http://www.islamonline.net/iol-english/dowalia/art-2000-August-03/art3.asp.

32. The cartoon, which appeared in a children's newspaper, depicted a child talking to a cockroach, and the cockroach answering in the language of the Azeris, who constitute about one-quarter of Iran's population and are frequent targets of ethnic jokes. Daryl Cagle, "Cartoons as a Measure of Freedom," *Daryl Cagle's Cartoon Web Log!,* June 29, 2006, http://cagle.msnbc.com/news/blog/June2006.asp.

33. http://www.goodreads.com.

34. Alana Semuels, "Internet: Unlikely Forum for Iran's Youth," *Los Angeles Times,* January 2, 2006.

35. http://www.mehrnews.com/en/NewsDetail.aspx?NewsID=602918.

36. After Iran organized a conference of the most notorious Holocaust deniers from Europe and America, an Israeli comics' cooperative, *Dimona*, gave the debate an appropriately satiric twist by organizing an anti-Semitic cartoon competition, with Art Spiegelman among the judges. *The Beat*, March 20, 2006. http://www.comicon/thebeat/2006/spiegelman_joins_antisemitic_c.html

37. http://www.wittyworld.com/news.html.

38. Nihad Awartani's cartoon appeared in *Ad-Dustor,* July 20, 2003. See Tom Gross, "Cartoons From the Arab World," http://www.tom grossmedia.com/ArabCartoons.htm.

39. Tom Gross, "Cartoons From the Arab World," cartoon appeared in *Al-Rai,* May 24, 2002.

40. Danny Rubenstein, "Drawn in Blood," *Haaretz,* October 5, 2005.

41. Tom Gross, "Cartoons From the Arab World," cartoon appeared in *Ad-Dustor,* October 19, 2003.

42. Tom Gross, "Cartoons From the Arab World," cartoon appeared in *Al Watan,* June 23, 2002.

43. Joel Kotek, "Major Anti-Semitic Motifs in Arab Cartoons," *Jerusalem Center for Public Affairs,* June 1, 2004.

44. See Tom Gross cartoon posted on April 6, 2003.

45. Talya Halkin, "Between Satire and Entertainment," *The Jerusalem Post,* December 9, 2004.

46. Lisa Alcalay Klug, "Drawing the Line," *Moment Magazine,* February 2005. A willingness by both sides to satirize their own society and to work toward Israeli-Palestinian cooperation is demonstrated by the *Israeli-Palestinian Comedy Tour,* founded in 2006 by Israeli and Palestinian comedians and joined by three American comedians. They have performed in Jerusalem, Haifa, and various American cities.

47. *Israeli Censorship of Arab Publications* (New York: The Fund for Free Expression, 1983.)

48. Hillel Nossek and Khalil Rinnawi, "Censorship and Freedom of the Press Under Changing Political Regimes," in *Gazette: The International Journal For Communication Studies* (London: Thousand Oaks and New Delhi, Vol. 65(2)).

49. Ibid., 196.

50. http://www.wittyworld.com/countries/israel.html.

51. http://www.wittyworld.com/countries/england.html. Who killed him is unknown. Syria's Ali Farzat has alleged that el-Ali had been warned by Arafat a week before he was killed that if he did not stop lampooning Arafat and his mistress, his life would be in danger.

52. The verdict was three years probation and a heavy fine for both, and a ban of two months for the magazine. However, this was less than the prosecution's proposed five years in jail and a permanent ban; and when the magazine was back in April, it sold out. See *The View from Fez,* "Nichane Trial to Get Underway," http://riadzany.blogspot.com/2007/01/nichance-trial-to-get-underway.html; Lalla Lilaini, "Nichane Update," http://www.lailalilaini.com/blog/archives/004584.html; Fadoua Benaich and Jesse Safe, "Morocco's serious humor gap," *Los Angeles Times,* January 15, 2007. See also "It Isn't Funny," *The Economist,* March 1, 2008, for an account of how satirist Ahmed Senoussi ("Bziz") was banned by Hassan II, unbanned, then banned again by Muhammad VI.

53. There are, however, a number of representations of Mohammed in some museums in Europe and the United States, and there is a stone frieze of the prophet as an ancient lawmaker in the U.S. Supreme Court. In Muslim countries depictions of Mohammed were common during the Ottoman Empire, though they are much less so today, especially among Sunnis.

54. "It's bizarre," said the author later. "I write a book to promote understanding between cultures and now I see Danish embassies burning in the Middle East." *London Times Online,* February 8, 2006.

55. Daryl Cagle and Brian Fairrington, eds., *The Best Political Cartoons of the Year, 2007 Edition* (Que Publishing, 2006), 8–11.

56. Ibid., 8.

57. Fleming Rose, "Why I Published the Muhammad Cartoons," *New York Times,* May 31, 2006.

58. However, Danish export losses in the Middle East were at least partly offset by increased sales in America, encouraged by right-wing groups. See Luke Harding, "How One of the Biggest Rows of Modern Times Helped Danish Exports to Prosper," *Guardian,* September 30, 2006.

59. "Smoking Dutch Cleanser," *New York Times,* February 11, 2008.

60. http:/news.bbc.co.uk/go/pr/fr/-2/hi/asia-pacific/4708216.stm-.

61. In the Netherlands in 2004 Theo van Gogh was murdered after he had made a movie critical of Muslims. In May 2008 a Dutch cartoonist was arrested, charged with drawing cartoons that incited hatred against Afro-Europeans and Muslims.

62. European Parliament resolution on the right to freedom of speech and respect for religious beliefs, B6-0138/2006.

63. Author's telephone interview with Kurt Westergaard, January 8, 2008; Cagle and Fairrington, *The Best Political Cartoons of the Year, 2007 Edition,* 9. Michael Kimmerman, "Outrage at Cartoons Still Tests the Danes," *New York Times,* March 20, 2008.

64. Of the three men accused of plotting against Westergaard, two were Tunisians, who would be subject to deportation, and the third was a Dane of Moroccan extraction who was released after questioning.

65. The message, which appeared on a militant Web site on March 20, 2008, was accompanied by an old image of bin Laden carrying an AK-47. On June 2, 2008, a bomb exploded in the Danish Embassy in Islamabad, killing at least six; http://www.guardian.co.uk/world/2008/mar/20/alqaida.eu/print.

66. Marc Lynch, in *Voices of the New Arab Public* (New York: Columbia University Press, 2006), speaks of a "new Arab public sphere" given voice by, for example, *Al-Jazeera,* with its "beautiful, unveiled anchorwomen."

CONCLUSION. STILL MORE SATIRE—AND WHY WE NEED IT

1. Freedom House, in its 2007 report ("Freedom in the World 2007," www.freedomhouse.org/uploads/press_release/fiw07_overview_final.pdf-) classified 90 nations, with 47 percent of world population in its "Free," or democratic, category.

2. Anatole France, *Penguin Island,* A. W. Evans, trans. (New York: The Heritage Press, 1947). The novel provides a sardonic assessment of law's origins in the protection of property, the causes of war, and the deep corruption in French officialdom.

3. *Le Canard Enchaîné* accepts no advertising or subsidy and exists entirely on its sales of a one-third to a half-million readers.

4. Havel was following in a great Czech satirical tradition, including Jaroslav Hasek's hilarious World War I novel, *The Good Soldier Schweik.* The novel was banned from the Czech army, then in Poland and Bulgaria, and burned by the Nazis in 1933. Joseph Heller said that he would never have written *Catch 22* had he not read *Schweik.*

5. Uys, cross-dressing as Evita Bezuidenhout, an Afrikaner ambassador to a mythical black homeland, got away with parodying the rulers' absurd rationalizations ("Democracy is too good to waste on just anyone"). There was even an 18-month uncensored run in Johannesburg of *Woza Albert* (Percy Mtwa, Mbongeni Ngema, and Barney Simon: Methuen Drama, 1983), a two-person anti-regime play (though during rehearsals the authors were arrested and held without charge for a month). Uys was not immune from censorship, however, for the frank sexual references in some of his plays resulted in cuts and periodic bans. Author's note, *Selle ou Storie* (Johannesburg: AD Donker, 1983), 79.

6. Calvin Trillin, "Gadfly," *The New Yorker,* May 10, 2004.

7. A popular Indonesian TV show, "Republik Mimpi" ("Republic of Dreams"), included an episode in 2008 in which two cast members mockingly impersonated the president and vice president. The show has met some political resistance and has twice had to switch channels, indicating that Indonesia is still some distance from being a "Republic of Dreams." Still, "lampooning those in authority would have been unthinkable during the earlier authoritarian rule of President Suharto," and Freedom House has rated Indoniesia the one "Free" country in Southeast Asia. See Kerry B. Collison, "Indonesia: Not Yet a Dream," *The Economist,* May 24, 2008.

8. The title, "Tragic ball at Colombey: 1 death," was a play on the death of 146 in a fire at a discotheque the same month as de Gaulle's death.

9. The French comedian, Dieudonné, son of a Frenchwoman and African father, faced criminal charges for "justifying terrorist acts" after 9/11 when he proclaimed in a French magazine that he preferred the charisma of Osama bin Laden to that of George Bush. Though he lost some lawsuits, he was not convicted on the criminal charges. However, TV stations were reluctant to give him airtime after he became rabidly anti-Semitic and ended one program by giving the Nazi salute and shouting "Isra-heil.". See Tom Reiss, "Laugh Riots," *The New Yorker,* November 19, 2007.

10. Later Graxi resigned in disgrace, but Grillo, still banned from TV, was limited to arena performances and a popular Web log. http://www.beppogrillo.it/eng/grillonews.html.

11. John Hooper, "Watch What We Tell You," *The Guardian,* November 27, 2003.

12. http://www.wittyworld.com/countries/japan.html, 2003.

13. http://www.wittyworld.com/countries/argentina.html.

14. *The Federation of Cartoonists' Organization,* www.fecoweb/Artists/ quinoeng.html. The persisting influence of the Catholic Church was made clear in 1989 when a television puppet show, *Kana K,* ran an episode in which a Pope John Paul II puppet said "Fuck you" in Italian. Complaints poured in, the network paid $1 million in fines, and the network president took the show off the air.

15. "Cartoon And Crisis," Elizabeth Farnsworth interview with Zapata, *The News Hour,* PBS, June 18, 2002.

16. Freedom House lists roughly 30 percent of nations in its "Partly Free" category.

17. In Freedom House's "Not Free" category.

18. See Robyn Dixon, "In Zimbabwe's Theater of Fear, Dissent Plays On," *Los Angeles Times,* November 19, 2007; Stanley Kwenda, "Zimbabwe: Mutare Police Block 'Final Puss' Play," *Financial Gazette (Harare),* November 15, 2007; *Artists for Democracy in Zimbabwe Trust,"* ADZT urges government to stop harassing innocent artists", http://www.adzt.org/news008.asp. Cont Mhlanga is another Zimbabwe satirist whose plays have been interrupted and closed down by the police.

19. Edgar Langeveldt, "I'm No Tool," *Zimbabwe Independent,* May 23, 2004

20. For example, Freedom House's report, "Freedom in the World, 2007," is subtitled "Freedom Stagnation Amid Pushback Against Democracy," and found that "the percentage of countries designated as Free has failed to increase for nearly a decade," with some countries actually slipping back.

21. Dario Fo, *Mister Buffo,* Ed Emery, trans. (London: Methuen, 1988).

22. Sigmund Freud, *Jokes and Their Relation to the Unconscious* (New York: WW Norton, 1960).

23. John A. Lent, "Political Adversaries and Agents of Change: Editorial Cartoonists in Southeast Asia," *Asian Thought and Society,* Vol. 19, No. 56, May–August 1994), 119; and Ranjini Obeyesekere, *Sri Lankan Theater in a Time of Terror* (Walnut Creek: AltaMira Press, 1999), 147.

24. Maureen Dowd, *New York Times,* November 28, 2004.

25. Humphrey Carpenter, *That Was Satire That Was* (London: Victor Gollancz, 2000), 326.

26. See Brandon Rottinghaus, Kenton Bird, Travis Ridout, and Rebecca Self, "It's Better Than Being Informed: College-Age Viewers of *The Daily Show,"* in Judy C. Baumgartner and Jonathan S. Morris, *Laughing Matters: Humor and American Politics in the Media Age* (New York: Routledge, 2008), 287–290. The Pew Research Center for Excellence in Journalism suggested the Jon Stewart's *Daily Show* "is clearly impacting American dialogue" and is "getting people to think critically about the public square." See Michiko Kakutani, "Is Jon Stewart the Most Trusted Man in America?", *New York Times,* August 17, 2008.

27. Whatever the short-term limits of political satire, it may at its best have a significant impact on the long-term climate of opinion. George Orwell's *1984* has become a definitive warning not only against Soviet tyranny but all of the emerging authoritarian trends in the western world: the ubiquitous security cameras reminding us of Big Brother; the demogaguery of sloganized language (Operation Iraqi Freedom); the use of Doublethink ("holding two contradictory beliefs in one's mind

simultaneously, and accepting both of them"); and the rewriting of the past—all captured in the constantly cited word "Orwellian."

28. "Censorship," http:/www.wittyworld.com/cnsrshp.html.

29. See Marcel Berline, "Borat's humor Is Immoral," *The Guardian,* November 29, 2006. Some Jewish organizations worried that the anti-anti-Semitism gags might be misunderstood as anti-Semitism. Kazakhstan, depicted as ludicrously mired in poverty and ignorance, complained that this was a gross distortion, which it was, and banned the movie. On the other hand, Kazakhstan, as an authoritarian state, needs more, not less, satire.

30. "The Right to Ridicule," *New York Review of Books,* March 23, 2006.

31. Though the previous riots erupted only in Muslim countries, there were concerns in the American and British media that they might be subjected to violent reprisals if they published the cartoons. A London magazine, *The Liberal,* did plan to publish the cartoons until warned by the police that they could not guarantee protection for the magazine's staff. And in February 2007 a Muslim man was convicted of stirring up racial hatred by leading a march on the Danish embassy in London protesting the Danish cartoons and shouting "Europe will pay with its blood," "7/7 on its way," and "bin Laden on his way."

INDEX

ABOUT THE AUTHOR

LEONARD FREEDMAN is Professor Emeritus of Political Science at the University of California, Los Angeles (UCLA), where he was Dean of the university's Continuing Education Division. He currently teaches political satire to UCLA undergraduates and extension students. He is the author of seven books, including *Power and Politics in America, Politics and Policy in Britain*, and *Tension Areas in World Affairs*. He wrote and narrated the National Public Radio series, *Power in America*.